W9-BCG-591

A Time
to Laugh

A Time to Laugh

The Religion of Humor

DONALD CAPPS

continuum

NEW YORK • LONDON

152.43
Capps

Unless otherwise indicated, Scripture quotations are taken from the New Revised Standard Version of the Bible, copyright 1989, Division of Christian Education of the National Council of the Churches of Christ in the United States of America. Used by permission. All rights reserved.

Scripture quotations marked RSV are taken from the Revised Standard Version of the Bible, copyright 1952 by the Division of Christian Education of the National Council of the Churches of Christ in the United States of America. Used by permission. All rights reserved.

Every effort has been made to trace the copyright owners of material included in this book. The author and publishers would be grateful if any omissions or inaccuracies in these acknowledgements could be brought to their attention for correction in any future edition. They are grateful to the following copyright holders:

Cartoons from *Never Eat Anything Bigger than Your Head* by B. Kliban, copyright © 1976 by B. Kliban. Published by Workman Publishing Company, New York. Permission sought.

"Stupid and Canny Jokes by Country" from *Jokes and their Relation to Society* by Christie Davies, copyright © 1998 by Christie Davies. Used by permission of Mouton de Gruyter, a division of Walter de Gruyter GmbH & Company.

"Therapeutic Humor Techniques" by Waleed Anthony Salameh, from *Handbook of Humor Research*, edited by Paul E. McGhee and Jeffrey H. Goldstein, copyright © 1983. Used by permission of Springer-Verlag.

"Further Thoughts" by Armand T. Ringer from *Martin Gardner's Favorite Poetic Parodies* by Martin Gardner, ed., copyright © 2001 by Martin Gardner. Published by Prometheus Books, New York. Used by permission.

"[Jesus smoking a cigar]" from *The Painted Towns of Shekhawati* by Ilay Cooper, copyright © 1994 by Ilay Cooper. Published in the United States by Grantha Corporation, Middletown, New Jersey, in association with Mapin Publishing Pvt. Ltd., Ahmedabad, India. Permission sought.

"Another Reason Why I Don't Keep a Gun in the House" and "Hopeless But Not Serious" from *The Apple That Astonished Paris* by Billy Collins, copyright © 1988 by Billy Collins. Reprinted by permission of the University of Arkansas Press.

Cover art by "The Reverend Will Bo Dunn" Doug Marlette

Cover design by Laurie Klein Westhafer

Library of Congress Cataloging-in-Publication Data

Capps, Donald.
    A time to laugh : the religion of humor / Donald Capps.
      p.   cm.
    Includes bibliographical references.
    ISBN 0-8264-1641-1 (hardcover)
    1. Wit and humor—Psychological aspects. 2. Psychology, Religious. 3. Wit and humor—Religious aspects. 4. Wit and humor—Religious aspects—Christianity. I. Title.
BF575.L3C37 2005
152.4'3—dc22
                                      2004023884

Printed in the United States of America

04 05 06 07 08 09   10 9 8 7 6 5 4 3 2 1

Contents

. . . a time to weep, and a time to laugh.
—*Ecclesiastes 3:4*

• • •

To Don Quixote
my alter ego

Acknowledgments

I especially want to thank Henry Carrigan for backing this particular expression of our shared belief that religion and humor should be friendly, not estranged bedfellows, and Ryan Masteller for shepherding it through the publication process. Joan Blyth, who has typed many of my manuscripts, has typed this one with her customary professional skill and graceful accommodation to my penchant for revising. Sang Uk Lee interrupted work on his doctoral dissertation at Princeton Theological Seminary to help me track down books and articles on the subject of humor. I rationalized my imposition on his time on the grounds that he too is a lover of humor. My colleague Abigail Rian Evans's poems in defense of Norwegians have inspired me to equal heights of earnest rebuttal. My wife, Karen, deserves a great deal of the credit and none of the blame for the very fact that this book got written at all. She has provided me with wonderfully funny accounts of the sayings and doings of her preschoolers, thus balancing my argument that male melancholic religion has its origins in boys' emotional separation from their mothers at ages three to five (Capps 1997a, 2002b) with empirical evidence that humor provides important compensations.

This book is dedicated to Don Quixote, who was Freud's rather implausible hero in his teens and early twenties and who became my no less plausible hero in my fifties. My biblical Burma-Shaves placed at ends of chapters make the point that I have made in a more formal way in my article on Don Quixote (Capps 1999) that the ability of religion to represent a golden age that never existed in fact is as valuable as its ability to envision a better future: Back in the 1940s, the Capps family, in our version of Quixote adventures, would travel from Omaha to St. Edward, Axtell, or Ogallala, Nebraska, to visit relatives, then continue on to Manitou Springs, Colorado, for summer vacations. The Burma-Shave signs along Lincoln Highway were virtually the only relief that the outside world afforded from the heat and close quarters inside our 1947 Frazer.[1] Several examples of these signs are reprinted in *The Norton Book of Light Verse* (Baker 1986, 239–40), two on biblical themes:

> Whiskers long
> Made Samson strong
> But Samson's gal
> She done
> Him wrong.
> *Burma-Shave*

> The Whale
> Put Jonah
> Down the hatch
> But coughed him up
> Because he scratched.
> *Burma-Shave*

My modest contribution to this venerable form of light verse is to provide titles that elucidate the deeper meaning of the biblical texts to which they refer.

Motoring through the Bible Belt

"Hey, Guys, Guess What I Just Saw!"

> Noah, a man of the soil, was the first to plant a vineyard. He drank some of the wine and became drunk, and he lay uncovered in his tent. And Ham, the father of Canaan, saw the nakedness of his father, and told his two brothers outside. Then Shem and Japheth took a garment, laid it on both their shoulders, and walked backward and covered the nakedness of their father; their faces were turned away, and they did not see their father's nakedness.
> *Genesis 9:20–23*

> Ham entered in
> To Noah's tent.
> He saw his beard
> And out he went.
> *Burma-Shave*

Introduction

A cheerful heart is a good medicine,
   but a downcast spirit dries up the bones.
   Proverbs 17:22

Like a maniac who shoots deadly firebrands and arrows,
so is one who deceives a neighbor
   and says, "I am only joking!"
   Proverbs 26:18

When I was a boy, I read the humor in *Reader's Digest,* the one magazine to which my parents subscribed on a regular basis. I enjoyed reading the humor sections "Life in These United States" and "Laughter Is the Best Medicine." Much of the humor was corny, but occasionally there would be a joke that was especially funny to me, and I would ask one of my brothers if he had seen it too. Humor was our primary avenue of brotherly bonding, and we had *Reader's Digest* to thank for this.

The idea that "laughter is the best medicine" became a conviction of mine from an early age, but I didn't give this particular belief much thought as I entered adulthood. Then along came Norman Cousins, who, in collaboration with his physician, checked himself out of the hospital and into a hotel room, where he improvised a therapeutic regimen that involved a lot of humor. His affliction was a degenerative disease, ankylosing spondylitis, an indication that the connective tissue in his spine was disintegrating (Cousins 1979, 30–31). His therapeutic regimen was a combination of vitamin C, the Marx Brothers, and episodes from the television series *Candid Camera*.

Cousins reported on this therapeutic regimen in his article "Anatomy of an Illness (As Perceived by the Patient)," published in 1976 in *The New England Journal of Medicine*. His book by the same title, published three years later, became a best seller, and Cousins was given a faculty appointment at the UCLA School of Medicine. He became an enormously popular speaker on medical matters from the patient's perspective. As Robert R. Provine points out in *Laughter: A Scientific Investigation* (2000), Cousins, later in life, "moderated his laugh-your-way-to-health message, noting that humor should be considered a metaphor for the entire range of positive emotions" (191). Critics suggested that he may simply have experienced a spontaneous remission of his symptoms, that he may not have had ankylosing spondylitis, and that vitamin C may not have had the presumed effect. But no one seems to have challenged his claim that ten minutes of laughter provided him at least two precious hours of pain-free sleep and other desirable health benefits. This claim seemed entirely plausible.

But why? Was it because we have been indoctrinated by *Reader's Digest*'s claim that laughter is the best medicine? Was it because it seems intuitively correct that, when one's very life is under threat, the Marx Brothers are better company than all those anonymous faces who comprise the hospital "health team"? Or is it because we ourselves feel better when we have had a good laugh? On the basis of his review of the research literature on the effects of laughter, Provine says that we should not *overemphasize* the positive effects of laughter. Attempts to replicate Cousins's self-experiment with a larger subject group have produced rather inconclusive results. The data from studies of the effects of laughter are difficult to interpret. Does laughter, a sense of humor, or a lighthearted personality have a positive effect on one's immune system, thus contributing to longer life expectancy? Unfortunately, the few studies that have claimed to demonstrate such effects used flawed research methods or had other problems, such as unconfirmed laughter, small sample size, or an inadequate control situation (198).

Studies seeking to demonstrate the pain-reducing effects of laughter have fared better, in Provine's opinion, but even here there are some nagging problems. Patients who watched comedies experienced no greater pain reduction than those who watched documentaries, suggesting that the pain relief was due to distraction or a related cognitive-behavioral process, not specifically comedy. Also, the intensity of the pain made a difference in the results. Intense pain tends to overwhelm subtler competing stimuli such as humor.

A problem inherent in all research studies of the effects of humor on health conditions is that the investigator, not the subject, selects the humor to which the subject will be introduced. Individual tastes in humor are extremely variable. What I think is funny may not be at all funny to you. If you or I were in Cousins's shoes, would we have taken videos of the Marx Brothers and *Candid Camera* with us to the hotel room? I can't speak for you, but these certainly would not have been my top choices. On the other hand, given my personal feeling that the

Marx Brothers and *Candid Camera* have a certain sadistic quality—enjoyment derived from causing someone else to suffer embarrassment or confusion—perhaps Cousins found them therapeutic because they enabled him to project his own sufferings onto the victims of the Marx Brothers and Allan Funt. Regardless, Provine's point is that researchers select the comedy to which subjects will be exposed, and based on the research studies I've read, this generally means they are exposed to stand-up comedians.

Provine concludes his review of the recent literature on a rather tentative note. The early optimistic assertions that humor has all sorts of health benefits has, more recently, given way to "a downward phase, as disillusioned investigators realize that the necessary science is neither as easy nor as obvious as first anticipated" (207). On the other hand, the mixed picture presented by the research to date is not, in his view, reason for outright skepticism concerning the idea that laughter has a medicinal effect. In any event, "the potential downside of laughter is small indeed, particularly if elected by patients. The promise of improved mood and quality of life without notable negative side effects is reason enough to implement experimental laughter or humor programs in health-care settings, even if welcome relief is provided only through placebo or distraction—there are worse outcomes than providing entertainment to patients desperately in need of it" (207). In other words, laughter is not necessarily the best medicine, but it cannot possibly be the worst.

Although I've begun this introduction with a brief discussion of the physical health benefits of laughter, this is not a book on wellness, wholeness, or any of the other terms currently employed by experts—and nonexperts—in the field of "spirituality and health." Rather, this book is concerned with the gifts that humor bestows on those who are receptive to it. The five chapters identify a handful of such gifts. As these gifts, whatever else they may be, are *psychological,* this is a book about the *psychology* of humor. I am aware that some people like psychology while others do not and that those who like it tend to like one psychological framework more than others. I use the word *psychology* here, however, in a very broad sense, defined by the dictionary as "the science dealing with the mind and with mental and emotional processes." This is as technical as this book gets with regard to psychology, so I hope that my attempt to give the book a locus will not discourage readers who care little for psychology from reading it. That this book is about *humor* should be motivation enough.

This is also, however, a book about *religion.* It reflects my personal belief that humor has a place in religion and that religion itself is impoverished when it fails to manifest and develop this aspect of itself. I am also aware that some people do not like the word *religion,* that this word has, for them, a negative connotation. They may associate it with their childhood experiences of ecclesiastical systems that were overtly or covertly abusive. They may prefer words such as *faith* or *spirituality* and use the word *religious* to communicate what they are not or have ceased to be. I happen to like the word *religion* because it is based on the Latin word *ligare,* which means to bind or bind together. This is the same

Latin word from which we get our English word *ligament,* which the dictionary defines as "a bond or tie connecting one thing with another" and "a band of tough tissue connecting bones or holding organs in place." The hymn "Blest Be the Tie That Binds" beautifully expresses this understanding of what religion is or is meant to be:

> Blest be the tie that binds
> Our hearts in Christian love:
> The fellowship of kindred minds
> Is like to that above.
>
> Before our Father's throne
> We pour our ardent prayers;
> Our fears, our hopes, our aims are one,
> Our comforts and our cares.
>
> We share our mutual woes,
> Our mutual burdens bear,
> And often for each other flows
> The sympathizing tear.
>
> From sorrow, toil, and pain,
> And sin we shall be free;
> And perfect love and friendship reign
> Through all eternity.
>   *—John Fawcett (1740–1817)*

Admittedly, a certain stretch of the imagination is required to view humor as a part of the "tough tissue" that "binds our hearts in Christian love" and maintains "the fellowship of kindred minds." The hymn itself emphasizes tears, not laughter. But this imaginative stretch is precisely what this book aims to be. In her poem "What the Figtree Said," Denise Levertov suggests that the fig tree recognized what the disciples who heard Jesus cursing it did not, namely, that Jesus, "who spoke in images," saw the barren fig tree as "a metaphor for their failure to bring forth what is within them (as figs were *not* within me)." Thus, Levertov writes from the fig tree's point of view, "My absent fruit stood for their barren hearts. He cursed not me, not them, but (ears that hear not, eyes that see not) their dullness, that withholds gifts *unimagined*" (1992, 6).

To be sure, Levertov is not referring here to the gifts of humor. Instead, she has in mind gifts of compassion and comprehension—compassion because the disciples fail to perceive Jesus' thirst and hunger, his innocent appetite; and comprehension because they, literal-minded, fail to see that the fig tree is a metaphor. I would not claim that humor is a more important gift than those of compassion and comprehension, but like these, it is a gift of the imagination, and the imagination is one of the ways in which we develop and maintain the ties that bind us together. As Levertov's poem shows, however, a general appeal to the imagination is not as effective as a case in point, that is, a fig tree. The dictionary definitions of imagination are unintentional testimony to this very fact, as they refer to the imagination as "the act or power of forming mental images of what is not actually present" and "the act or power of creating mental images of what has never been actually experienced." I suspect that most of us are likely to be rather suspicious of a creative act that produces something that is not really there or never experienced until we are presented with the thing itself—a painting, a poem, or a joke. Then we are likely to accept the truth of the definition—the joke relates an event that didn't really happen—but at the same time we are also back on solid ground, as the joke is something that really is there, something that is part of our everyday experience—sitting in a doctor's office, entering a crowded restaurant, driving a car. Even jokes about situations that are not part of our everyday experience—meeting St. Peter at the pearly gates—describe this experience in ways that are familiar to us, as though we were at the registration desk of a hotel or being interrogated by an official at a border crossing between two countries. True, in a literal sense, the events that jokes recount rarely if ever happen. But in another, more metaphorical sense, they happen time and time again. So this book has its locus in the interplay of psychology, religion, and imagination, and humor is the connecting link between these three.

This interplay, however, raises an interesting issue. Whether or not humor has direct physical benefits, there can be little doubt that it has psychological benefits. Research studies have in fact shown that humor is a moderator of life stress (Lefcourt and Martin 1986; Bizi et al. 1988; Abel 1998); that it reduces some forms of anxiety (Smith et al. 1971; Yovetich et al. 1990; Thorson and Powell 1993); that it has some effect on depression (Porterfield 1987; Nezu et al. 1988; Deaner and McConatha 1993); and that it shares with worry the ability to help persons cope with their problems (Kelly 2002). The interesting issue is that these are some of the psychological benefits that religion also seems to offer, so what is to prevent individuals from turning to humor exclusively and abandoning religion entirely? Alternatively, if religion has these beneficial effects, why turn to humor? After all, if religion does what humor does and so much more, humor is at best superfluous and at most a distraction from what is more important. What I hope to show in the course of this book, however, is that humor need not be viewed as a competitor, much less an enemy, of religion. On the contrary, religion itself is impoverished when it fails to manifest its own historical association with humor, an association that may be traced back to the biblical tradition itself and to the simultaneous emergence of religion and humor in the development of the child. Thus, I am not primarily concerned with what religion may do to humor, for humor can take care of itself. Rather, my concern is that religion loses something when it fails to include humor in its inventory of the ties that bind our hearts in Christian love and maintain the fellowship of kindred minds.[1]

Thus, if this book presents the view that humor has a handful of gifts to offer religion in friendship, affection, and support, it also laments the fact that some of religion's most influential voices have viewed humor as the proverbial gift horse, insisting on looking into its mouth to determine its age by the condition of its teeth.[2] But religion too is rather elderly by now, and humor would have every right to cast a critical eye at *its* stablemate and wonder if it has the energy to rouse itself, shake the lethargy from its aging limbs, and burst through the barn doors, whip-snorting its way down the garden path. Instead, humor nuzzles its old partner and asks, in a voice grown tender with age, "Why the long face?"[3]

Motoring through the Bible Belt

Levite Priest Reassures Terrified Boy

When a man or woman has a disease on the head or the beard, the priest shall examine the disease.
Leviticus 13:29–30

Be calm, my son,
Don't think it's weird
That your mother has
A full-grown beard.
Burma-Shave

1. Humor as Saving Psychic Resources

Sigmund Freud's first solo-authored book, *The Interpretation of Dreams* (1965), first published in 1899, is now considered a major classic. His second book, *Jokes and Their Relation to the Unconscious* (1960), first published in 1905, is a very different story. Those who know that Freud wrote an important book on dreams often are surprised to learn that he also wrote a book on jokes. They are even more surprised to learn that he believed that dreams and jokes have a great deal in common. In *The Interpretation of Dreams*, he observes that dreams use the following devices to disguise their deeper meanings: *representation* (the presentation of dream-thoughts in sensory form), *condensation* (the compression or abbreviation of dream-thoughts), and *displacement* (the condition of things of minor importance occupying a central position while things of high importance are relegated to the dream's periphery). In the sixth chapter of his book on jokes, Freud contends that jokes use these very techniques to mask their meanings, implications, and so forth. Thus, dream work and joke work have much in common, and if it requires some exercise of our cognitive abilities to "get" a joke, so it requires the exercise of our analytical powers to discover the "meaning" of a dream.

One factor that led to Freud's decision to write a book on jokes was a remark by his friend Wilhelm Fliess that Freud's interpretations of dreams were like someone's attempts to explain a joke (Freud 1925/1952, 125). This made Freud's point that dreams and jokes have much in common. But Freud's theoretical interest in jokes predated the publication of *The Interpretation of Dreams* by several years. In an 1897 letter to Fliess, he quoted a joke about two Jewish beggars and then confessed that for some time he had been putting together a collection of Jewish anecdotes. This collection no longer exists, but scholars have estimated that it included some two hundred jokes. As we will see, Freud's interest in jokes at this point in his life was prompted by various anxieties, personal and professional.

I will not attempt here to summarize Freud's major points in his book on jokes. However, I want to comment briefly on an important similarity between dreams and jokes. Even though we know that a dream is not real, we tend to want to share a dream with someone else. At times we do this at some risk because the dream may reveal some things about our unconscious or even conscious thoughts that trouble or disturb the other person. We may even tell the dream in order to disturb the other person: "Guess what? I dreamed last night that I was making love to your sister!" As Genesis 37:5 reports, "Once Joseph had a dream, and when he told it to his brothers, they hated him even more." We find it hard to believe that he was oblivious to the fact that his dream would make them upset with him.

Similarly, in the fifth chapter of his book on jokes, Freud discusses the fact that jokes involve a social process. While one can enjoy comedy by oneself, a joke must be told to someone else. If someone makes up a joke, the joke process is not complete until he or she communicates the joke to someone else. The same is generally true of a joke that we read or that someone else tells us. We seem to have a need to pass it along to somebody else. Thus, jokes get circulated, and because they do, we might say to someone as we begin to tell a particular joke, "Stop me if you've heard this before." Of course, such admonitions are rarely acted upon because the hearer may be wondering if the present joke has a different punch line from the one he or she is already familiar with.

But if jokes are shared, what intrigues Freud is that we usually do not laugh when we tell someone else a joke. Rather, we usually adopt a rather serious tone or look, and if we begin to laugh before we finish telling it, we may well spoil the whole effect, especially if our own laughter gets in the way of our telling the joke. In contrast, the person who hears the joke is expected to laugh, and if this person does so, the joke teller experiences pleasure. If, however, the other person does not laugh or even expresses displeasure, the joke teller feels deflated. The joke, we say, has "fallen flat." The expected pleasurable interchange has not occurred.

On the other hand, if the joke does evoke laughter in the hearer, the hearer has experienced pleasure without having to work for it. In Freud's view, therefore, jokes are an important means by which we save in "psychical expenditure" (182). This is an important feature of his theory of jokes, one that I want to explore throughout the course of this chapter. Thus, the first gift of humor is that it saves in the expenditure of valued but limited psychical resources.

Freud's Economic Theory of Humor

In a little-known article titled "Thoughts for the Times on War and Death" (1915), Freud observes that we humans tend to live beyond our psychic means. This is the price we pay for the fact that we live in civilized societies. Neuroses occur because we live beyond our psychic means, and the very prevalence of neuroses indicates that this borrowing against the future is widespread. In the same way that we become anxious if we are living beyond our economic means, so we become prone to anxiety if we are living beyond our psychic means, and anxiety is at the root of all neuroses (Freud 1926/1989). Thus, humor, viewed very broadly, is much more important in a civilized society than we might think, for it enables us to avoid the expenditure of psychic means that we otherwise would be spending.

In the book's final chapter, "Jokes and the Species of the Comic," Freud suggests that humor saves the expenditure of three forms or expressions of psychic resources. These are *painful emotions, costly inhibitions,* and *difficult thinking.* He suggests a link between humor and an economy in the expenditure of painful emotions, between jokes and an economy in the expenditure of costly inhibitions, and between the comic and an economy in the expenditure of difficult thought or ideas. Thus, the book ends with the following conclusion:

> We are now at the end of our task, having reduced the mechanism of humorous pleasure to a formula analogous to those for comic pleasure and for jokes. The pleasure in jokes has seemed to us to arise from an economy in expenditure upon inhibition, the pleasure in the comic from an economy in expenditure upon ideation . . . and the pleasure in humor from an economy in expenditure upon feeling. In all three modes of working of our mental apparatus the pleasure is derived from an economy. All three are agreed in representing methods of regaining from mental activity a pleasure which has in fact been lost through the development of that activity. For the euphoria which we endeavor to reach by these means is nothing other than the mood of a period of life in which we were accustomed to deal with our psychical work in general with a small expenditure of energy—the mood of our childhood, when we were ignorant of the comic, when we were incapable of jokes and when we had no need of humor to make us happy in our life. (293)

While clear distinctions between humor, jokes, and the comic are somewhat difficult to maintain, humor, for Freud, has much to do with temperament and mood, so we often use the phrase "good humor" to refer to persons who remain cheerful or upbeat even when things are going against them or when they have good reason to be down in the dumps. Jokes are funny anecdotes designed to make another person laugh and often are fabricated to circumvent one or another form of censorship or prohibition. If, as Freud observes, dreams circumvent such censorship, so do jokes, and the types of inhibitions they circumvent are typically sexual and aggressive. The word *comic* has various meanings, but what Freud especially has in mind when he uses the word here is nonsense, which may include words or actions that convey an absurd meaning or no meaning at all, or things of little or no importance, especially trivialities that are

represented as having great importance or significance. Thus, if being in society requires that we engage in rational thought and make a serious effort to think
in a logical and sensible manner, the comic expresses a sort of vacuity of thought
and honors the illogical, the irrational, the stupid, and the dimwitted. A common phrase that captures Freud's sense that we often live beyond our thinking
resources or means is "at one's wit's end," a situation in which one's mental
resources have been exhausted.

Unlike *The Interpretation of Dreams,* which Freud continued to expand and
modify in subsequent editions, his *Jokes and Their Relation to the Unconscious* was
hardly touched in subsequent editions. James Strachey, the editor of his collected works, suggests that Freud was disinclined to revise the book because it lies
somewhat apart from the rest of his writings. In fact, Freud comments in his
Introductory Lectures on Psychoanalysis (1917/1966) that the writing of his book
on jokes temporarily diverted him from his main path (292), and in his *Autobiographical Study* (1925/1952), he made a somewhat depreciatory mention of it,
remarking that he "set a higher value upon [his] contributions to the psychology
of religion, which began in 1907 with the establishment of a remarkable similarity between obsessive acts and religious practices or ritual" (125). But after an
interval of more than twenty years, he returned to the topic of humor with a
short essay simply titled "Humor" (1927/1963).

The Kinder, Gentler Side of the Superego

Like his earlier book on jokes, Freud's essay "Humor" has not received much
attention. It is important, however, because in this essay Freud augments his
economical view of humor with a perspective based on his theory of the mind.
That is, the development of his theory of the structure of the mind, which ante-
dated the writing of his earlier book on jokes, plays a vital role in the essay. This
is his well-known theory that the mind consists of three agencies: the id, the ego,
and the superego.

The title "Humor" alerts the reader that this essay concerns the savings in the
expenditure of painful emotions and does not primarily concern the savings in
the expenditure of costly inhibitions and difficult thinking. On the other hand,
the essay builds on his earlier discussion of jokes as a social process. After a brief
introductory paragraph in which he explains that he considered humor from an
economic point of view in his earlier book, he begins the second paragraph with
the observation that there are two ways in which the social process of humor may
take place: "Either one person may himself adopt a humorous attitude, while a
second person acts as spectator, and derives enjoyment from the attitude of the
first; or there may be two people concerned, one of whom does not take any
active share in producing the humorous effect, but is regarded by the other in a
humorous light" (263). To illustrate the first type, Freud tells the story of a criminal who, as he is being led to the gallows on a Monday morning, quips, "Well,
this is a good beginning to the week."

Freud had related this same joke in his book on jokes, and it was accompanied by another joke about a criminal who was being led to the place of execution and asked for a scarf for his bare throat so as not to catch cold. Freud observes that this was "an otherwise laudable precaution but one which, in view of what lay in store so shortly for the neck, was remarkably superfluous and unimportant" (285). On the other hand, there is something admirable about "the man's tenacious hold upon his customary self and his disregard of what might overthrow that self and drive it to despair" (285). Freud adds, "This kind of grandeur of humor appears unmistakably in cases in which our admiration is not inhibited by the circumstances of the humorous person" (285), that is, our disapproval of the man for his criminal acts.

Returning to the criminal who comments on the fact that his execution will occur at the beginning of the week, Freud suggests that this criminal gains a certain personal satisfaction from creating this bit of humor, but he also spares the eyewitnesses to his execution the expenditure of their own painful emotions. Hearing the criminal make light of his predicament, the other person's expectations are nullified. The other person anticipates "that the victim will show signs of some affect; he will get angry, complain, manifest pain, fear, horror, possibly even despair. The person who is watching or listening is prepared to follow his lead, and to call up the same emotions. But his anticipations are deceived; the other man does not display any affect—he makes a joke. It is from the saving in expenditure in feeling that the hearer derives the humorous satisfaction" (264).

Thus, as in his earlier book, Freud is interested here in joking as a social process. However, his subsequent discussion in the essay focuses on the person who, in making the joke, adopts a humorous attitude with respect to his own situation. How does the criminal in this case arrive at this mental attitude? What is the *internal* dynamic process that underlies the "humorous attitude" that he is able to adopt? This question can be answered only by having recourse to Freud's theory of the mind. To answer it, however, he suggests that we first need to identify the fundamental characteristics of humor. One is that it is *liberating*, in that it expresses "the ego's victorious assertion of its own invulnerability," its refusal "to be hurt by the arrows of reality or to be compelled to suffer," and its insistence that "it is impervious to wounds dealt by the outside world, in fact, that these are merely occasions for affording it pleasure" (265). There are, however, a couple of ways in which one might assert that one is invulnerable to the wounds dealt by the outside world. One of these is *resignation*, which might take the following form: "It doesn't worry me. What does it matter, after all, if a fellow like me is hanged? The world won't come to an end." This way of putting it is an assertion of the ego's invulnerability, but being resigned, it is not humorous but matter-of-fact. *Humor*, because it is rebellious, is the second way in which one might assert one's invulnerability. Being rebellious, it signifies the triumph of the ego, even as the resigned attitude did, but it also expresses the victory of the pleasure principle, which opposes the reality principle in Freud's thought. That is, the *resigned* response is an acceptance of the reality of the situation, that the criminal will not get out of it alive. The *humorous* response does not deny this reality—it is not, after all, based on false illusions and is certainly not delusional. The criminal knows that his situation is quite hopeless. But he is determined not to let his desperate situation get the better of him and refuses, in a sense, to allow the reality principle to have the last or final word. Invoking the pleasure principle, the criminal says, in effect, "You can kill me, but you can't hurt me." If this sounds nonsensical, it is because one is viewing the situation from the perspective of the reality principle only.

Because it asserts the triumph of the pleasure principle over the reality principle, such humor appears to approximate the regressive processes that are typically found in psychopathology. But it differs from psychopathology, or even, for that matter, from alcoholic intoxication, because it does not take leave of the real world. Instead, it simply upholds the pleasure principle and asserts its victory over the reality principle.

How do we account, psychodynamically, for this refusal to be hurt by the arrows of reality? Rather surprisingly, Freud suggests that the answer lies with the superego, which, in much of his thought, involves the internalization of parental voices, sociocultural laws and maxims, and so forth. It is the locus of conscience and conscientiousness. At this point in the essay, he makes a brief allusion to his chapter "Jokes and the Species of the Comic" in his book on jokes in which he explored the relationship between the child and the comic. While children as children do not normally strike us as comic, they *do* have a comic effect on us when they conduct themselves not as children but as serious and thoughtful adults. When we adults watch a child who is engaged in serious thought, with brow furrowed, we may chuckle to ourselves because we are aware of the incongruity between the expenditure of thought and the relative insignificance, in the larger scheme of things, of what is being thought about. Or consider this example derived from Freud's book on jokes: A brother and sister are performing a drama they have composed before an audience of uncles and aunts. The scene is a hut by the seashore. In the first act, the two author-actors, a poor fisherman and his honest wife, are complaining about their hard times and small earnings. So the husband decides to cross the wide seas in his boat to seek his fortune elsewhere, and after tender farewells between the two of them, the curtain falls.

The second act takes place a few years later. The fisherman has returned a wealthy man with a big bag of money, and he tells his wife, who has awaited his arrival outside the hut, what good fortune he has encountered in foreign lands. His wife interrupts him proudly, "I too have not been idle," and she opens the door of the hut and points to twelve large dolls lying asleep on the floor. Freud reports that at this point in the drama, the actors are interrupted by a storm of laughter from the audience that they are unable to understand. They stare disconcertedly at their fond relatives, who have behaved properly up to this point and have listened with eager anticipation. The laughter of the adults "is explained on the supposition that the audience assumed that the young authors still knew nothing of the conditions governing the origins of young children and were therefore able to believe that a wife could boast of the offspring born during her husband's long absence and that a husband could rejoice with her over them" (228).

A joke that plays on a similar naivete is this one from a book on Norwegian humor: "Lena and Ole stood up for the wedding of Lars and Helga. Shortly after the wedding, the newlyweds moved away. Ole and Lena didn't see their friends for six years, and at the reunion at their home in Wisconsin, Lars and Helga showed off their five children. Helga was so proud, and as she confided to Lena: 'Yah, Lena, it sure vas lucky I got married six years ago because as it turned out, I vas chock full of babies'" (Stangland 1979).

There are, of course, situations in which children laugh at the serious behavior of adults. In the instance Freud reports, however, it was the adults who laughed at the serious efforts of the children. They were not mocking the children or merely having fun at the children's expense. Instead, their laughter derived from their recognition of their own naivete as children, and in Freud's view, this very recognition was the source of their pleasure. In a word, they reconnected with the child in themselves. In his essay on humor, however, Freud takes this point a step further and relates it to the role of the humorist in adult society. The humorist adopts the attitude of the adult who recognizes and smiles "at the triviality of the interests and sufferings which seem to the child so big" (266). Thus, the humorist assumes the role of the adult and assures the audience that their anxieties are unfounded. If, however, the humorist is able to address the anxieties and worries of other members of the society, this is because of an awareness of similar anxieties of one's own. In other words, the original situation in humor is one in which a person "adopts a humorous attitude towards himself in order to ward off possible suffering" (266). In effect, this person is assuming two positions at once, namely, treating himself like a child and at the same time playing the part of the superior adult in relation to the child.

If this is what is going on, then, in Freud's view, the distinction between the ego and the superego provides an explanation for it: "Generally, the superego inherits the parental function; it often holds the ego in strict subordination, and still actually treats it as the parents (or the father) treated the child in his early years" (266). Thus, under many conditions, the superego is the part of our minds that holds us to strict rules of behavior and, in serving as our conscience, often demands more from us than our parents did. But, in humor, a very different side of the superego manifests itself. Instead of holding the ego in strict subordination, the superego, in effect, says to the ego that its anxieties are ill-founded: "Look there! This is all that this seemingly dangerous world amounts to. Child's play—the very thing to jest about!" (268).

Freud acknowledges that this is a side of the superego to which psychoanalysis has not paid much attention, and therefore, he writes, "If it is really the superego that, in humor, speaks such kindly words of comfort to the intimidated ego, this teaches us that we have still very much to learn about the nature of that energy" (268).[1] Nonetheless, one thing seems clear, namely, that "if the superego does try to comfort the ego by humor and to protect it from suffering, this does not conflict with its derivation from the parental function" (269).

This more genial side of the superego has important implications for religion. If, in Freud's understanding, the superego and religion are mutually supportive, as both are concerned with morality, his essay on humor invites the conclusion that religion's social role need not be limited to its endorsement and support of conscience. If it is true that the superego has a more genial side, one that assures the ego that this seemingly dangerous world is "child's play, the very thing to jest about," there is no reason in principle that religion could not endorse and support this side of the superego as well. Freud admits that "we know that the superego is a stern master"; therefore, "it may be said that it accords ill with its character that it should wink at affording the ego a little gratification." Nevertheless, "in bringing about the humorous attitude, the superego is in fact repudiating reality and serving an illusion," which has "a peculiarly liberating and elevating effect" (268). No doubt, the criminal who is being led to the gallows to pay for his crimes with his life has felt the condemnation of his superego during the time he has been in prison. But now, the morning he is being led to the gallows, the superego comes to his aid in the form of a humorous attitude toward the event that is about to occur. He will pay for his crimes, but he will be spared the expenditure of painful emotions and the costly inhibitions that the superego normally exacts.

One suspects that the superego can show this genial side of itself because it knows that its stern side has, in reality, prevailed. A humorous attitude will not produce a stay of execution. So the superego can allow the ego a little leeway. As Freud points out, humor is rebellious, but it is not revolutionary; that is, it reflects the ego's acceptance of the fact that the superego is more powerful than itself, that the superego cannot be demolished. In this sense, the humorous attitude is conservative as it supports the superego and its moralities, and this is why the superego can afford to endorse the humorous attitude. Even so, we should not minimize the fact that the superego, so often associated with religion, does allow the ego the leeway that humor reflects, while it would be not nearly so tolerant of a direct assault on its rules and prerogatives. A teacher may punish a student for insulting remarks but tolerate and even secretly enjoy a witty comment that is no less rebellious in spirit.

Finally, Freud mentions that "it is not everyone who is capable of the humorous attitude: it is a rare and precious gift, and there are many people who have not even the capacity for deriving pleasure from humor when it is presented to them by others" (268–69). In suggesting that humor is a gift, he returns, at the very end of his essay, to the economic theory of humor with which his book on humor ended and his essay on humor began. As he contended in the book, humor saves in the expenditure of painful emotions, costly inhibitions, and difficult thinking. In this sense, psychodynamically speaking, humor is like money in the bank. On the other hand, it is not a mere commodity that is subject to strict economic laws of exchange, of supply and demand. To be sure, it has its producers and its consumers, but it belongs not to the world of business and bargaining but to the world of gift giving as a way of showing friendship, affection, and support. Perhaps this is why the inability or refusal to derive pleasure from the humor produced by others has a deflationary effect on its producers. The comedian who complains that his audience is tough to please is a case in point.

In the world of humor, the inability or refusal to be amused is akin to the refusal of a gift, and it is experienced by the one who proffers the gift as a means to maintain power, control, and superiority. This may explain, in part, why the most famous statement of nonamusement was that of a queen: "We are not amused" is the side of the superego that exercises power and control over the rebellious ego, not the side of the superego that recognizes the ego's vulnerability and gives it license to joke about its largely hapless situation. Thus, a major contrast may be drawn between the savings in expenditure of psychic resources that humor affords and the psychic miserliness of those who will not derive pleasure from humor when it is presented to them by others. They are like the folks that Levertov's poem "What the Figtree Said" describes as withholding the gift of imagination.

Freud's Interest in Beggar Jokes

This consideration of humor as a form of gift giving leads us back to Freud's book on jokes and, specifically, to a type of joke that actually involves gift giving. Discussion of these jokes will enable us to make more concrete his economical theory of humor as a savings in the expenditure of limited psychic resources. Two types of jokes seem to loom especially large in his book. These are jokes about the Jewish beggar and jokes about the Jewish marriage broker. I will focus here on the Jewish beggar jokes because they are the clearest illustration of his economic theory of jokes.

We may look at these jokes in one of two ways. The first is to take much the same approach that Freud himself takes with the joke about the criminal who is about to be hanged. This involves simply asking how the primary character in the joke saves an expenditure, in this case, of painful emotions. As we have seen, however, Freud is also interested in the spectators and in the way that the criminal's quip saves *them* the expenditure of painful emotions. Since jokes involve a social process, this suggests to him that we should focus our attention on the joke's *listeners* and ask how the joke affords the listener a savings in expenditure of his or her psychic resources. Thus, a second way to approach the issue is to ask why Freud himself turned to these types of jokes at this point in his life. How did they save *him* the expenditure of painful emotions, costly inhibitions, and even difficult (i.e., rational and logical) thinking?

In *The Jokes of Sigmund Freud: A Study in Humor and Jewish Identity* (1984), Elliott Oring takes this second approach. He suggests that Freud's project of collecting Jewish humor was psychologically motivated. In Oring's view, Freud was experiencing a great deal of professional struggle at the time, some of which was related to the fact that, because he was Jewish, his medical career was virtually at a standstill. Promotions that would have been automatic had he not been Jewish were being denied him. Thus, Oring focuses on the person who responds to a joke or set of jokes and, in effect, asks the question, "What does this person get out of these jokes?" As mentioned, the general answer that Freud himself gives to this question is that he or she gains a savings in the expenditure of painful emotions, costly inhibitions, and/or difficult thinking. But this is only a general answer to the question. What these emotions, inhibitions, or thought processes may be will depend on the individual and the challenges or difficulties one is facing at this time in one's life.

In Oring's view, Jewish beggar jokes were included among the jokes Freud was collecting at this time because this was, in fact, his own painful situation. He had borrowed significant amounts of money to support his medical education, and this borrowing created an indebtedness that he resented as it limited his independence of thought and action. Moreover, he was the eldest sibling and only son in the family, and his father was a notoriously poor provider for the family. Freud would therefore give some of the money he borrowed to his family, thus adding significantly to his own indebtedness while also assuming the role of benefactor to his family. Another reason for borrowing large sums of money was so that he could arrange to visit with his fiancée. While his benefactors, wealthy Jewish men, assured him that these were gifts and that they did not expect to be repaid, Freud himself viewed them as loans. Oring observes, however, that in at least two instances, his benefactors died before he had opportunity to repay the loans in full.

Oring cites a letter that Freud wrote to his fiancée, Marthe Bernays, in which he first refers to his shame in having to rely on others for financial assistance and then resolves to accept his indebtedness without feeling a sense of personal obligation. The benefactor in this case was his old Hebrew teacher, Samuel Hammerschlag, who had invited Freud to his home and, after describing his own situation of poverty in his youth, offered him fifty florins with no strings attached. Freud wrote Bernays:

> I intend to compensate for it by being charitable myself when I can afford it. It is not the first time the old man has helped me in this way; during my university years he often, unasked, helped me out of a difficult situation. At first I felt very ashamed, but later, when I saw that [Josef] Breuer and he agreed in this respect, I accepted the idea of being indebted to good men and those of our faith without the feeling of personal obligation. (Oring 1984, 16)

He goes on to tell Bernays that he made it clear to Hammerschlag that he would spend the money on his family. Hammerschlag, however, vigorously opposed this idea, indicating that Freud was working very hard and could not at the moment afford to help others. But Freud did make it clear to Hammerschlag that he would have to spend at least half of the money in this way. Oring notes that when Freud, years later, was in more comfortable circumstances himself, he liberally provided his children with money and generously contributed to the support of needy friends and acquaintances, thus remaining true to his intention to "compensate for it by being charitable myself when I can afford it."

However, at the time he needed to rely on others for support, his intention to be charitable toward others when he was in a position to do so and the fact that he gave half of the loan to his family were insufficient to enable him to put his sense of shame to rest. In fact, to the extent that the shame we feel for our family is greater than the shame we feel for ourselves, his announced intention to give his family much of the proceeds added to his shamefulness. This was almost certainly a sense of shame that was focused on his father, whose own inadequacies as a provider were a major reason Freud needed to borrow money in the first place.

How he resolved to deal with the painful emotions of shame evoked by such situations as the meeting with Hammerschlag is indicated in the sentence, "I accepted the idea of being indebted to good men and those of our faith without the feeling of personal obligation" (16). As Oring points out, the beggar jokes that Freud includes in his book on jokes express a similar resolve, and it is the fact that the beggar does not feel any personal obligation to his benefactor that accounts for the humor. We normally feel that a person who is indebted to another would at least feel he had some personal obligation, if not to repay the lender (after all, the lender considered it a gift), then at least to spend the funds prudently. Or, if not that, to express his undying gratitude to the person who helped him in a time of distress and need. But this is precisely what the beggar in at least two of the beggar jokes in Freud's book does not express. Here is one of the beggar jokes:

> A *Schnorrer* [Jewish beggar] approached a wealthy baron with a request for the grant of some assistance for his journey to Ostend. The doctors, he said, had recommended him sea-bathing to restore his health. "Very well," said the rich man, "I'll give you something towards it. But must you go precisely to Ostend, which is the most expensive of all sea-bathing resorts?"—"Herr Baron," was the reproachful reply, "I consider nothing too expensive for my health." (Freud 1905/1960, 63–64)

Freud comments, "This is no doubt a correct point of view," that is, that one should spare no expense where one's health is concerned. It is not, however, "correct for a petitioner. The answer is given from the point of view of a rich man. The *Schnorrer* behaves as though it was his own money that he was to sacrifice for his health, as though the money and the health were the concern of the same person" (64). Thus, instead of expressing feelings of personal obligation, the beggar shamelessly acts as though he is entitled to the money, that in a certain sense, it was his money all along to spend however he saw fit. Moreover, if the funds were a gift, what right does the benefactor have to dictate how the beggar spends them?

Here is another beggar joke that expresses a similar absence of the feeling of personal obligation and a sense, instead, of entitlement:

> An impoverished individual borrowed 25 florins from a prosperous individual with many asseverations of his necessitous circumstances. The very same day his benefactor met him again in a restaurant with a plate of salmon mayonnaise in front of him. The benefactor reproached him: "What? You borrow money from me and then order yourself salmon mayonnaise? Is *that* what you've used my money for?" "I don't understand you," replied the object of attack, "if I haven't any money I *can't* eat salmon mayonnaise, and if I have some money I *mustn't* eat salmon mayonnaise. Well, then, when *am* I to eat salmon mayonnaise?" (56).

In commenting on this joke, Freud notes that the beggar's reply has the form of a logical argument but that it is, in fact, illogical: "The man defends himself for having spent the money lent to him on a delicacy and asks, with an appearance of reason, *when* he is to eat salmon. But that is not the correct answer. His benefactor is not reproaching him with treating himself to salmon precisely on the day on which he borrowed the money; he is reminding him that in his circumstances he has no right to think of such delicacies *at all*" (57). Thus, the beggar "disregards this only possible meaning of the reproach, and answers another question as though he had misunderstood the reproach" (57).

Thus, here again, the beggar refuses to act as one who has any personal obligation to his benefactor. He fails to observe the expectation that he would spend the money given to him in a prudent, sensible manner, and he responds to his benefactor's reproach with an air of indignation and affront. If the joke reflects a refusal to feel the painful emotion of indebtedness and the shame that accompanies it, it carries off this refusal by means of the appearance of logic and therefore reflects another form of psychic savings, that of difficult or rational thinking. The response appears logical, but is, in fact, quite specious. It is an exercise in "faulty reasoning" (64; also 253).

Later, Freud returns to this joke and comments on the moral issue that the beggar chooses to ignore (130). There is, he suggests, a sort of epicureanism implied in the joke. The beggar rejects the appeal to virtuous renunciation and instead says that if he doesn't eat salmon mayonnaise when he has some money, he may never get to eat it. Viewed as a rejection of the idea of the fruitfulness of virtuous renunciation now so that a higher goal might be attained later, the joke is also a savings in costly inhibition, the kind of inhibition to which Freud, a struggling young doctor, would have been expected to subscribe.

This joke, therefore, reflects a saving in the expenditure of all three types of psychic resources that Freud identifies in the concluding pages of his book on jokes: of painful emotions (in this case, shame for accepting a handout and feelings of gratitude toward one's benefactor), of difficult thinking (the obligation to engage in genuine rational discourse with another person), and of costly inhibition (the deferring of one's gratification for a later, more obviously moral purpose). In a sense, then, the salmon mayonnaise joke is illustrative of Freud's view that jokes work against the power of civilized society to create neurotic personalities. The beggar may not be a pleasant individual to be around and to have dealings with, but he seems remarkably free of neuroses. We might say that he is behaving like a child, for as Freud writes in the concluding paragraph of his book on jokes,

> all three [economies] are agreed in representing methods of regaining from mental activity a pleasure which has in fact been lost through the development of that activity. For the euphoria which we endeavor to reach by these means is nothing other than the mood of a period of life in which we were accustomed to deal with our psychical work in general with a small expenditure of energy—the mood of our childhood, when we were ignorant of the comic, when we were incapable of jokes and when we had no need of humor to make us feel happy in our life. (Freud 1905/1960, 293)

This beggar joke, therefore, recalls a period in our lives when we were not spending our psychic resources like drunken sailors. What the beggar lacks in economic prudence he more than regains in the conservation of psychic energy. In this sense, he is the richer of the two men in the story. The benefactor expends his psychic resources when he reproaches the beggar for misspending the money he has given him and when he is infuriated (we assume) by the beggar's cavalier response. Also, since the beggar appears to have the last word, the benefactor inhibits any violent action he might wish to take against the beggar. Instead of acting impulsively, he thinks better of it and exercises the good judgment that is expected of a man of his status and breeding. Thus, here again, the joke illustrates the expenditure of painful emotions, costly inhibitions, and difficult thinking.

Freud relates another beggar joke, however, in which the situation is reversed, and it is the benefactor who spares himself some painful emotions. This is his story of the baron who, deeply moved by a beggar's tale of woe, rings for his servants. When they appear, he says to them, "Throw him out! He's breaking my heart!" (135). Here, the baron saves himself the painful emotions of sympathy and pity, but we also sense that a savings in costly inhibition is involved, as he derives some satisfaction from being able to act on the impulse that he has certainly felt on other occasions when similarly importuned to tell the beggar to go to hell. By employing illogic or irrational thinking, however, he achieves this outcome while seeming to have great pity and sympathy for the man.

Another story in the same vein is told by Theodor Reik, an early associate of Freud's, in his book *Jewish Wit* (1962). The beggar complains to a rich man that he has not eaten for three days, to which the millionaire responds, "Sometimes one has to force oneself" (76). Here again the benefactor spares himself the pain of empathizing with the beggar's plight by "misunderstanding" the reason the beggar hasn't eaten.

Freud relates another joke that plays more directly on the issue that he himself commented on in his letter to Bernays, that of resolving not to feel a personal obligation to his benefactors. This time, however, the shoe is on the other foot, for there was also the belief in the Jewish community of Freud's day that the one whom the beggar importunes is in the beggar's debt because the beggar gives his benefactor the opportunity to be charitable toward someone who is less fortunate.

> A *Schnorrer* on his way up a rich man's staircase met a fellow member of his profession, who advised him to go no further. "Don't go up today," he said, "the Baron is in a bad mood today; he's giving nobody more than one florin"—"I'll go up all the same," said the first *Schnorrer*. "Why should I give him a florin? Does he give *me* anything?" (Freud 1905/1960, 135)

Freud considers this an especially ingenious joke because it "employs the technique of absurdity, since it makes the *Schnorrer* assert that the Baron gives him nothing at the very moment at which he is preparing to beg him for a gift. But the absurdity is only apparent. It is almost true that the rich man gives him nothing, since he [the rich man] is obliged by the Law to give him alms and should, strictly speaking, be grateful to him [the beggar] for giving him an opportunity for beneficence" (135). But the baron, who is in a bad temper, refuses to feel this way. To be sure, he gives the beggar a florin, but without feeling any sense of gratitude to the beggar for enabling him to act charitably toward one who is less fortunate.

Reik discusses this joke under the general heading "The Sacred Duty of Charity." He writes:

> It has often been said that the Jewish giver does not bestow benefits on the poor in giving him money, and his actions do not deserve the name of goodness or kindness. He simply fulfills his religious duty, and the beneficiary need not, in the strict sense of the word, be grateful to him. On the contrary, the donor owes some gratitude to the receiver because the beneficiary gave him an opportunity to high religious merit. This is the meaning of the countless anecdotes of the Schnorrers, of their grasping and insolence and of their claims on the donor of alms. These Schnorrers sometimes treat their benefactors as if the roles were reversed, as if they were doing them a favor in accepting money. There is an old anecdote of the beggar who is advised not to visit the rich man one day because he was in a bad mood. The beggar, full of indignation, says: "What do you mean, should I make him a present of the money? Does he give me anything?" (Reik 1962, 75)

Thus, if the rich man treats the beggar in a niggardly way, it is as if the beggar were being compelled to give the rich man money as this is money that the beggar had coming to him. There may be another, subtler implication here that if the beggar does not go up to claim his measly florin, he, in effect, is donating his florin to the rich man, and why in heaven's name should he do that? After all, it makes no sense that a poor man would make a donation to a rich man.

Finally, Freud relates a joke that has direct bearing on his own habit of giving to his family a portion of the money he received from a benefactor.

> A *Schnorrer*, who was allowed as a guest into the same house every Sunday, appeared one day in the company of an unknown young man who gave signs of being about to sit down to table. "Who is this?" asked the householder. "He's been my son-in-law," was the reply, "since last week. I've promised him his board for the first year." (Freud 1905/1960, 134)

Here, the beggar acts as though it is his prerogative to play the benefactor with the householder's resources. This story takes us back to Freud's letter to his fiancée in which he reports that his old Hebrew teacher objected to his intention of spending the money on his family. The older man's objections had some effect, but in the end, Freud reserved the "right" to spend the money as he saw fit despite the fact that it was not his money: "I did make it clear to him that I must spend at least half the money in this way" (Oring 1984, 16). We might ask what right Freud has to determine how the money will be spent, but what his response to Hammerschlag and the joke have in common is that the expenditure of costly inhibitions will be avoided. Freud will stand up to the older man even at the risk of seeming disrespectful and ungracious. As Oring points out, "the gifts and loans that he received from his benefactors generated in Freud feelings of indebtedness, dependence, and resentment" (17–18). At the same time, Freud knew that such feelings would inhibit his ability to pursue his own independent ways of thinking. This, after all, was also the time when he was beginning to focus on the role of sexual repression in the formation of psychopathologies, a pursuit that his friend and benefactor Josef Breuer could not accept or endorse. This may help to explain why Freud considered jokes to be especially relevant to the saving of the expenditure of costly inhibitions. Certainly the beggar jokes that appear in his book are more illustrative of an attitude of uninhibitedness than of liberation from painful emotions, as it is the beggar's disregard of the usual proprieties expected of a beggar—gratitude, deference, etc.—that makes these jokes amusing.[2]

Humor and Saving the Expenditure of Painful Emotions

On the other hand, Freud thinks of humor, broadly understood, as primarily a savings in the expenditure of painful emotions. In the concluding section of the last chapter of his book on jokes, he focuses on the ways in which humor spares us "distressing affects" or emotions, and it is here that he cites the "gallows humor" already mentioned. Also, noting that an "economy of pity is one of the most frequent sources of humorous pleasure," he cites several of Mark Twain's stories about his family that "work with this mechanism." For instance, in an account of his brother's life, Twain tells us how his brother

> was at one time employed on a great road-making enterprise. The pre-mature explosion of a mine blew him up into the air and he came down again far away from the place where he had been working. We are bound to have feelings of sympathy for the victim of the accident and would like to ask whether he was injured by it. But when the story goes on to say that his brother had a half-day's wages deducted for being "absent from his place of employment" we are entirely distracted from our pity and become almost as hard-hearted as the contractor and almost as indiffer-ent to possible damage to the brother's health. (286)

In a world of limited psychic resources, we welcome this distraction from our pity, and laughter replaces our expressions of concern—"Was your brother all right? Did he suffer irreparable damage? Did he need to be hospitalized?"

In another story that Twain tells about his brother, it is not the listener but the brother himself who fails to exhibit the expected emotion. In this case, Twain describes how his brother

> constructed a subterranean dwelling, into which he brought a bed, a table and a lamp and which he roofed over with a large piece of sailcloth with a hole in the middle. At night, however, after the hut was finished, a cow that was being driven home fell through the opening of the roof on to the table and put out the lamp. His brother patiently helped to get the beast out and put the establishment to rights again. Next night the same interruption was repeated and his brother behaved as before. And so it was every following night. Repetition makes the story comic, but Mark Twain ends it by report-ing that on the forty-sixth night, when the cow fell through again, his brother finally remarked: "The thing's beginning to get monotonous." (287)

Freud comments: "At this our humorous pleasure cannot be kept back, for what we had long expected to hear was that this obstinate set of misfortunes would make his brother *angry*. And indeed the small contributions of humor that we produce ourselves are as a rule made at the cost of anger—instead of getting angry" (267). Thus, while the repetition of the same scene every night has a comedic element, the brother's response makes the story more deeply humorous. What humor achieves is a kind of displacement, "by means of which the release of affect that is already in preparation is disappointed and the cathexis diverted on to something else, often on to something of secondary importance" (289).

Such a diversion is reflected in the story of the man who is about to be exe-cuted when he takes note of the fact that it happens to be Monday, the first day of the week, or in the story of the man who is being led to his execution on a frigid day without a scarf. The painful affect is avoided by focusing on some feature of the situation that should not, under ordinary circumstances, attract attention at all. The incongruity of making something of secondary importance into something of primary importance—Monday, scarf—creates the humorous effect. Yet as Freud points out in his essay on humor, one does not thereby take leave of reality (e.g., through some form of delusion or ecstasy) or anesthetize oneself from reality (e.g., through alcoholic intoxication). Rather, one pays attention to a feature of the real situation that seems inconsequential or unimportant. This is what gives humor an air of absurdity. But such apparent absurdity is, in fact, meaningful if it enables one to cope with a situation in which one might otherwise lash out in a hapless gesture of revenge, succumb to a helpless sense of fear, or yield to a mood of hopeless despair. The title of a book by Paul Watzlawick, *The Situation Is Hopeless, but Not Serious* (1983), expresses the idea that through the gift of a humorous attitude, one may experience a sort of triumph in what are clearly dire circumstances. The following poem by Billy Collins (1988, 56) suggests that there are days when the situation is so hopeless that there isn't much point in taking anything that happens that day seriously:

HOPELESS BUT NOT SERIOUS

These days every morning begins like a joke
you think you have heard before,
but there is no one telling it whom you can stop.

One day it's about a cow who walks into a bar,
then about a man with a big nose on his honeymoon,
then about a kangaroo who walks into a bar.
Each one takes up an entire day.

The sun looks like a prank Nathanael West
is pulling on the world; on the drive to work
cars are swinging comically from lane to lane.
The houses and lawns belong in cartoons.

The hours collapse into one another's arms.
The stories arc over noon and descend
like slow ferris wheels into the haze of evening.
You wish you could stop listening and get serious.

Trouble is you cannot remember the punch line
which never arrives until very late at night,
just as you are reaching over for the bedside lamp,
just before you begin laughing in the dark.

Jokes Relating to Death Anxiety

I have focused in this chapter on Freud's interest in beggar jokes to illustrate his idea that humor offers a savings in the expenditure of psychic resources. As Oring has shown, it would be possible to make a similar case concerning Freud's use of various other joke types in his book, including jokes about marriage brokers, the Jewish outsider, traveling to other European countries, and the rabbi who claims to have mystical powers. But another way to make use of Freud's theory is to shift the focus from the jokes that particularly interested him to other types of jokes that confirm his general theory that humor saves the expenditure of psychic resources in three important ways, namely, the expenditure of painful emotions, costly inhibitions, and difficult thinking. One type of joke that he does not consider are jokes about death.

A research study by James Thorson and F. C. Powell (1993) demonstrates that humor may have a slight effect on death anxiety. Their study, however, involved the use of questionnaires and did not include exposure to humor relating to death. Whether this would have made any difference in the results, producing, for example, a more robust association between humor and reduction of death anxiety, is of course impossible to say. Nonetheless, the very fact that there are a great many jokes relating to the threat of death is prima facie evidence that humor is one of the ways in which we try to shield ourselves from painful emotions, costly inhibitions, and difficult thinking about death.

There are at least five types of humor relating to death anxiety. There are jokes in which a doctor informs a patient or a family member of the patient that he or she has only a short time to live; jokes involving a deathbed scene; jokes involving funerals and wakes; jokes relating to the afterlife; and jokes focusing on what the deceased loved ones, especially the spouse, intend to do after the death has occurred. These five types cover most if not all of the bases as far as death anxiety is concerned. Many examples of each type could be presented here, but the following selection will serve to illustrate the type and also support the idea that one of the ways in which we may neutralize the threat of death is to resort to humor. We are all familiar with Dylan Thomas's recommendation that we "rage" against death, against the "dying of the light," but the very fact that jokes about death are so abundant suggests that humor is another important way in which we challenge the ability of death to upset and demoralize us, treating it, as Freud suggests in his article on humor, as mere "child's play."

Jokes about Impending Death. Jokes in this category usually involve doctors reporting to their patients that they are in much worse condition than they thought or imagined, and that death is quite imminent. Here's a variation on the popular formula of "good news/bad news" jokes:

> "Yeah, Doc, what's the news?" answered Fred when his doctor called with his test results. "I have some bad news and some really bad news," admitted the doctor. "The bad news is that you only have twenty-four hours to

live." "Oh my God," gasped Fred, sinking to his knees. "What could be worse news than that?" "I couldn't get hold of you yesterday."

Here's another "you don't have much time to live" or "you are already living on borrowed time" joke:

After his annual physical examination, an elderly patient asked his doctor, "Tell me, how long am I going to live?" "Don't worry," his doctor replied, "You'll probably live to be eighty." "But, Doctor, I *am* eighty!" The doctor cheerfully replied, "See, what did I tell you?"

A variation on this "you don't have much time to live" joke involves a doctor informing his patient that *if* he doesn't change his ways, he will almost certainly die in a matter of weeks or months:

Upon completing his examination of the patient, the doctor told him to get dressed. "I'm afraid your condition is fairly poor." The doctor sighed. "The best thing for you to do would be to give up liquor, stop smoking, give up all that rich food you've been eating at fancy restaurants, and stop seeing all those young women who keep you out until all hours." The patient thought for a moment. "What's the next best thing?"

Here's a joke in which the patient learns indirectly that he is terminally ill. It too has a good news/bad news format:

An artist asked the gallery owner if there had been any interest in his paintings that were on display. "I have some good news and bad news," the owner replied. "The good news is that a gentleman inquired about your work and wondered if it would appreciate in value after your death. When I told him it would, he bought all fifteen of your paintings." "That's wonderful," the artist exclaimed. "What's the bad news?" "The gentleman was your doctor."

Here's another one:

Ole and Lars were crazy about baseball. They even speculated on the possibility of baseball being played in heaven. So they made an agreement. Whoever went first would find a way to tell the other back on earth whether or not baseball was played in heaven. Lars was the first to go, and one day as Ole was walking down the street, he felt a slight tap on his shoulder. "Is dat you, Lars?" asked Ole. "Yah, it's me, Ole. I've got some good news and some bad news." "Vell," said Ole, "let's have da good news first." "Da good news, Ole," said Lars, "is dat yes, dere is baseball in heaven." "OK," responded Ole. "Now what is da bad news?" "You're scheduled to pitch next Tuesday."

If one of the preceding jokes involves the patient's own need to change his lifestyle if he wants to prolong his life, in the following joke, his survival depends on his wife's cooperation:

Ole hadn't been feeling well and hated to go to a doctor. Lena finally talked him into getting a physical by agreeing to get one herself. After they both had been checked over, the doctor called Lena aside and said, "I'm afraid Ole has a very serious illness. In fact, it might be fatal. There are two things that might save his life. First, you will have to fix him three home-cooked meals a day for the rest of his life. And second, you must make love to him every day without fail. Lena pondered a bit and announced, "I'll break the news to Ole." So she stepped across the physician's waiting room where Ole was sitting, waiting for the diagnosis. "Ole," said Lena, "guess what? You're gonna die."

Failing to assist her husband in staying alive is one thing. Murdering him is quite another. Here is one example:

The Norwegian lady discovered that her husband, Bjarne, was fooling around. She called the undertaker, saying, "I vant you to come and pick up my husband's body." Inquired the undertaker, "When did he die?" She answered, "He starts tomorrow."

Here's another joke in the same vein:

Father O'Grady was saying his good-byes to his parishioners after Sunday morning services as he always did when Mary Clancy came up to him in tears. "What's bothering you, dear?" inquired Father O'Grady. "Oh, Father, I've got terrible news," replied Mary. "What is it, my child?" asked the priest. "Well, my husband, Mr. Clancy, passed away last night, Father." "Oh, Mary," said the priest, "that's terrible. Tell me, did he have any last requests?" "Well, yes, he did, Father," replied Mary. "What did he ask?" She replied, "He said, 'Please, Mary, put down the gun . . .'"

Finally, here is a joke in which the one who is supposed to die has no plans or intentions of doing so:

One year a Norwegian gave his mother-in-law a cemetery plot for her birthday. The next year he gave her nothing. When his wife asked him why not, the Norwegian answered, "Vell, she didn't use da present I bought her last year."

A common theme in these jokes is that one is near death, but there are other subthemes as well, such as the fact that informing the person who is dying is no easy task, and this leads the informer to employ a great deal of indirect and mis-leading communication; the fact that one might be able to forestall death if one is prepared to make some difficult life changes, changes that the victim thinks may result in a life that is tantamount to death itself; and suspicions that one's loved ones are not as invested in keeping one alive as they should be. Thus, these jokes address some rather common anxieties about death, especially anxieties relating to the timing and circumstances of death, and they concern both the dying persons' anxieties and those of others—doctors, loved ones, etc.—who must either inform the dying that their death is imminent or bear the burden of caring for the dying until death comes to claim them.

Deathbed Scenes. There are many jokes involving the conversations that occur around the bedside of a dying man or woman. Here's one in which the dying man is hedging his bets:

A priest was preparing a man for his long day's journey into night. Whis-pering firmly, the priest said, "Denounce the devil. Let him know how lit-tle you think of his evil!" The dying man said nothing. The priest repeat-ed his order. Still the dying man said nothing. The priest asked, "Why do you refuse to denounce the devil and his evil?" The dying man said, "Until I know where I'm heading, I don't think I should mix in."

In the following joke, the dying man thinks the two men who have come to bid him farewell have less than honorable motives:

Tom O'Leary was in his bed dying, slipping in and out of consciousness. His wife came into the room with his doctor and the parish priest. "Mrs. O'Leary, you realize that the bill for my services is one thousand dollars," the doctor said. "Fine," said the woman. "I'll see to it that it's paid from the insurance." "And don't forget, Mary, the funeral and casket will cost one thousand dollars," the priest said. "Don't worry, Father, I'll see to it that you're paid as well." The three walked over to the bed. The doctor stood on one side of Mr. O'Leary and the priest stood on the other. Tom opened his eyes and saw the two men there and said, "Father, would you tell the people at my funeral that I died as Jesus died?" "Do you mean pure of heart and poor in spirit, Tom?" "No, I mean between two thieves!"

Freud has a version of the "two thieves" joke that, while not directly concerned with death anxiety, is worth repeating here, if only to illustrate how long this joke and its variations have been around:

Two not particularly scrupulous businessmen had succeeded, by dint of a series of highly risky enterprises, in amassing a large fortune, and they were now making efforts to push their way into good society. One method, which struck them as a likely one, was to have their portraits painted by the most celebrated and highly paid artist in the city, whose pictures had an immense reputation. The precious canvases were shown for the first time at a large evening party, and the two hosts themselves led the most influential connoisseur and art critic up to the wall upon which the portraits were hanging side by side, to extract his admiring judgment on them. He studied the works for a long time, and then, shaking his head, as though there was something he had missed, pointed to the gap between the pictures and asked quietly, "But where's the Savior?" (Freud 1905/1960, 87)

As Freud points out, the technique employed in this joke is actually reflected in its content, for there is "something missing" in the joke itself—the observation that the critic wanted to say but could not say, namely, "You are a couple of rascals" (88).

Funeral Jokes. Jokes about amusing or whimsical happenings at funerals are abundant. In fact, it's hard to imagine anything that could conceivably occur during a funeral that has not already been thought of in the funeral joke tradition. Here's one involving that familiar clergy trio, a minister, a priest, and a rabbi:

A minister, a priest, and a rabbi die in a car crash. They go to heaven for orientation. They are all asked, "When you are in your casket, and friends, family, and congregants are mourning over you, what would you like to hear them say?" The minister says, "I would like to hear them say that I was a wonderful husband, a fine spiritual leader, and a great family man." The priest says, "I would like to hear that I was a wonderful teacher and a servant of God who made a huge difference in people's lives." The rabbi replies, "I would like to hear them say, 'Look, he's moving.'"

Part of the humor of this joke is that the rabbi, unlike the minister and priest, places much greater value on his survival than on his exemplary reputation. Another part is the fact that clergy are supposed to represent the theological view that the next life is much to be preferred over the present one.

The following joke addresses the dilemma of how to give a man a decent burial when no clergy are around to officiate:

Ole and Lars were shipwrecked on a small island in the Pacific. Also stranded was an Irishman named Kelly. As time went on, the men grew accustomed to being marooned and led a good life on the island. Finally, the Irishman died. The two Norwegians were puzzled about how to give Kelly a proper funeral since he had been a Catholic. Ole volunteered to do the service if Lars would dig the grave. Ole said he had once listened to a Catholic church service, so after Lars dug a big hole, Ole put on his best ministerial tone: "In da name of da Father, the Son, and [shoving Kelly's body with a foot] in da hole he goes!"[3]

Here is another joke about things going wrong at a funeral:

> A new business was opening, and one of the owner's friends sent flowers for the occasion. But when the owner read the card with the flowers, it said, "Rest in peace." The owner was a little peeved, and he called the florist to complain. The florist apologized, "Sir, I'm really sorry for the mistake, but rather than getting angry, you should imagine this: Somewhere there is a funeral taking place today, and *they* have flowers with a note saying, "Congratulations on your new location."

Or this darker one:

> Minutes before her husband's funeral, a widow took one last look at his body. To her horror, she saw that he was wearing a brown suit whereas she had issued strict instructions to the undertaker that she wanted him buried in a blue suit. She sought out the undertaker and demanded that the suit be changed. At first, he tried to tell her that it was too late, but when he could see that she wasn't going to back down, he ordered the mortician to wheel the coffin away. A few minutes later, just as the funeral was about to start, the coffin was wheeled back in and the corpse was now wearing a blue suit. The widow was delighted and, after the service, praised the undertaker for his swift work. "Oh, it was nothing," he said. "It so happened there was another body in the back room and he was already dressed in a blue suit. All we had to do was switch heads."

Then there is the issue of how to conduct oneself at a funeral. You should not, for example, punch the body and tell people that he hit you first, ask someone to take a snapshot of you shaking hands with the deceased, take a flower from the wreath as a buttonhole, or go around telling people that you've seen the will and they're not in it.

Because comments about the appearance of the deceased lying in the casket—"She looks so nice" or "He seems to be at peace"—are common at funerals, it was perhaps inevitable that jokes like the following would occur: "Two Norwegians attended the funeral of their friend Nels. 'He sure looks good,' said Ole. 'He should,' responded Lars. 'He yust got out of the hospital.'"

Or consider the following comment by an observant Norwegian lady:

> Lena was happily married to Gundar and they had five children. Then Gundar died. Shortly, Lena married Sven and they had four children. Then Sven died. Before long, Lena married Ole and they had five children. Then Ole died. Then it wasn't long before Lena died. At the funeral, friends filed past the casket. One lady murmured, "See how nice she looks, and isn't it nice they are together again?" The lady behind her asked, "Who do you mean? Lena and Gundar?" "No," said the lady. "Vell

den, you mean Lena and Sven?" "No," answered the lady. "Den you must mean Lena and Ole?" "No," said the lady, "I mean her knees."

This joke plays on the fact that funerals are liminal experiences, and the participants find themselves in a sort of no-man's land between the realities of earth and the superlatives of heaven.

The Afterlife. The most common type of joke about the afterlife are "pearly gate" jokes. The premise of these jokes is that admission is not automatic but that the criteria for admission are somewhat arbitrary, as the rules that are in place at any given time cannot be anticipated in advance. On the other hand, St. Peter is a decent fellow, so his rules are not very strict and, as the following joke indicates, he is generally willing to negotiate:

> Eddie died and was waiting at the pearly gates while St. Peter leafed through his big book to see if Eddie was worthy. St. Peter went through the book several times, furrowed his brow, and said to him, "You know, I can't see that you ever did anything really bad in your life, but you never did anything really good either. If you can point to even one *really* good deed, you're in." Eddie thought for a moment and said, "Yeah, there was one time when I was driving down the highway and saw a giant group of bikers assaulting this poor girl. I slowed down my car to see what was going on, and sure enough, there they were, about fifty of them, tormenting this terrified young woman. Infuriated, I got out of my car, grabbed a tire iron out of my trunk, and walked up to the leader of the gang, a huge guy with a studded leather jacket and a chain running from his nose to his ear. As I walked up to the leader, the bikers formed a circle around me. So I ripped the leader's chain off his face and smashed him over the head with the tire iron. Laid him out flat. Then I turned and yelled at the rest of them, "Leave this poor innocent girl alone! You're all a bunch of sick, deranged animals! Go home before I teach you a lesson in pain!" St. Peter, impressed, says, "Really? When did this happen?" "Oh, about two minutes ago."

Presumably, his one really good deed in life was too recent to have been recorded in St. Peter's big book.

In the following joke, there is a link between what kind of car you drove on earth and your prospects for getting into heaven:

> St. Peter stood at the pearly gates and examined those who would enter. One of the questions he seemed to think important related to automobiles. "What kind of car did you own?" he asked the first man. "A Packard," the man replied. "I'm sorry," said St. Peter, "but that does not help you. You will have to go down." "Did you have an auto?" he asked the second man. "I did, sir—a Pierce-Arrow." "Too bad," said St. Peter.

"Please press the lower button." "And you, did you own a machine?" he asked the third fellow. "Yes, sir, I did." "What was it?" "A Ford," the man replied." "Come in," said St. Peter, throwing open the gates. "You've had your hell on earth."

It may be worth noting that many pearly gates jokes involve elevators manned by St. Peter himself or one of his faithful assistants.

A joke of more recent vintage involves the vehicle that one will be supplied to get around heaven:

Three guys were met at the pearly gates by St. Peter. He told them, "I know that you guys are forgiven because you're here. Before I let you into heaven, I have to ask you something. Your answer will depend on what kind of car you get. You have to have a car in heaven because heaven is so big." Peter asked the first guy, "How long were you married?" The first guy replied, "Twenty-four years." "Did you ever cheat on your wife?" Peter asked. The guy said, "Yeah, seven times, but you said I was forgiven." Peter said, "Yeah, but that's not too good. Here's a Pinto for you to drive." The second guy got the same question from Peter. He replied, "I was married for forty-one years and cheated on her once, but that was our first year and we really worked it out well." Peter said, "I'm pleased to hear that; here's a Lincoln for you." The third guy walked up and said, "Peter, I know what you're going to ask. I was married for sixty-three years and didn't even look at another woman. I treated my wife like a queen!" Peter said, "That's what I like to hear. Here's a Jaguar for you." A little while later, the two guys with the Pinto and the Lincoln saw the guy with the Jaguar crying on the golden sidewalk. They went over to see what was the matter. When they asked the guy with the Jaguar what was wrong, he said, "I just saw my wife. She was on a skateboard!"

Then there are jokes in which two applicants for admission discover, through conversation, that their deaths were related:

Two men waiting at the pearly gates struck up a conversation. "How'd you die?" the first man asked the second. "I froze to death," said the second. "That's awful," says the first man. "So how did you die?" asked the second man. "I had a heart attack. You see, I knew my wife was cheating on me, so one day I showed up at home unexpectedly. I ran up to the bedroom and found her alone, knitting. I ran down to the basement, but no one was hiding there. I ran up to the second floor, but no one was hiding there either. I ran as fast as I could to the attic, and just as I got there, I had a massive heart attack and died." The second man shook his head. "That's so ironic," he said. "What do you mean?" asked the first man. "If only you had stopped to look in the freezer, we'd both still be alive."

These two men, lamenting their deaths on earth, have not yet discovered what an elderly couple have learned, namely, that trying to prolong their lives on earth was an understandable but dumb mistake:

> An eighty-five-year-old couple, married for almost sixty years, died in a car crash. They had been in good health the last ten years, mainly as a result of her interest in health food and exercise. When they reached the pearly gates, St. Peter took them to their mansion, which was decked out with a beautiful kitchen and a master bath suite with a sauna and Jacuzzi. As they oohed and aahed, the old man asked Peter how much all this was going to cost. "It's free," Peter replied. "This is heaven." Next they went to survey the championship golf course that their home backed up to. When the old man asked the price of the green fees, St. Peter replied, "This is heaven; you play for free." Next they went to the clubhouse and saw the lavish buffet lunch with the cuisines of the world laid out. "How much to eat?" asked the old man. "Don't you understand yet? This is heaven. It's free," Peter replied with some exasperation. "Well, where are the low-fat and low-cholesterol tables?" the old man asked timidly. Peter lectured, "That's the best part. You can eat as much as you like of whatever you like and you never get fat and you never get sick. This is heaven." With that, the old man threw down his hat, stomped on it, and began cursing. Peter and his wife both tried to calm him down, asking him what was wrong. The old man looked at his wife and said, "This is all your fault. If it weren't for your lousy oatmeal, I could have been here ten years ago!"

Finally, there's the fellow who was quite literally in limbo:

> St. Peter became aware of a man pacing up and down outside the pearly gates. "Can I help you?" asked St. Peter. The man looked at his watch impatiently. "No, it's OK. I won't be long." Five minutes later, St. Peter looked out again and saw that the man still seemed agitated about something. "What is it?" asked St. Peter. The man stopped his pacing. "Look," he said, "you know I'm dead, and I know I'm dead. So will someone please tell the cardiac arrest team?"

There are, of course, many jokes about hell, and the reasons for why one might end up there range from the rather obvious explanation that he was a politician or a lawyer to the more obscure fact that his wife's name (e.g., Penny, Sherry, Brandy, and the inevitable Fanny)[4] reveals his life's preoccupations. In this type of humor, Jesus' camel's eye analogy applies especially to lawyers.

The Surviving Spouse. The following jokes convey the idea that there won't be a great deal of grieving following the death of a husband or wife. The joking tradition has little sympathy or patience for the idea that the survivor would be emotionally devastated by the death of the other, and that it will take months or even years to adjust to the loss. In the following example, the surviving spouse takes the death in stride:

Two old ladies met in the park. After inquiring about each other's health, the topic of conversation turned to their respective husbands. "Oh," said one. "Harry died last week. He went out to the garden to dig up a cabbage for dinner, had a heart attack, and dropped dead in the middle of the vegetable path." "Oh my," said the other, "what did you do?" "I opened a can of peas instead."

In the following joke, the wife is quite open about her plans following her husband's demise:

Ole entered a funeral home. "What can we do for you?" the undertaker asked. Ole replied, "I vant to make arrangements for my funeral. I vant to be buried at sea." "Why would you want to be buried at sea?" asked the puzzled undertaker. "Did you serve in the Swedish Navy?" "Naw, it's nuthin' like dat. I vant to get back at my vife. She said dat vhen I died, she was going to dance on my grave!"

In this joke, it's the husband who inadvertently reveals his intentions after his wife's death:

Lena was dying, and in her final hours, she sympathetically wished her husband a happy life when she was gone. "In fact, Lars," she said, "When I am gone, I tink you should get yourself anudder vife. And you can even give her my dresses." "Von't work," answered Lars. "She's a 6 and you're an 18."

The implication, of course, is that physically speaking, "she" is a vast improvement over his present wife.

Humor for Chronic Death Anxiety

The jokes presented here are just a few of the many jokes about death and the afterlife that have been published and republished in humor books. As suggested earlier, they represent one method that we have at our disposal for taking some of the sting out of death. More specifically, the five types of jokes identified here address the most prominent and perennial anxieties that death evokes, including anxiety over the announcement that one has a terminal illness or only a short time to live, over the deathbed vigil and the inevitable ambiguities that it manifests, over the funeral as a public event and how the bereaved will comport and compose themselves, over the question of what we may expect to happen to us and our loved ones after death, and over the future lives of those who are left behind. Thus, the joking tradition recognizes that death anxiety is complex, that it has many faces and facets. It is a tribute to this tradition that it has addressed all of the major stages in the death and dying process, from the moment when the impending death is announced to the period after the death has occurred and the survivors are faced with the task of continuing on in their loved ones' absence. Thus, the joking tradition has its own stage theory, one that is unlikely to displace other theories and models (e.g., Kübler-Ross 1969) yet has the virtue of a certain concreteness that other theories lack. Its role, as Freud suggests, is a savings in the expenditure of our psychic resources. In its performance of this role, humor makes a valuable contribution to our capacity to cope with the anxieties that death evokes and provokes in us. Obviously, some of our most painful emotions are associated with death. But as the forgoing jokes also suggest, however indirectly, death exacts costly inhibitions and virtually demands that we engage in difficult thought and reflection. Humor, therefore, offers a welcome respite from the expenditure of our limited psychic resources, resources that are vulnerable to being used up by our anxieties relating to death.

The point of this consideration of jokes about death is not, however, that they may help someone who is currently grieving the loss of a loved one. Nor is it to make a case for the use of humor in funerals when this can be done with sensitivity, a case that is nicely made in a short article by Kenn Filkins (1994) titled "Funeral for a Funny Lady: Humor and the Funeral Message." Filkins contends, and I agree, that "humor in a funeral can be a balm or a bomb—a healing salve or a painful stab. Healing humor comes intrinsically from the personal stories, but humor hurts if it is a joke 'to ease the tension of the audience or speaker.' Jokes appear crass or trite to the mourners. By humor I'm not suggesting that you take a Pearly Gates joke (of someone standing before Gabriel) then rewriting it with the deceased as the main character" (25). The jokes that I have presented here would be totally inappropriate at a funeral or in conversation with a person who is grieving.

Instead, their value relates to the fact that we all have anxieties about death—we would not be human if we did not—and that such anxieties are never very far from our consciousness. I have heard persons say that never a day goes by that they do not think about death—either their own or a loved one's—in a deeply personal way. We humans are forward-looking by nature, a function, perhaps, of the fact that we have eyes in the front of our heads, and we naturally, therefore, think a great deal about the future. In the psychological literature on anxiety disorders, anxiety has been defined as "anticipatory dread." It also has been contrasted with fear, for in fear we know what is threatening us, whereas in anxiety we have a diffuse and vague sense of uneasiness. Where fear involves fright leading to flight, anxiety involves foreboding that tends to stop us in our tracks.

I suggest, therefore, that humor is useful for our more chronic state of death anxiety, and the very fact that it is *not* recommended, or is recommended with great caution, in situations of acute grief implies its value for the more chronic state of death anxiety that hovers around us even when—or perhaps especially when—we are happy and contented, when we find ourselves thinking to ourselves or exclaiming to one another, "If only this happiness and contentment could last forever!" The painful emotions that humor in this case may spare us are not, therefore, the stabbing pains of grief but the more persisting helpless awareness that this happy state cannot last forever.

The Price of Costly Inhibitions

By focusing in this chapter on jokes relating to death anxiety, I have necessarily given primacy to Freud's view that humor saves in the expenditure of painful emotions. On the other hand, many of the jokes I have just presented on death also illustrate Freud's point that humor saves in the expenditure of costly inhibitions, including the inhibition to mention or talk about the subject of death itself. I would like, however, to conclude this chapter on Freud with a brief consideration of the costly inhibition theme, as the psychic costs of inhibition (especially of sexual and aggressive desires) were a major concern of his, and he viewed jokes, the form of humor he selected for his major treatment of humor, as especially designed to counter such inhibitions.

In conversations with students, I have gained the distinct impression that where borderline humor is concerned, they are far more conflicted about sexual humor than about aggressive humor. They know that they do not appreciate aggressive or "sick" humor, but they are unsure whether they should—or should-n't—laugh at humor that has a sexual theme. This uncertainty is, in some cases, exacerbated by their sensitivity to gender issues, especially issues relating to the treatment of women as sex objects. It is not, therefore, simply or perhaps even primarily due to the more puritanical inhibitions to which earlier student populations were subject.

One of the ways that I have attempted to elicit this conflict so that it might be talked about more openly is by presenting students with several pages of limericks on "mishaps, misunderstandings, miscreants, and misconduct." In several cases the misconduct involves a religious professional, and these cases include the additional concern of clergy sexual misconduct, an issue that I myself take very seriously (Capps, 1993, 1997b). Here's an example:

> A handsome young monk in a wood
> Told a girl she should cling to the Good.
>   She obeyed him, but gladly,
>   He repulsed her, but sadly,
> And said she had misunderstood.

Here's another:

> There was a young monk from Siberia,
> Whose morals were very inferior;
>   He did to a nun
>   What he shouldn't have done,
> And now she's a Mother Superior.

I suggest to students that the very fact one *does* take an issue seriously gives one a certain license to enjoy humor, such as these limericks, that makes light of it. After all, Freud was concerned for those—himself included—who suffered precisely because they took moral precepts and prohibitions seriously. Thus, humor

that plays on the violation of such precepts implicitly acknowledges one's pre-
disposition not to violate them in real-life situations. This is much like the occa-
sional holiday that acknowledges and even reinforces the idea that most of our
days are to be devoted to work and other social obligations.

I also have a page of limericks that bears the heading "The Limerick: A
Debased and Perverse Poetic Form." It is designed to aid students in acknowledging the uneasiness they experience concerning humor that nonetheless provides valuable if necessarily transient release from their own expenditure of costly inhibitions. An example of this type of limerick is the following:

> The limerick's callous and crude,
> Its morals distressingly lewd;
>   It's not worth the reading
>   By persons of breeding—
> It's designed for us vulgar and rude.

And this one by Morris Bishop:

> The limerick is furtive and mean;
> You must keep her in close quarantine,
>   Or she sneaks to the slums
>   And promptly becomes
> Disorderly, drunk, and obscene.

Such limericks simply declare that the limerick form is one in which the usual
inhibitions of morality and good taste are set aside. A variation recognizes that
the reader expects a limerick to be "callous and crude" or "furtive and mean" and
then undercuts this very expectation. For example, consider the following limerick by Stanley J. Sharpless:

> There was a young lady . . . tut, tut!
> So you think that you're in for some smut?
>   Some five-line crescendo
>   Or lewd innuendo?
> Well, you're wrong. This is anything but.

Or this:

> A bather whose clothing was strewed
> By winds that left her quite nude,
>   Saw a man come along,
>   And unless I am wrong,
> You expected this line to be rude.

These two limericks address the very internal conflict that one may be experiencing over whether to retain the "inhibition" or relinquish it. On the same page, I include a couple of my own limericks that have a similar intent, as they create the expectation that the poet will use an obscene word, and then they back off, employing a completely inoffensive rhyme instead.

There was a young friar named Tuck
Who lured Marian into his truck.
    If you're wanting to know,
    Did they give it a go?
I'm sorry, you're just out of luck.

There was a philosopher named Descartes
Who heard beans are good for the heart.
    He ate a whole can,
    Then fetched a hand fan,
And waited for something to start.

The second of these two limericks shifts the focus from sexual misbehavior to bodily functions that are considered inappropriate in certain social contexts (e.g., when eating in a restaurant, sitting in church, or discussing one's course load with the academic dean). Jim Dawson's *Who Cut the Cheese? The Cultural History of the Fart* (1999) is an invaluable resource for enabling students to discuss this issue together in class. I recommend Dawson's book to doctoral students who are beginning to think about their dissertation topic because, like most dissertations, it manifests impeccable research methods applied to a rather dubious topic. Another topic that also addresses the problem of costly inhibitions is male genitalia, especially the theme of penis anxiety among men, the corollary of Freud's hotly contested theory of penis envy among women. (A valuable counterpart to Dawson's book is David M. Friedman's *A Mind of Its Own: A Cultural History of the Penis* [2001], which asserts that of all the bodily organs, the penis especially forces men to confront the mysteries and contradictions of human life.) A limerick that never fails to get a laugh from students—both women and men—is the following:

An old archaeologist, Throstle,
Discovered a marvelous fossil.
    He knew from its bend
    And the knob on its end
'Twas the peter of Paul the Apostle.

This limerick works with seminarians because it has a religious theme, but also because it makes fun of biblical archeology and employs alliteration in the final line, thus making light of the scholarly pretensions of biblical scholars and the elocutionary talents of rhetorical preachers.

This limerick, though, is only, as it were, the tip of the iceberg, for the deeper reality that seems to haunt males from early childhood through old age concerns the fate and function of their penises. Anxieties relating to penises include their relative size; their vulnerability to injury and attack (e.g., the fairly recent case of John Bobbitt whose wife took a knife to his penis while he was asleep); their involuntary discharges during sleep (a worrisome event for adolescent boys as well as the early church fathers); their reliability during sexual intercourse (the "erectile dysfunction" issue that Bob Dole has made a household word); malfunctions associated with aging (e.g., urine retention); and worst of all, prostate cancer. Two jokes that play on the issue of penis anxiety while affording the opportunity to reflect on that age-old controversy—secular medicine or religious healing?—are the following.

First, the secular approach: An eighty-year old guy asked his doctor for a prescription for Viagra. The doctor gave him a knowing look and wrote out the prescription, but warned him about the dangers of too much excitement for his rather weak heart. Later, the old guy was hanging out in a bar with a couple of his buddies. While they were sipping their beers, he casually took out his pocket knife and his Viagra bottle and began cutting all the tablets into four pieces. His friends observed this strange behavior with puzzlement until one of them thought he had it figured out. He said, "What's the idea? Do you really think you can achieve with one-quarter dose what it takes better men than you a full dose?" The old guy replied, "Oh, I've long since given up on that. I just need enough so that I'll quit pissing on my shoes."

Here's the religious approach: A new priest at his first mass was so nervous he could hardly speak. After mass he asked the monsignor how he had done. The monsignor shook his head and replied, "When I get nervous in the pulpit, I replace the water glass with a glass of vodka. If I start to get nervous, I take a sip." So the next Sunday the priest took the monsignor's advice. At the beginning of the sermon, he got so nervous he downed the whole glass. He proceeded to talk up a storm. Upon returning to his office following mass, he found the following note from the monsignor on the door: "Sip the vodka; *don't* gulp it. There are ten commandments, not twelve. There are twelve disciples, not ten. Jesus was consecrated, not constipated. Jacob wagered his donkey; he did not bet his ass. We do not refer to Jesus Christ and his disciples as JC and the Sunshine Boys. David slew Goliath, he did not kick the shit out of him. We do not refer to the cross as the Big T. The recommended grace before a meal is not 'Rub-a dub-dub, thanks for the grub. Yeah, God!' Next Sunday there will be a taffy-pulling contest at St. Peter's, not a peter-pulling contest at St. Taffy's."[5]

Conclusion

In *Inhibitions, Symptoms and Anxiety* (Freud 1926/1989), Freud presented his argument that anxiety leads to costly inhibitions which then manifest themselves in various psychological symptoms. By studying the symptoms and what they mean to the patient, the psychoanalyst seeks to uncover the original cause or source of the anxiety that led to the inhibition. One of his earlier cases illustrates how this works: An unmarried woman had been going on walks with her sister's husband when her sister was ill and bedridden. Just before her sister died, she had a momentary thought that her sister's husband was now free to marry. Feeling deeply guilty for having thought this, she repressed it. Shortly thereafter, she developed a paralysis in her legs that rendered her unable to walk. Through psychoanalysis, Freud was able to make a psychodynamic connection between her paralysis, the guilty thought, and her walks with her sister's husband. When she eventually acknowledged the guilty thought, her symptoms began to disappear. Freud cautioned her against a romantic attachment to her sister's husband, as he felt this would reevoke her guilty feelings, and instead encouraged her to find another man. The case concludes with Freud's account of his attendance at a dance where he saw the young woman swirling around the dance floor with another man, her husband-to-be (Freud 1895/1953, 135–85).

Freud does not explore the possible use of humor in this case, but his essay on "Humor," written many years later, suggests this possibility: Instead of dealing with her guilty thought by repressing it, she might have dealt with it instead via humor. That is, she could have viewed her thoughts about her sister's husband's availability now that her sister was dead as something to joke about: "Of all the available men, why would anyone in her right mind want to marry her sister's husband?" Am I *this* desperate?" What began as a guilty thought thus becomes a laughing matter. Her superego has forgiven her momentary lapse— "Now that my sister is dead, I can have her husband"—and has suggested that this thought is more ludicrous than shameful. That the idea of marrying her sister's husband occurs to her during the deathbed scene makes it seem especially comical, and she can imagine that had her sister known her thoughts, the two of them would have had a good laugh together. In fact, we can imagine her sister making a joke of it, perhaps at her husband's expense.

This case illustrates the fact that painful emotions and costly inhibitions often occur together. And where these two are gathered together, we should not be surprised—or disturbed—if humor is somewhere in the midst of them.

Motoring through the Bible Belt

Check beneath the Covers before You Move the Bed

Saul sent messengers to David's house to keep watch over him, planning to kill him in the morning. David's wife Michal told him, "If you do not save your life tonight, tomorrow you will be killed." So Michal let David down through the window; he fled away and escaped. Michal took an idol and laid it on the bed; she put a net of goats' hair on its head, and covered it with the clothes. When Saul sent messengers to take David, she said, "He is sick." Then Saul sent the messengers to see David for themselves. He said, "Bring him up to me in the bed, that I may kill him." When the messengers came in, the idol was in the bed, with the covering of goats' hair on its head.

1 Samuel 19:11–16

Saul grabbed his hair
To slit his throat
But 'twasn't David,
'Twas a goat.
Burma-Shave

2. Humor as Stimulus to Identity Creation

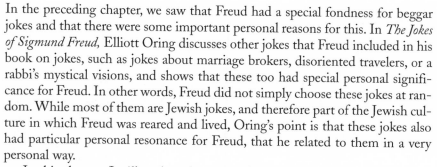

In the preceding chapter, we saw that Freud had a special fondness for beggar jokes and that there were some important personal reasons for this. In *The Jokes of Sigmund Freud,* Elliott Oring discusses other jokes that Freud included in his book on jokes, such as jokes about marriage brokers, disoriented travelers, or a rabbi's mystical visions, and shows that these too had special personal significance for Freud. In other words, Freud did not simply choose these jokes at random. While most of them are Jewish jokes, and therefore part of the Jewish culture in which Freud was reared and lived, Oring's point is that these jokes also had particular personal resonance for Freud, that he related to them in a very personal way.

In this chapter, I will explore the personal significance of jokes by focusing on Norman N. Holland's *Laughing: A Psychology of Humor* (1982). Holland, an English professor at the University of Buffalo at the time he wrote this book, begins it with a quotation from a poem by Denise Levertov: "She continued to laugh on some days, to cry on others, unfolding the design of her identity" (9). His thesis is that we are attracted to certain types of humor or certain joke themes because they relate to our personal identity. In enjoying a cartoon or a joke in private, we, in a sense, "recreate" our own identity. In passing a joke along to someone else, we share our identity with the other. Jokes are not unique in this regard. A favorite poem, novel, or film serves the same purpose. It's just that we don't usually think of jokes in this way because we view them as a rather trivial art form.

Holland devotes the first half of his book to theories about humor. He concludes that these theories, ranging from those of Aristotle to those of late-twentieth-century experimental psychologists, "almost seem to form a coherent system," a system in which the stimulus for laughter is some form of *incongruity*, and the nature of laughter is some form of *catharsis*. Yet none of these theories "seems to apply to all laughers, nor do they explain why one person laughs at a certain joke and another doesn't. Nor do several different theories combine to form one large explanation. We could apologize for the whole package as the curate did for his egg in the old *Punch* cartoon: 'Parts of it are excellent!' Yet a theory, like an egg, ought to satisfy throughout" (155–56).

What to do about this problem? Holland suggests that we need to turn "from theories and some presumed *we* to real laughers" (116). Since the two hundred theories he reviewed mostly ask, "Why do we laugh?" Holland decided to change the question to, "Why does he or she or I—somebody in particular—laugh?" To explore this question, he gave a group (seven) of his students at the University of Buffalo six cartoons by B. Kliban and asked them to record their reactions and allow him to convey these to the readers of his book. They were to write what, if anything, they found humorous in the cartoons, why they thought they had laughed (or hadn't), and what associations they had with the cartoons.

When all of the students' reports were in, Holland organized them by cartoon. What was especially apparent when he did so was that sometimes two or more students would express a common theme, but more often their responses were highly divergent. This led him to conclude that the theories of humor he had reviewed tend to focus on what the responses to a cartoon or joke have in common, and ignore the responses that are unique to a particular individual. This may explain why theories of humor have emphasized that humor is stimulated by incongruity. A picture of an angular Don Quixote on a horse accompanied by an overweight Sancho Panza riding a donkey seems inherently incongruous, especially when we know some of the historical background of this particular knight's errand. In a sense, recognition of incongruity is the one thing that can be said about all of the persons who laughed at or found a particular cartoon humorous. Recognition of incongruity may also be proposed as the basis for dividing laughers from nonlaughers. The former recognized the incongruity. The latter did not and hence didn't "get" the joke.

But what interested Holland much more was the fact that there was so much divergence in the responses of the seven students. It was as if each student had a different basis or reason for laughing at the same cartoon. He also found that as an individual student moved from one cartoon to another, certain themes repeated themselves. For example, one student, whom Holland names Serge, consistently responded to the puncturing of external authorities or his own assumptions. For example, this is what he wrote about a cartoon depicting an ordinary woman mistakenly crowned the King of Norway: "Very funny. How ludicrous pomp and ceremony are. Military/political/church all represented. What weight does authority hold?" This is his response to a cartoon depicting a man ordering food in a restaurant for himself and his companion, an oversized fly: "The verbal humor is based on the abrupt transition from choice food to trash (as seen in human terms) but both are to receive what they value. Also, how men treat their wives when out: ordering for them, perhaps even commenting on how women were assumed to have little knowledge of fine foods, implying that the woman has no taste" (121). Here, it is the "authority" of the male connoisseur of fine food that is being punctured. (See cartoons on page 44.)

To demonstrate that Serge's responses relating to the puncturing of authority were unique to him, Holland cites the response of another student (whom he names Silas) to the second cartoon: "Here the fly is a dinner guest. Usually the situation is one where the fly is uninvited ["Waiter, there's a fly in my soup"], but in Kliban's world flies are appropriate companions at mealtime and may even be great conversationalists." And here is what a third student, Sherry, had to say about the first cartoon: "It suggests the desire for women to be recognized in what they recognize to be a man's world. Some women are better at achieving male recognition than others. Is it necessary for a woman to be crowned a king to have really been successful? Rewards are sexually defined."

These responses by Silas and Sherry confirm that Serge's responses to the two cartoons, ones that centered on the puncturing or deflating of authority, were uniquely his. By the same token, Silas's response to the "Cynthia Is Mistakenly Crowned King of Norway" cartoon is thematically similar to his response to the "I'll have the Gazpacho" cartoon: "The absurdity makes us laugh because Cynthia walking to her car with a bag full of groceries could be anyone we know . . . when suddenly, she is thrust into royalty. . . . I see this as a psychic projection of a woman who wished secretly to be a man, or is at least envious of men, men who achieve high social status as kings and in her daydream Cynthia becomes king, not queen. She is not only king, while performing mundane chores, but has six men following her to do her will" (122). The similarity in Silas's two responses is that he, unlike Serge, does not focus on the pompous males in the cartoons, but on the one who is in the least dominant position (the fly, the woman carrying groceries). He wants to bestow on this less dominant figure an ascribed or desired dignity. If Serge sees Kliban cutting pompous men down to size, exposing the absurdity of their pomposity, Silas sees the same situations from a different angle, from that of the aspirant to the "high social status" that men represent and enjoy.

The reader of *this* book may wonder why I focused, initially, on Serge's responses to the two cartoons and why I focused on these two cartoons and not the other four. After all, Holland presents the responses of several students to all six cartoons. What was it about Serge's responses to these two cartoons that attracted my attention? And why did I give priority to his responses, over, say, those of Silas, which are no less valid? I believe the reason is that I personally identified with what Serge had to say about the two cartoons. For me, he hit the nail on the head when he pointed to the pomposity of the male diner and the "ludicrous" nature of the "pomp and ceremony" presented in the crowning of Cynthia, King of Norway. I have no reason to doubt that the two cartoons also invite Silas's explanation for why they are amusing, but Serge's responses come much closer to explaining why I too laughed at these two cartoons.

This, to me, is an important point, as it suggests that Serge and I share in common an "identity theme" of enjoying "the puncturing of external authority or [one's] own assumptions." I believe, further, that I chose these two cartoons because they invite this interpretation in ways that the other four cartoons do not. This point is supported by the fact that Serge and I seem to have trouble discovering what is funny about two other cartoons for which Holland supplies Serge's responses. In the first case (a cartoon captioned "Carl Meets His Match in Ramon"), Serge does not say why he thinks the cartoon is funny but instead asks, "Why should I find this funny? Carl—hard sound. Ramon—soft sound. Understatement? Culture versus brutality?" It seems clear that Serge is struggling to make a case for why this cartoon is humorous. Its humor is not nearly as self-evident to him as in the case of the other two cartoons. Similarly, in response to a cartoon captioned "Short on Brains, but a Terrific Dancer," Serge poses a question: "My central question here would be, 'Who is the caption referring to?' Is that what the two central figures think of each other?" Again, he is preoccupied with the question of what he is to make of the cartoon. Why *should* he find it funny? One might view his responses to these two cartoons as negative identity themes, for here he seems to be deferring to external authorities, or trying to, rather than following his own instincts. He seems to be saying, "Tell me why this cartoon is funny." (See cartoons on page 46.)

Perhaps too he is having trouble with these cartoons because they evoke disturbing thoughts within himself. Two other students, Sherry and Sid, commented on the theme of competition in the first of these cartoons. Sid, for example, notes that it portrays "petty academic/silly rivalries." Does this mean that Serge has difficulty with the theme of competition, possibly because it *is* important to him? On the other hand, Sid is able to enjoy "Cynthia Is Mistakenly Crowned King of Norway" for reasons that approximate Serge's reasons for enjoying it, though he seems in the following response to draw a moral from the mistaken crowning of Cynthia that Serge does not draw:

> Very funny. For all the results we get from our elected or crowned officials, it might as well happen in this fashion: I mean on a street corner, haphazardly like this. [Cynthia's] expression as the [archbishop] places the crown on her head seems to sum it all up: "What are they all about, anyway? I'm just trying to get these heavy packages home, and now they place this dumb, heavy crown on my head?" Blind justice, no? But just one question: how did Richard Nixon or Hitler attain power, if not a case of blundering blindness on we the people's part? (122)

Holland points out that "Serge thought the cartoon was a spoof of authority" while "Sid contrasted the randomness of official power with Cynthia's purposeful shopping" (123). Yet both Serge and Sid judge this cartoon to be "very funny" and give as their reason for this judgment that, as the caption suggests, there is something "mistaken" about the way authority works. In short, Serge, Sid, and I

Carl Meets His Match in Ramon

Short on Brains, but a Terrific Dancer

might form a joking community around the Cynthia cartoon, while Serge and I would excuse ourselves with regard to "Carl Meets His Match in Ramon," around which Sid and Sherry might form a joking community.

By the same token, I doubt that either Serge or I would be able to form a joking community with Sherry insofar as "Cynthia Is Mistakenly Crowned King of Norway" is concerned because he and I seem to take a very different view from Sherry's concerning the "authority" represented in this cartoon. As we have seen, Sherry views the cartoon as "suggesting the desire for women to be recognized in what they recognize to be man's world." If one views the cartoon as one that "punctures" authority as Serge and I do, it strains the imagination to think that Cynthia, or any other woman, would actually desire the sort of recognition that the cartoon portrays. Who would deem it an honor to be crowned by these mountebanks?

Up to this point, I have been emphasizing Serge's—and my—recognition of the "fact" that the first two cartoons have a common theme of "puncturing authority." "I'll Have the Gazpacho" does it by making fun of the man who orders delicacies for himself and excrement for his table companion, while "Cynthia Is Mistakenly Crowned King of Norway" does it by poking fun at a formal ceremony, the crowning of royalty. But Holland also wants to make the case that there is much more to our response to a cartoon or joke than a theme such as "puncturing authority" suggests. Or, to put it another way, the theme of "puncturing authority" has for Serge, me, and anyone else for whom it may function as an identity theme some highly individualized meanings and associations. Holland therefore devotes a whole chapter of his book to an analysis and interpretation of why a single individual, Ellen, laughed at Kliban's cartoons.

I will not discuss this analysis in detail, but it centers around Holland's identification of a central, perhaps *the* central, identity theme in Ellen's life, namely, "I give to myself so that another self will give to me" (146). He admits that this statement expresses the identity theme in a very abstruse and formulaic way, but he goes on in the chapter to show how it plays itself out in Ellen's life. He makes clear, for example, that this theme is not, for her, a matter of careful calculation. Instead, it is one in which she "imagines the other to be a freely bountiful source. To make it so, Ellen gives food and belief, but, most interestingly, intelligence, work, wit, imagination, and even play-acting" (147–48). He discerns in her playful giving that "Ellen's own joking and laughing fulfilled a cluster of deep needs, that is, Ellen sought to transform the *missed* other by *giving* and being given to. Her wit was one important way she gave" (148). Thus, humor, as noted earlier, is a gift, but for Ellen it is more than that, as it is integral to her understanding of herself as a person.

Significantly, Ellen personally identified with Cynthia, the woman who is mistakenly crowned King of Norway. This was probably because the cartoon, when viewed from Cynthia's own perspective, is about being given to, but in a way that does *not* meet her needs. Unlike Sherry, who viewed the cartoon as suggesting "the desire for women to be recognized in what they recognize to be a man's world," Ellen sees Cynthia as a woman who is simply interested in getting through her day and is interrupted in the middle of her routine. She seems to be saying, "For heaven's sake, they're crowning me King of Norway again. They make these mistakes all the time." Thus, Ellen finds in this cartoon a humorous commentary on her own central identity theme, as if to say, "Like Cynthia, I give of myself so that another self will give to me. But what happens? What do I actually receive? A gift I cannot use, a gift that is totally irrelevant to me, one that does not begin to meet my deepest needs" (150).

Ellen's response may therefore illustrate Freud's point that humor may save us the expenditure of painful emotions, here the sense that the expected reciprocity of giving and being given to does not occur. But Holland's concerns are different. In his view, humor provides Ellen a valuable stimulus to "recreate" her identity. As he puts it, "We are all confirming and recreating our identities all the time" (170). While there are many stimuli besides humor for engaging in this continual act of self-recreation, one of the things that humor does especially well is put one's identity into "playful question." By seeing herself in Cynthia, Ellen could laugh at her own way of approaching life in which she gave of herself with the expectation that her giving would elicit the self-giving of others in return.

Holland's analysis and interpretation of Ellen's "sense of humor," however, raises an interesting question. How conscious is Ellen of the fact that this *is*, for her, a central, perhaps *the* central, identity theme of her personality and life? And how conscious is she of the fact that a cartoon like the crowning of Cynthia enables her to place this theme into playful question? I think that her own "theory" of humor—her theory about what makes this and other cartoons humorous—tends to obscure rather than illustrate the fact that the cartoon enables her to deal playfully with her own identity theme. In her comments on this cartoon, she emphasizes the incongruity that occurs when the "mundane" and the "high" are juxtaposed:

> One of the things about this book [of Kliban's cartoons] I really like is they take just totally mundane things and take something really high, put it next to it, and—I mean, the caption makes the story, and also she's carrying groceries and they mistakenly crown her King of Norway. . . . That they should take the entire apparatus—and it looks like the pope or some archbishop or something—walking down the middle of the street and find this lady carrying groceries and mistakenly crown her King of Norway. You wonder who they were looking for? (150)

This comment may help to explain why the most popular theory of humor is that humor derives from situations of incongruity. Ellen recognizes this incongruity in the juxtaposition of a woman carrying a bagful of groceries and the entire "apparatus" of the ecclesiastical, military, and political system. While this incongruity is certainly present, Holland is asking us to center on a more personal sense of incongruity between our own central identity theme or themes and experiences in ordinary life relating to this theme or themes. Invoking a theory about humor may be one of the ways in which we defend against the insights into ourselves that humor itself offers to us.

Having a theory about humor, however, is only one of the ways in which we may erect such defenses. Serge seems to have had trouble seeing the humor in "Carl Meets His Match in Ramon" because he was reluctant to recognize the theme of competition to which others, such as Sherry and Sid, responded without difficulty. In this case, it was not a theory about humor that served a defensive purpose, but the fact that something in the content of the cartoon itself evoked painful or troubled emotions. On the other hand, our awareness of our tendency to erect such defenses may itself be a means of gaining greater insight into our identity themes. As Holland suggests in his concluding chapter, "Why the Rest of Us Laugh," humor enables us to engage "the familiar psychoanalytic terms [of] fantasy and defense" (180). By "defense" Holland means what one admits in from the not-self and how one shapes it in order to admit it, and by "fantasy" he means the clusters of wishes and fears that one projects from the inner world of self onto the outer worlds of the cartoons (180). These two processes closely resemble one another, for "our defensive and adaptive strategies must gratify needs and give pleasure as well as ward off anxiety. Otherwise we would find other defenses and adaptations that do" (181–82).

Holland further suggests that out of this give-and-take between defense and fantasy, some "transformation" may occur, and "transformation" in this context means the discovery of a variation of one's identity theme or themes (180). Thus, a cartoon or a joke, insignificant as it may seem, may have a transformative effect that carries well beyond its immediate stimulus to laughter. This transformative effect, it seems, is exactly what Freud experienced when the beggar jokes that he was studying enabled him to "accept the *idea* of being indebted to good men and those of our faith without the *feeling* of personal indebtedness" (my emphasis). That is, he could accept the idea of indebtedness in principle but refuse to apply it to himself. These jokes were transformative because they released him from the painful emotions and costly inhibitions that typically accompany a sense of personal indebtedness.[1]

Animal and Bird Jokes

Small children take special interest and delight in stories about animals and birds. This is partly because these creatures are inherently interesting and arouse a child's natural curiosity. It is also, however, because the stories deal with issues that concern children, especially issues that they are anxious about. While few adults read children's stories about animals and birds for their own sake, adults *do* seem to like jokes about birds and animals, especially birds and animals that behave like humans. I suggest that these animal and bird jokes are especially useful for exploring our identity themes.

In *Young Man Luther* (1958), Erik H. Erikson, a psychoanalyst who coined the term "identity crisis," suggests that "in Luther's rich personality there was such a soft spot for the sow so large" that it may be considered "one of Luther's identity elements" (33). While it may seem a bit odd to claim that one of the elements of a man's own identity is his soft spot for a sow, we rarely stop to question the common assertion that a man's best friend is his dog, an assertion that has produced various jokes that play on the ambiguity in the statement that a man's wife was caught sleeping with his "best friend." In any event, the evidence for Erikson's assertion that Luther's soft spot for the sow was integral to his identity is the following quotation from a pamphlet that Luther wrote in which he was trying to make clear that there is a prereligious state of mind. He bids his readers to consider in this light the sow who

> lies in the gutter or on the manure as if on the finest feather bed. She rests safely, snores tenderly, and sleeps sweetly, does not fear king or master, death nor hell, devil or God's wrath, lives without worry, and does not even think where the clover might be. And if the Turkish Caesar arrived in all his might and anger, the sow would be much too proud to move a single whisker in his honor. And if at last the butcher comes upon her, she thinks maybe a piece of wood is pinching her, or a stone. (32)

The sow, in her prereligious state of grace, "has not eaten from the apple, which in paradise has taught us wretched humans the difference between good and bad" (32–33).

Thus, if the book of Proverbs advises, "Go to the ant, you lazybones; consider its ways, and be wise" (6:6), Luther advises us to consider the sow who is much too proud to move a single whisker in an invading conqueror's honor, and faces her death with equanimity, thinking that the lethal knife the butcher wields is a chunk of wood or perhaps a stone that is causing her some slight discomfort. She refuses to be hurt by the arrows of reality or to be compelled to suffer. Her attitude—and Luther's identification with her—is comparable to Freud's triumphant prisoner whose humor has a liberating and elevating effect: "Look here! This is all that this seemingly dangerous world amounts to. Child's play—the very thing to jest about!" (Freud, 1927/1963, 268)[2]

Erikson's view that a soft spot for the old sow was one of Luther's identity elements suggests that jokes about animals and birds may be especially useful stimuli for recreating one's identity in the ways that Holland suggests. As Erikson mentions in his book *Identity and the Life Cycle* (1959), published a year after *Young Man Luther* appeared in print, our identity is comprised largely of our identifications and of how we synthesize these into a hopefully coherent whole (Erikson 1959, 120–22). Thus, in Erikson's view, there was a sense in which Luther identified with the sow, that his soft spot for her was a soft spot in himself, a soft spot, that is, for his own "prereligious state of mind," or his sense that there was something in himself that predated, as it were, his awareness of the difference between good and bad. It was a state of blissful innocence, a state of prevenient (i.e., antecedent to human action) grace.

It is also clear that Luther intends his reference to the sow to be humorous, and this, of course, is typically the view that humans have of pigs and hogs. There is something inherently comical about pigs. Other animals may be used for comic purposes, but the comedy usually has to be supplied by the human who constructs the scene or story. The pig, by virtue of its appearance, provides a comic effect without special human invention or contrivance. Luther certainly understood this fact of nature, and it may have been the very basis of his view that salvation is not something we can earn or purchase for ourselves, but is instead a matter of grace, a gift that derives from the fact that we are the children of God. So, as Erikson recognizes, there was for Luther a link between the sow, grace, and humor, and following Holland, we may view this trio as an important identity theme for Luther.[3]

To test the idea that bird and animal jokes may be the royal road to identity creation, I presented fifteen jokes involving birds and animals to a few family members and friends and asked them to identify any jokes that they could "relate to" and, if so, to explain why. I used the phrase "relate to" in preference to the phrase "identify with" because it is somewhat vaguer and allows more interpretive latitude. On the other hand, "relate to" is more focused than asking individuals to indicate what joke they found the funniest and to explain why. As Holland discovered, the students who participated in his studies often related to cartoons that they did not find especially funny or witty, and this was often due to the fact that the cartoon had some association with their personal experience, values, etc. Because there were quite a number of jokes, I did not try to make anything out of the fact that a joke was *not* selected. I focused only on those that *were* selected.

I tried the test out on my wife, Karen, first. She identified two jokes to which she could relate. One was a joke about two bats:

> At two o'clock in the morning, two bats were hanging upside down in their cave. The first bat turned to the other and said, "How about getting some nice tasty blood for an evening snack?" "Where are we gonna find blood at this time of night?" asked the other. "All right," said the first, "I'll go off by myself." Half an hour later, the first bat returned with blood dripping from his mouth and covering his body. "Wow," said the second bat, "where did you get all that blood?" "See that tree over there?" "Yeah." "Well, I didn't!"

The other was about two dachshunds: "Two dachshunds were chatting. 'I can't figure it out,' said the first dog. 'I'm in perfect shape but I'm constantly anxious.' 'Why don't you go to a psychiatrist?' said the second. 'How can I? I'm not allowed on the couch.'"

Karen related to these two jokes in her role as a preschool teacher. In the first joke, it was the "naivete" of the bat that caught her attention. She explained, "You can be having a morning when the kids get you upset, and then, all of a sudden, one of them does something that reminds you how naive they are. You don't want to laugh, because it isn't funny to them, but it really *is* funny."[4] As for the joke about the two dachshunds, Karen related this to small children being told they have to abide by the rules that the adults have established, especially situations in which one child will remind another of these very rules. So she derived pleasure from the fact that one dachshund informed the other that he couldn't act on his very reasonable suggestion because this would mean violating the rules. When I suggested that there might be a connection between the first dachshund's anxiety and being rule-bound, she didn't disagree, but what she related to in the joke was the fact that the two dogs were having a serious conversation, "just like listening in on the children as they work or play together."

I think we could conclude that Karen has a "soft spot" for very young children, and that this is one of her own identity elements. When I asked her if she personally identified with the bat or the dachshund, she said that she didn't think so, that what she related to was their association with the children. She later mentioned that she also related to the following joke about a tiny turtle:

> A tiny turtle began to climb a tree very slowly. Three hours later, it reached the top, climbed out onto an outside branch, jumped into the air waving its front legs, and crashed to the ground. Saved by its shell, the tiny turtle started to climb the tree again. Four hours later, it reached the top, climbed onto a branch, jumped into the air waving its front legs, and crashed to the ground. Undaunted, the tiny turtle tried again. This time it took five hours to climb to the top of the tree. Once there, it stumbled onto an outside branch, jumped into the air waving its front legs, and crashed to the ground. As the tiny turtle dusted itself off for yet another laborious ascent of the tree, two birds were watching from above. The female bird turned to the male and said, "Darling, don't you think it's time we told him he's adopted?"

Karen observed that the tiny turtle "struggled so hard to succeed at the task despite the fact that it was so unnatural." Here again, we see an association with three- to four-year-olds who are confronting many challenges for the very first time. Parts of their bodies are being required to perform feats that seem very unnatural to them.

As our conversation drew to a close, Karen said, "I'd be interested to know what jokes *you* pick out." I told her that I'm the investigator, not the subject, and in my case, I already know all the jokes. She suggested that my first reason was a cop-out and that the second one was not a problem because the question I was asking did not require a total unfamiliarity with the jokes, although she acknowledged that another reason she liked the joke about the bats was that she didn't "anticipate the ending." Could this also be an identity element, namely, that she likes to be surprised, especially when it involves a situation in which the use of imagination is involved?

So I acceded to her wishes and found that I related to a joke about a parrot and one about a cat being accidentally shot by a Norwegian. Here's the parrot joke:

Bob received a parrot for his birthday. The parrot was fully grown, with a bad attitude and worse vocabulary. Every other word was an expletive. Those that weren't expletives were, to say the least, rude. Bob tried hard to change the bird's behavior and was constantly saying polite words, playing soft music, doing anything he could think of to try to set a good example. Nothing worked. He yelled at the bird, and the bird got worse. He shook the bird, and the bird became angrier and ruder. Finally, in a moment of desperation, Bob put the parrot in the freezer. For a few moments he heard the bird squawking and cursing—and then suddenly there was quiet. Bob was afraid he had actually hurt the bird and quickly opened the freezer door. The parrot calmly stepped out onto Bob's extended arm and said, "I'm sorry that I might have offended you with my language and actions and ask for your forgiveness. I will endeavor to correct my behavior." Bob was astonished at the bird's change in attitude and was about to ask what had prompted such a drastic change when the parrot said, "Sir, may I ask what the chicken did?"

I related to the implication that the parrot was prepared to adopt the behavior that was expected of him but that he was not, it would seem, inwardly changed. The formality of his apology and the fact that he now calls Bob "sir" suggests that he is being deferential but only because he doesn't want to be placed in the freezer again. Also, his question about the chicken may be taken various ways, but when I thought of this question in light of the assignment, I detected a note of sarcasm in the parrot's query, a sarcasm disguised by the formality of the question: "Sir, may I ask . . . ?"

I suspect that the pretense of compliance with the directives of others is one of my own identity elements and that this would be consistent with my previous acknowledgment that I share Serge's positive response to spoofs on the authority of others. Such spoofs, which the parrot exhibits in this joke, are different, in my view (and in my sense of myself), from complaining about the errors and mistakes of those who are in power and from participating in efforts to make them more accountable for their actions. To me, the parrot's query about what the chicken did to deserve his fate has less of a sense of moral indignation and more of the tone of feigned curiosity. In this sense, I identify with the parrot who does not share Bob's own reformist identity element. Bob succeeded in making the parrot conform outwardly to Bob's own sense of propriety, but the parrot is just as rebellious, inwardly, as before. And I identify with *that*.

Here is the second joke:

Ole and Lena had the Torkelsons over for lutefisk and lefse. Torkelson liked his lutefisk with plenty of melted butter and pepper. Lena couldn't find the pepper, so she rummaged through the cupboard and found a container she thought was pepper. The next day Ole and Lena discovered it was actually gunpowder. So Ole called Torkelson on the phone and told him of the mistake. "Vell, I'm glad to find out what happened, becoss ven ve got home last night, I leaned over to tie my shoes and I accidentally shot da cat."

I related to the theme of the unintended consequence of the simple act of leaning over to tie his shoes. This entirely innocent act set off a series of events that had cat-astrophic consequences. The identity element here is one of interest in the laws of causation, or why one thing leads to another to another. Torkelson seems less concerned about the sad fate of the cat than about how it happened that he accidentally shot the cat, but this figured less in my relating to the joke than the fact that the Torkelsons were likely to pay a price for accepting a dinner invitation from that infamous couple in the Norwegian and Swedish joking tradition, Ole and Lena. So I related to this joke as one who takes interest in the laws of causation because I hope that my awareness of them may enable me to avoid the pain that I might otherwise experience at the hands of other persons whose ability to inflict pain may be predicted in advance. I am also aware, however, of how erratically I actually act on this interest. Thus, I find myself guessing that, should Ole and Lena invite the Torkelsons over for dinner again, Torkelson probably will accept and will do so against his better judgment.

If Karen were looking over my shoulder as I write this, she might ask me if this identity element works the other way, if others should be equally wary of my capacity to inflict pain on them. My answer to this question would be, "Unfortunately, yes." But I would add that the fact that I am aware that others need to be wary of the pain I may cause them is not an identity element of mine, whereas my own pain-avoidance is. This, I believe, points up the fact that my identity elements are more self-protective than altruistic. Put otherwise, I have a soft spot for the boy who lives inside of me who wondered, from an early age, about how he might protect himself from inflictions of pain that are, or appear to be, unintentional.

Subsequently, I also found myself relating to a third joke, one about a dog who plays poker:

Three men and an Irish setter were sitting at a table playing poker. The stakes were high and an onlooker was amazed to see the dog win two hands in a row. "That's incredible," said the onlooker. "I've never seen such a smart dog." "He ain't that smart," whispered one of the players. "Whenever he gets a good hand, he wags his tail."

To me, this joke is a significant improvement on the version I heard as a boy, and the nature of this improvement is what enabled me to relate to it. Here is the original version:

John saw Bill studying a chess board. Opposite him sat a dog. "What's going on?" asked John. "Just playing chess with my dog," answered Bill. "You're kidding!" exclaimed John. "Who ever heard of a dog who could play chess? That's the smartest dog I've ever seen." "Oh, I don't know about that," said Bill. "I've beaten him three games out of four."

In the version involving the poker game, the issue is not merely which player wins more than the other. More important is the skill employed in maintaining a "poker face," namely, not revealing one's hand by one's facial expression. The dog would seem to have the advantage here, as his facial expression is not nearly as variable as a human's, but this advantage is offset by a major disadvantage, namely, that dogs have expressive tails. The implication is that the dog will never be a great poker player until he can develop, as it were, a "poker tail."

I relate to this joke because I want to be more like the dog who *hasn't* learned to disguise his happiness over his good fortune. I am more like the human poker players who have learned that there are advantages to keeping one's elation to oneself—the poker face routine—and like the player who whispers that the dog is not so smart, I tend to think critically of those who talk about their good fortune, as I view this, rightly or wrongly, as bragging, and I tend to believe that no one likes a braggart. This joke, however, is not about chess, a game largely of skill, but about poker, a game in which luck plays a major role. So when the dog wags his tail, he is exulting in his good fortune, and to the other players, this very exultation is an indication that he is *not* as skillful as the others. Thus, "tail wagging" in this case signals that one has been dealt a "good hand" and is grateful for it. Perhaps the dog knows Psalm 16:6, "The boundary lines have fallen for me in pleasant places," and thanks God for this. In any event, this identity element reflects a desire to behave differently and may therefore challenge my earlier assertion that I do not share the parrot owner's "reformist" identity element. On the other hand, I think that this desire to change would not normally be viewed as an improvement, but rather as a regression to a less mature form of self-expression. After all, I am relating not to the humans in the joke but to the dog.

These accounts of Karen's and my responses to the animal and bird jokes in light of how we related to them suggests that one is likely to find two or three jokes out of a selection of fifteen that do in fact have relevance to Holland's idea that jokes are a stimulus to identity creation. This identification with two or three jokes has largely been the case with the friends and family members who have responded to my invitation—not unlike Ole and Lena's invitation to the Torkelsons to come over for lutefisk and lefsa!—to engage in the exercise. I will not report on all of these responses, but the following response from our son John, who is a philosophy professor, indicates that he, like his father, related to the joke about the foul-mouthed parrot who was placed in the freezer. He also related to another parrot joke and one about a rabbit. The parrot joke:

A lady bought a parrot from a pet store, only to find after taking the bird home that the bird would say nothing but "My name is Mary and I'm a whore." Weeks of trying to teach the bird other phrases proved useless. The bird still dropped the same line, usually at the most inopportune moments, much to the lady's embarrassment. One day her parish priest dropped by for a visit, and sure enough, while he was there the parrot squawked out the only words it would say. After apologizing profusely to the priest, the lady explained that her bird resisted all efforts at reformation. The priest offered to take the bird to visit the two birds he had, as all his birds would say were Hail Marys while clutching rosaries in their claws. He was certain they would have a good influence on the lady's bird. So he took the parrot to his house and put it in the cage with his two birds, and the first words out of the newcomer's mouth were, "My name is Mary and I'm a whore." The priest, being most anxious to see what would happen, was dumbfounded when one of his birds said to the other, "Throw that damned rosary away! Our prayers have been answered!"

And here is the rabbit joke:

A rabbit escaped from the research laboratory where he had been born and bred. On his first taste of freedom, he met a group of wild rabbits frolicking in a field. "Hi," he said, introducing himself, "I've escaped from the laboratory and I've never been outside before. What do you rabbits do all day?" "See that field over there?" They said. "It's full of plump, juicy carrots. Care to try some?" So they all went off and ate some carrots. "That was great," said the escaped rabbit afterwards. "What else do you do?" "See that field over there?" they said. "It's full of fat lettuces. Care to try some?" So they all went off and devoured the lettuces. "This is wonderful," said the escaped rabbit. "I really love it out here in the wild." "So are you going to stay with us?" they asked. "I'd really like to, but I've got to get back to the laboratory. I'm dying for a cigarette."

John began his response by observing that he related to these three jokes because the animals acted the most humanlike in comparison with the animals in the other jokes. In the two parrot jokes, the parrots draw inferences from what happens. Their conclusions are based on faulty assumptions but are rational nonetheless. Bob's parrot assumes that if he was put into the freezer for his bad behavior, then the same goes for the chicken. Similarly, the parrot in the second joke assumes that the parrot named Mary has come as an answer to prayer, while the real reason she has been placed there is that the priest believed the two male parrots would have a positive influence on her. Thus, where I had related to what I considered the feigned reformation and the note of sarcasm in Bob's parrot's query about the chicken, John related to what he felt was the parrot's understandable but erroneous assumption that the chicken had been placed in the freezer for the same reason that he had been put there, that is, for punishment and, hopefully, reformation.

As for the rabbit joke, John mentioned that the rabbit is, of course, addicted to cigarettes but seems to have some self-consciousness of the sacrifices that this addiction entails, and this too seems very human.

As he thought further about these three jokes, John also found himself relating to "their almost political sensibility," as they poke fun at people who have meat in their freezer, at laboratories that conduct animal research, and at the hyper-religious: "So maybe I relate to the first parrot joke in agreeing with the parrot: 'So what did the chicken ever do to you?' " Likewise, the second parrot joke suggests "that the Lord may work in mysterious ways, and not always in the ways predicted by his ardent believers." In these further reflections on why he related to these particular jokes, John shifts somewhat from his earlier theme of "faulty albeit rational reasoning" and introduces a new identity theme of "political sensibility," which relates to inhumane treatment of animals but which he also extends to religion. He indicates that he does not identify with "ardent believers" (this may be viewed as a negative identity theme), but he does resonate with the idea that God works in mysterious ways, that is, in ways that these ardent believers would not have predicted. In this sense, the "ardent believer"—the parish priest—is the one who engages in "faulty reasoning," mistakenly assuming that his two male parrots are truly devout and will have a positive moral effect on the female parrot.

John concluded his reflections with this comment: "I'm worried that I might have wandered into some cliché or trap, but that's where I am right now." This comment—which may itself reveal an identity theme of wariness of empirical research studies—may be another reason he liked the rabbit joke, and also why he suggested that I should pay him for his willingness to participate in *my* research project.[5]

With a bit of cajoling, I was also successful in getting Evelyn, John's wife, also a philosophy professor, to read through the fifteen jokes and tell me the ones to which she related. She selected the bat joke to which Karen related *and* to the joke about the poker-playing Irish setter to which I related. Evelyn related to the joke about the bat flying smack-dab into the tree because she relates to "people who are clumsy," and she related to the joke about the tail-wagging dog because she relates to "people who are smart in some ways but not in others due to their natural make-up." Her use of the word *people* in reference to the bat joke suggests that she does not, as did Karen, associate the hapless bat with small children who collide into objects because their minds are focused on something else. Rather, she associates the bat with persons who are clumsy at what they do, and presumably, clumsiness might include a whole range of missteps, including physical but also mental and perhaps social clumsiness as well. As Evelyn also observed that she appreciates jokes that are at one's own expense more than jokes that are at another's expense, we are probably justified in assuming that she relates to the bat joke both because she feels for others who are "clumsy" and because she identifies with them in some ways. They are not objects of ridicule or scorn, but of empathic understanding. So in effect, an identity theme of hers is empathy toward anyone, including herself, who displays a certain clumsiness in situations in which adroitness is prized and rewarded by others.

As for the joke about the dog who wags his tail, Evelyn's grounds for relating to it are quite similar to my own, as she too notes that in this case, the dog's "natural make-up"—the tendency of his tail to wag when he is happy—works against him in a situation that calls for an implacable demeanor. But she takes this observation further and notes that she relates to "people who are smart in some ways but not in others due to their natural make-up." This seems to suggest an empathy for persons who are betrayed, more or less, by aspects of themselves over which they have relatively little control. It may also be significant that she picks up on the word "smart" in the joke itself, and relates to this way of characterizing the dog's abilities and disabilities. Only a smart dog could play poker in the first place, but a dog whose tail gives himself and his hand away isn't as smart as he needs to be if he wants to be a consistent winner at playing poker. "Smart" in this case does not mean the same thing as "smart" in the intellectual sense but has to do with the ability to function effectively in a situation in which social skills are especially required. Thus, it may be that social acumen is one of Evelyn's identity themes and that she relates to the dog in this joke because he is able to perform in a social world that is not considered his own by natural or ascribed right or prerogative.

Her identification with the dog's social acumen may, however, point to another identity theme, that of an awareness that the cards are, quite literally, stacked against her and others like her because, as the joke suggests, the other players take advantage of the fact that the dog has a natural characteristic—a wagging tail—that would not be a liability in his own context. How, in other words, would the humans in this joke function if the issue were that of skill in fetching sticks or, more to the point of the joke itself, in welcoming a dog who has returned home after a grueling business trip or a tough day at work? Would the human be as skillful in demonstrating his happiness that his Rover has returned home safe and sound? Thus, as in John's relating to certain jokes, Evelyn seems also to be relating to the jokes she has selected with a degree of "political sensibility," and it is perhaps worth noting that such sensibility is less evident in the ways in which Karen and I related to the jokes that we selected.

I noted earlier that I tried this set of fifteen animal and bird jokes out on a few friends as well. One friend, Carl, looked the jokes over and commented that he doesn't like jokes that "anthropomorphize" animals, so most of his responses focused on why the jokes were not very funny to him, how one might "fix" those whose humor does not depend on such anthropomorphizing, and what "pet lovers" (a group to which he does not belong) would think about these jokes: "I bet they'd find them funny or offensive depending on how the animals and birds made out."

His only comment that seems close to a "relating to" response is in reference to the following joke:

A boy called on his girlfriend at her tenth-story apartment in readiness for their date. While she was getting dressed, he played ball in the lounge with her small dog. Unfortunately, the door to the balcony was open, and when the ball bounced out the door and over the ledge of the balcony, the little dog followed it. A few moments later, the girl appeared. The boy asked, "Have you noticed your dog has been acting depressed lately?"

After noting that this joke "almost works," Carl added, "We can imagine a dog being, at least, sad. And we can absolutely imagine a kid trying to work his way out of that kind of dilemma." The identity theme here might be that of working one's way out of a tough spot or dicey situation that one has gotten oneself into. As Carl held a high managerial position prior to his retirement, I am aware from the stories he has told me that this was a skill he had difficulty developing, largely because he felt it was incumbent on him to be straightforward and honest with the people he worked with. If he had been the boy, he probably would have said, "Guess what? I was playing ball with your dog, and the door to the balcony was open. Your dog chased the ball, and both he and it fell over the ledge. See that blob on the pavement below? That's him!" He might even have added, "Want me to go down and retrieve your ball?"

Conclusion

I have emphasized in this chapter *personal* or *individual* identity themes because this is the focus of Holland's own studies of humor and identity. Whether any attempt to identify significant personal identity themes by means of animal and bird jokes is highly illuminating or a colossal waste of time is up to the reader to judge, but at least there is something to be said for focusing on the identity themes of *individuals* when more and more complaints are being expressed that the individual doesn't seem to count for much anymore. As William James observed more than a hundred years ago:

> The first thing the intellect does with an object is to class it along with something else. But any object that is infinitely important to us and awakens our devotion feels to us also as if it must be *sui generis* and unique. Probably a crab would be filled with a sense of personal outrage if it could hear us class it without ado or apology as a crustacean, and thus dispose of it. "I am no such thing," it would say; "I am MYSELF, MYSELF alone." (1902/1982, 9)

On the other hand, humor also might be employed to identify *group* identity themes, and jokes about ethnicity (which will be introduced in chapter 3 and discussed in greater detail in chapter 4) are especially relevant in this regard. Yet here too animal and bird jokes may be useful, as they may help to identify some of the more informal ways in which two or more individuals share identity themes. An illustration of this shared identity are those of us who don't use personal computers and therefore are unable to communicate via e-mail. We rely instead on the telephone and what some computer users refer to disparagingly as "snail mail" (i.e., the U.S. Postal Service). This reliance on "snail-mail" raises the issue of how group identities often are formed over against what the majority of persons value or, in this case, devalue, namely, communicating via letters that are placed in envelopes, stamped, and dropped into the corner mailbox.

Three snail jokes appear as a group in Ted Cohen's *Jokes: Philosophical Thoughts on Joking Matters* (1999, 39). Notice that two of them also involve turtles.

What does a snail say when riding on the back of a turtle?
"Whee!"

A turtle was mugged and robbed by a gang of snails. When the police asked for a description of the villains, the turtle replied, "I'm sorry, but I just don't know. It all happened too fast."

One evening a man hears a faint tapping at his front door. When he opens the door he sees no one, and then he notices a snail on the ground. He picks up the snail and heaves it as far as he can across the lawn. A year later he hears a tapping at the door again, and again when he opens the door nothing is there except the snail, who says, "What the hell was that all about?"

These snail jokes betray a certain affection for the slow-moving and slow-to-react snail. They imply, by their rather gentle tone, that there is something about the snail that deserves our admiration. The snail is blessed with antennae that enable him to chart his way, and though certainly slow, he knows where he is going and is quite methodical about getting there. I have spoken with other nonusers of e-mail, and while they do not all share my dislike for the very phrase *snail mail*, they do share in common with one another the belief that faster is not always better. This, it seems to me, is a *group* identity theme, and while it is not unique to nonusers of e-mail, it is nonetheless one that makes for a common bond between us. I conclude this chapter with my favorite snail joke, one that suggests that snails have a great deal to teach us anxiety-ridden humans.

A wife and her husband were having a dinner party for some important guests. The wife was very excited about this and wanted everything to be perfect. At the very last minute, she realized that she didn't have any snails for the party, so she asked her husband to run down to the beach with a bucket to gather some fresh ones. Very grudgingly, he agreed. He took the bucket and walked out the door, down the steps, and out to the beach. As he was collecting the snails, he noticed a beautiful woman strolling alongside the water just a little farther down the beach. He kept thinking to himself, *Wouldn't it be great if she would just come down and talk to me?* He went back to gathering the snails. All of a sudden, he looked up, and the beautiful woman was standing right over him. They started talking, and eventually she invited him back to her place. They ended up spending the night together. At seven o'clock the next morning, he woke up and exclaimed, "Oh, no! My wife's dinner party!" He gathered all his clothes, struggled into them quickly, grabbed his bucket, and ran out the door. He ran along the beach all the way to his apartment and began running up the stairs. He was in such a hurry that when he got to the top of the stairs, he dropped the bucket of snails, scattering them all the way down the stairs. Just then, the door opened; his very angry wife stood in the doorway wondering where he'd been all this time. He looked at the snails all down the steps; then he looked at her, then back at the snails, and he said, "Come on, guys, we're almost there!"6

As my friend Carl might say, "We can imagine a cadre of snails needing some encouragement to complete an arduous journey. And we can absolutely imagine a guy trying to work his way out of that kind of dilemma."

Motoring through the Bible Belt

Stop That Mule!

Absalom happened to meet the servants of David. Absalom was riding on his mule, and the mule went under the thick branches of a great oak. His head caught fast in the oak, and he was left hanging between heaven and earth, while the mule that was under him went on.
2 Samuel 18:9

Absalom had
A smooth-shaved chin,
'Twas his head of hair
That did him in.
Burma-Shave

3. Humor as Expression of Intimacy

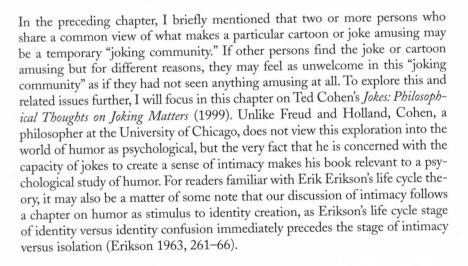

In the preceding chapter, I briefly mentioned that two or more persons who share a common view of what makes a particular cartoon or joke amusing may be a temporary "joking community." If other persons find the joke or cartoon amusing but for different reasons, they may feel as unwelcome in this "joking community" as if they had not seen anything amusing at all. To explore this and related issues further, I will focus in this chapter on Ted Cohen's *Jokes: Philosophical Thoughts on Joking Matters* (1999). Unlike Freud and Holland, Cohen, a philosopher at the University of Chicago, does not view this exploration into the world of humor as psychological, but the very fact that he is concerned with the capacity of jokes to create a sense of intimacy makes his book relevant to a psychological study of humor. For readers familiar with Erik Erikson's life cycle theory, it may also be a matter of some note that our discussion of intimacy follows a chapter on humor as stimulus to identity creation, as Erikson's life cycle stage of identity versus identity confusion immediately precedes the stage of intimacy versus isolation (Erikson 1963, 261–66).

Anecdotal and Formulaic Jokes

Cohen begins his book with the observation that we should not take as a matter of course "the fact that there is a kind of story meant to make us laugh. The fact of jokes—the fact that there are such things—is something of note, something worth thinking about" (1). He also emphasizes that his book is only about the type of humor known as "jokes." Thus, his book may be viewed as having more in common with Freud's book, which focuses on jokes, than with Holland's book, which focuses on cartoons. He mentions, further, that the jokes he has in mind are of two kinds: "One is the kind of joke that is a very short story—fictional, beginning with a description of people, then things, and then actions, and ending with a very concise conclusion (usually a single sentence) called 'the punch line'" (1–2). This type of joke typically begins with openings such as, "The Pope decides to have a garden made inside the Vatican," "A priest in a small parish in the south of Ireland found that paganism had appeared among his parishioners," or "A Jew was called to serve in the army." The last of these three openings is from a joke that occurs in Freud's book on jokes. This is the version that Freud tells:

> Itzig had been declared fit for service in the artillery. He was clearly an intelligent lad, but intractable and without any interest in the service. One of his superior officers, who was friendly disposed to him, took him on one side and said to him, "Itzig, you're no use to us. I'll give you a piece of advice: buy yourself a cannon and make yourself independent!" (Freud 1905/1960, 64)

Freud suggests that this advice "is obvious nonsense. Cannons are not to be bought and an individual cannot make himself independent as a military unit—set himself up in business, as it were" (65). Elliott Oring suggests, however, that making himself independent is "just the way Freud wished he could behave" at the time he wrote his book on jokes (22). If so, Freud's pleasure in this joke supports Holland's idea that jokes involve a dialectic of defense and fantasy, the defense being expressed in Freud's reluctance to submit to the confining viewpoints of his chosen profession, and the fantasy being expressed in the idea that he might, in fact, go independent, which is largely what he *did* do when he formed his own psychoanalytic association.

The second kind of joke is more obviously formulaic. Examples are lightbulb-changing jokes, knock-knock jokes, elephant jokes, and the like. These jokes typically begin with a question—"How many Christian Scientists does it take to change a lightbulb?"—but not always. Such formulaic jokes typically involve a task and an agent. In some, the task (i.e., changing the lightbulb) is held constant. In others, the agent (e.g., bureaucrats, Nebraskans, poets, White House aides, etc.) is held constant. In still others ("Why did the chicken cross the road?") the task and agent are held constant, but the motive changes.

Cohen observes that the distinction between short story and formulaic jokes is often blurred. This happens, for example, in the question "How many Jewish mothers does it take to change a lightbulb?" This, he proposes, is destined to be both a lightbulb-changing joke and a Jewish mother joke. It also may be noted, though Cohen does not make this point, that two forms of one of these types of jokes may occur in the same joke. For example, "A minister, a priest, and a rabbi go into a bar. The bartender asks, 'Is this some kind of a joke?'" The ingenuity behind this joke is that a "minister, priest, and rabbi" story is wedded to the "a guy goes into a bar" story.

Problem-solving Jokes

Cohen further notes that many jokes may be thought of as solutions to problems. Lightbulb-changing jokes are cases in point. The solution in this case is purely mechanical, one of replacing the old bulb with a new bulb. But then the human element enters in, and this complicates matters. The following joke is an example of misguided problem solving:

> A couple of New Jersey hunters are out in the woods when one of them falls to the ground. He doesn't seem to be breathing, and his eyes are rolled back in his head. The other guy whips out his cell phone and calls the emergency services. He gasps to the operator, "My friend is dead! What can I do!" The operator, in a calm, soothing voice, says, "Just take it easy. I can help. First, let's make sure he's dead." There is a silence, then a shot is heard. The guy's voice comes back on the line. He says, "OK, now what?"[1]

Freud's Itzig story also may be viewed as a problem-solving joke. While officially declared fit for artillery service, Itzig was clearly unfit due to his intractibility and lack of interest in the service. But how to excuse him from the service in a way that would be responsible to the service yet kindly toward him? This is just one of the many jokes that plays on the difficulty of communicating bad news to someone else. The jokes are based on the idea that one should save as much expenditure of painful emotions as possible.

Freud's "marriage broker" jokes fall into the same category of problem solving. These jokes are based on the following formula: The prospective groom is introduced to the prospective bride by the broker, the prospective groom takes the marriage broker aside and expresses his objections to the proposed match, and the broker responds to the objections by claiming that they are immaterial or, in fact, points in favor of the match. For example,

> The would-be bridegroom complained that the bride had one leg shorter than the other and limped. The *Schadchen* [marriage broker] contradicted him: "You're wrong. Suppose you marry a woman with healthy, straight limbs! What do you gain from it? You never have a day's security that she won't fall down, break a leg, and afterwards be lame all her life. And think of the suffering then, the agitation, and the doctor's bill! But if you take *this* one, that can't happen to you. Here you have a *fait accompli*." (72)

In the following example, the marriage broker takes a different tack:

> The *Schadchen* was defending the girl he had proposed against the young man's protests. "I don't care for the mother-in-law," said the latter, "She's a disagreeable, stupid person." "But after all, you're not marrying the

mother-in-law. What you want is her daughter." "Yes, but she's not young any longer, and she's not precisely a beauty." "No matter. If she's neither young nor beautiful, she'll be all the more faithful to you." "And she hasn't much money." "Who's talking about money? Are you marrying money then? After all, it's a wife you want." "But she's got a hunchback too." "Well, what *do* you want? Isn't she to have a single fault?" (71)

There is a similar defense in the following example:

The bridegroom was paying his first visit to the bride's house in the company of the broker, and while they were waiting for the family to appear, the broker drew attention to a cupboard with glass doors in which the finest set of silver plate was exhibited. "There! Look at that! You can see from these things how rich these people are." "But," asked the suspicious young man, "mightn't it be possible that these fine things were only collected for the occasion—that they were borrowed to give an impression of wealth?" "What an idea!" answered the broker protestingly. "Who do you think would lend these people anything?" (75)

Sometimes, however, the marriage broker forgets himself and unintentionally supports the prospective bridegroom's objections:

The bridegroom was most disagreeably surprised when the bride was introduced to him, and drew the broker on one side and whispered his remonstrances. "Why have you brought me here?" he asked reproachfully. "She's ugly and old, she squints and has bad teeth and bleary eyes. . . ." "You needn't lower your voice," interrupted the broker. "She's deaf as well." (74–75)

In the following version, the marriage broker's assistant undermines the case the broker is attempting to make on behalf of the proposed match:

A marriage broker had brought an assistant with him to the discussion about the proposed bride, to bear out what he had to say. "She is straight as a pine tree," said the *Schadchen*. "As a pine-tree," repeated the echo. "And she has eyes that ought to be seen!" "What eyes she has!" confirmed the echo. "And she is better educated than anyone!" "What an education!" "It's true there's one thing," admitted the broker. "She has a small hump." "And *what* a hump!" the echo confirmed once more. (74)

These marriage broker stories illustrate Cohen's point that many jokes involve solutions to problems and that they may well be created in this way. In this respect, he argues, "they bear a faint resemblance to problems of simultaneous equations in elementary algebra. Find x and y, when $x + y = x - y = 3$" (3).

But they also illustrate another, more central point of his analysis, namely, that the success of a joke depends on the hearer's knowledge or awareness of the *conditions* that it presupposes (3). These conditions are usually implied, for to state them or make them overt would ruin the joke. The more the hearers are aware of these conditions, the more likely they will be to recognize the humor involved. Freud suggests, for example, that the "condition" these marriage broker jokes addressed was the institution of arranged marriages (see Orring 1984, 28). Yet for Freud, this formal "condition" is perhaps the most superficial one. More important is the fact that this social institution is based on duplicity, deception, and exploitation. Thus, what attracts his attention is the fact that the marriage broker "accidentally" says what one is not supposed to say and thus finds a way around a costly inhibition, one that is detrimental to the individuals involved and to the society that agrees to look the other way. He writes:

> In any case, if our marriage-broker anecdotes are jokes, they are all the better jokes because, thanks to their facade, they are in a position to conceal not only what they have to say but also the fact that they have something—forbidden—to say. The continuation of this interpretation—and this uncovers the hidden meaning and reveals these anecdotes with a comic facade as tendentious jokes—would be as follows. Anyone who has allowed the truth to slip out in an unguarded moment is in fact glad to be free of pretense. This is a correct and profound piece of psychological insight. (126)

Significantly, it is the marriage broker himself who lets the truth slip out in an unguarded moment, and this, in Freud's view, "converts the laughable figure of the *Schadchen* into a sympathetic one, deserving of pity. How happy the man must be to be able at last to throw off the burden of pretense, since he makes use of the first chance of shouting out the very last scrap of truth!" (126).

Freud goes on to suggest that the marriage broker allows the truth to come forth "as soon as he sees that the case is lost" (126–27). Then, and only then, does he betray another concealed defect that has escaped notice ("She's deaf as well!") or

> express his contempt for the people he is working for: "I ask you—who would lend these people anything?" The whole of the ridicule in the anecdote now falls upon the parents, barely touched on in it, who think this swindle justified in order to get their daughter a husband, upon the pitiable position of girls who let themselves be married on such terms, and upon the disgracefulness of marriages contracted on such a basis (127).

Thus, it is the marriage broker himself who "inadvertently" exposes the deception and deceit in the practice of arranged marriages, and he is the right man to express such criticisms, for he knows most about these abuses; but he must not say them aloud, for he is a poor man whose existence depends on exploiting them. The popular mind, which created these stories, and others like them, is torn by a similar conflict; for it knows that the sacredness of marriages after they have been contracted is grievously affected by the thought of what happened at the time when they were arranged. (127)

Perhaps the closest analogy to the marriage broker in our society is the used-car salesman.

The Conditionality of Jokes

In my view, Freud's psychological analysis of the conditions that underlie marriage-broker jokes successfully challenges the argument that he was wrong to include these jokes in his book on the grounds that they are unfavorable toward women. But I leave this to the reader to decide. For our purposes here, these marriage-broker jokes illustrate Cohen's point that it helps to know the conditions that the joke assumes or takes for granted, and that the more knowledgeable one is with regard to these conditions, the more likely it is that the hearer will not only "get" the joke but also find it amusing. Cohen notes that some of the most conditional jokes are ones involving the topics and jargon of a professor. To "get" the joke, you may need to know some things about this particular professor that only a member of the profession knows. On the other hand, for most of the professional jokes that are told, one needs only to know the assumed or attributed characteristics of members of this profession. Jokes about lawyers who have no heart and no principles are examples of this.

Cohen cites the following joke to explain that in some cases one needs to know two conditional facts:

> Early one morning a man awoke in a state of terrible anxiety because of the dream he had been having. He immediately called his psychiatrist, and after making a special plea because of his distress, he was granted an appointment that morning even though it was not the day for seeing his psychiatrist. When he arrived in the doctor's office, he said, "I had the most awful dream you can imagine. In it I raped my mother, killed my wife, and seduced my daughter, and more things worse than those. I woke up shaking and sweating, and I called you immediately. Then I had a quick piece of toast and some coffee, and ran down here to see you." "What?" said the psychiatrist. "You call that a breakfast?" (14–15)

What one needs to know is "the exceptionally high proportion of Jews among psychiatrists, and to know the commonplace about Jewish mothers that they are excessively concerned, especially about food" (15). A third "condition" adds another basis for enjoyment of this particular joke. In Cohen's view, "The joke is deeper for those who believe it an occupational hazard of psychiatry that its practitioners tend to look for deep and convoluted explanations when simple and direct ones would do, and, conversely, that they tend to look only at the surface in the few cases in which something hidden is at work" (15).

Cohen emphasizes that the teller or hearer of the joke does not actually need to believe the "condition" that underlies it. One only needs to be acquainted with the idea. While someone else might refer to these as "stereotypes," he prefers to call them "commonplaces." Thus, the joke "The thing about German food is that no matter how much you eat, an hour later you're hungry for power" requires that one knows "the old chestnut about Chinese food invariably leaving one hungry soon after eating, whether one believes that about Chinese food or not," and that one also knows "the commonplace about Germans that they long to control others, to have and to wield power" (21). Cohen also suggests that "it makes some difference whether one only knows this commonplace, or whether one knows it and believes it to be true. And finally, it matters whether one has negative feelings about Germans on that count, or doesn't. If it offends one to have Germans represented in this way, then the amusement may be lost altogether" (21–22).

Having mentioned the importance of knowledge of the conditions underlying the joke in order to "get" and also appreciate it, Cohen takes up the question, "If jokes rely for their success on the hearer knowing the conditions that they assume, why not include these conditions in the joke itself?" He answers this question in this way: First, when the joke is encumbered in this way, it seems labored and even contrived. While there are exceptions, good jokes tend to be concise. But conciseness as such is not the essential point. A second and more fundamental point is that the overt statement of the underlying conditions of the joke is unnecessary because the hearer already knows them or is assumed to know them. They therefore can go unsaid, and this fact—that something goes unsaid—is typically what makes the joke funny or amusing.

Joking as a Communal Act

The very fact that the joke's underlying conditions can go unsaid leads Cohen to suggest that "a deep satisfaction in successful joke transactions is the sense held mutually by teller and hearer that they are joined in feeling" (25). This means that the teller of the joke begins "with an implicit acknowledgment of a shared background, a background of awareness that you both are already in possession of and bring to the joke. This is the foundation of the intimacy that will develop if your joke succeeds, and the hearer then also joins you in a shared response to the joke" (28). Thus, if you *have* to explain or make a direct reference to the conditions that the joke assumes, you are probably telling the joke to the wrong hearers and setting yourself up for a deflating reaction. And when this happens, the joke teller has no reason to condemn the hearer, to claim, for example, that the hearer is a humorless clod: "All you can say of the fellow who doesn't laugh at your joke . . . is that *he is not like you*, at least not in regard to the dynamics of your joke" (26, Cohen's emphasis).

On the other hand, the fact that the hearer did not laugh at your joke is not an insignificant fact, for what has happened in this case is the failure of "the effort to achieve an intimacy between teller and hearer. It is a failure to join one another in a community of appreciation. It is exactly this community that begins to be marshaled when conditional jokes are told" (26–27). Thus, on the plus side, when the hearer does join you in a shared response to the joke, the *intimacy* that results is "the shared sense of those in a *community*. The members know that they are in this community, and they know that they are joined there by one another" (28, Cohen's emphasis). This intimacy has two constituents. One is a shared set of beliefs, dispositions, prejudices, preferences, and so forth—a shared outlook on the world, or at least part of such an outlook. The other is a shared feeling—a shared response to something. Both may be cultivated without jokes, but jokes exemplify the second constituent—shared feeling—by means of the first—shared beliefs and so on—and this, Cohen suggests, "is a very curious and wonderful fact about jokes" (28).

He admits that he may be overvaluing the intimacy made available through joke telling. Still, he is confident that this is an intimacy that we should not underestimate. After all, "when we laugh at the same thing, that is a very special occasion. It is already noteworthy that we laugh at all, at anything, and that we laugh all alone. That we do it *together* is the satisfaction of a deep human longing, the realization of a desperate hope. It is the hope that we are enough like one another to sense one another, to be able to live together" (29, Cohen's emphasis).

But what about jokes for which the teller and the hearer do not share the relevant background? He calls these jokes "asymmetrical" and cites the example of adults urging a child to tell a joke the child does not understand, "thinking it somehow cute that the child tells a good joke without understanding it" (32). More complex examples are ethnic jokes that are told in settings in which shared beliefs and feelings are absent. If the requisite conditions are not met, then the teller is engaged "in a kind of fraudulence, and as with all kinds of lying, deceit, and fraudulence," is "subject to moral appraisal" (35). Put otherwise, "an insincere, hollow intimacy" is worse than stiff formality (35).

Moral Considerations in Joke Telling

Cohen explores the issue of morality in joke telling in his concluding chapter "Taste, Morality, and the Propriety of Joking." He confesses at the outset, "I believe jokes and joke-telling are wonderful and can be very serious, but I am also aware of the danger in too much joke-telling and joke-telling when it is out of place" (p. 69). He further acknowledges that by and large, men are more likely to tell jokes to one another than women are likely to tell jokes to one another, which may be because women "have other conversational devices for establishing and maintaining intimacy," whereas for men "joke-telling is a primary device of this kind" (69). There is nothing inherently wrong with this, but he cautions against joke telling "when it is a kind of avoidance." For example, telling a joke about death can be a way of dealing with death, but it can also be a way of avoiding death. He admits that he is one of those who tends to tell too many jokes, too often, and in too many kinds of situations. (He manages to pack 166 jokes into a book of only 99 pages.) Cohen and others like him usually get away with it because the laughter and ostensible humor are considered good things, even if they come at the cost of other good things. But he feels that he and others like him really shouldn't get away with it, at least not as much as they do, "because a laugh is not always worth it, not if it is a deflection from something else that needs to be done" (70).

From this more general point about the "propriety" of joke telling, Cohen moves to the subject of humor that is offensive to someone. There are jokes that poke fun at a certain group of people and are not offensive, but there are others of this type that *are* likely to give offense. Cohen doubts that there is any easy formula to tell us which jokes are offensive or when it is the wrong time to put forth a particular joke, but he thinks it may be possible to explain what has gone wrong when these transgressions occur.

Taking ethnic jokes as an example, he suggests that there is a kind of so-called ethnic joke in which the ethnicity of the characters is not essential to the joke. For example, a joke about a person who is inept or stupid might begin, "There was an Irishman who . . . ," but the joke could just as well be told about a Swede, or an Italian, or someone from New Jersey. Here's a joke I sent to my wife's mother, who is ninety years old, when she left the apartment she had been living in for twenty-five years and moved to a retirement home:

> Ole had been placed in a nursing home, and before long, things got boring. So Ole made a sign by hand that read: Whoopee on the bed, $20; on the chair, $10; on the floor, $5. He put the sign outside his door, but nothing happened until three days later, when there was a rap on his door. There stood a little old lady with a $20 bill in her hand. "Oh," said Ole, "I suppose you want one on the bed?" "No," said the old gal, "I want four on the floor."

Ole, of course, is a Scandinavian name, and I suspect that the fact my wife's mother is Norwegian added to her enjoyment of the story. But the implied message in my sending this joke to her had less to do with Ole's ethnic background and more to do with the fact that she was entering a retirement home for the first time in her life. I also sent her this Ole joke:

> Ole came home to his apartment one night, snorting, "Dat janitor, what a bragger. He claims he's made love to every voman in dis apartment building except one." "Humph," said Ole's wife, "must be that snooty Mrs. Peterson on third floor."

She liked this joke too, and no doubt the fact that it contains Scandinavian names added to her appreciation of it. But both jokes could be adapted to virtually any ethnic group, and it seems unlikely that any such adaptation would give offense to whatever ethnic group this happened to be.

In Cohen's view, however, there are other jokes in which the ethnicity itself is a substantial element of the joke. He tells this Irish joke, which he notes is also an English joke:

> An out-of-work Irishman went walking around London until he found a construction site with a sign announcing that workmen were being hired. When he applied for the job, it was his bad luck that the foreman in charge was an Englishman with a dismal view of the Irish. "So, Paddy, you think you can do the work?" asked the foreman. "Oh, yes," said the Irishman, "I've been doin' construction for thirty years." "Then you really understand construction?" asked the foreman. "Of course," said the Irishman, "I can do it all—the plumbin', the electric, the carpentry." "Then you wouldn't mind if I gave you a bit of a test?" asked the foreman. "No, no. Test away." "Then tell me, Paddy, what is the difference between a joist and a girder?" "It's too easy," said the Irishman. " 'Twas the former wrote *Ullyses*, whilst the latter wrote *Faust*." (71)

Cohen suggests that this joke plays on the perception of the Irish as excessively literary and the perception that the English "don't care much for the Irish" (72). This joke may or may not be offensive when told to someone Irish or English, but Cohen's point is that ethnic commonplaces are integral to the joke itself. Change the ethnicity of the out-of-work construction worker to an Australian, Swede, or Iranian, and the joke loses its point.

While some people think it is wrong to tell jokes that make use of these ethnic commonplaces because they reflect false or inaccurate stereotypes, Cohen disagrees. Jokes that make use of the "putative characteristics" of the person in the story, like the one about the Irish workman who knows his Joyce and Goethe, are, if not better, at least "richer and subtler" than jokes in which the ascribed ethnicity is irrelevant to the humor involved, and "they are devices for achieving considerably greater intimacy" (75). Conversely, "if the only point in making a character in a joke Polish is to signal that he will be inept," then "some potential 'material' in the joke has gone unused, and this seems somehow a waste" (75). Furthermore, another reason for preferring a Polish or Irish joke in which it really matters that the character is Polish or Irish "is that such jokes require more of the hearer, involve him more intimately, and give him greater opportunity for self-congratulation in his appreciation of the joke. They involve a bigger and richer contribution from the hearer" (75).

Cohen acknowledges, however, that the very fact ethnic commonplaces are relevant to the meaning of a joke also creates a problem. In an important sense, the better such a joke might be, the more danger that it may be offensive or be considered "in bad taste." Admitting that it is exceedingly difficult to draw the line between what is and is not objectionable, he cites several jokes that he thinks cross the line. The reason may be that they purvey disagreeable stereotypes, but in his view, this is not a very reliable indicator of what is and is not offensive. In fact, he finds some jokes that are flattering to Jews to be more offensive than jokes that present Jews in an unflattering light. A more reliable guide is the feeling of *uneasiness* one has when hearing or reading the joke. To the extent that Cohen is able to probe his own uneasiness, he does not think that it has to do with the possibility that either he or the joke teller will begin to *believe* the conditions that the joke assumes, but neither does he think that if someone could *prove* these jokes have no pernicious effects that this would make the telling of them acceptable. What he finally concludes is that one should not—cannot—invoke some "moral theory" and then show that an implication of the theory is that this particular joke is bad. This is not because Cohen has no moral standards as far as jokes are concerned. If this were true, he would not be discussing the issue. Rather, it is because a moral theory usually needs to make the case that a certain behavior does genuine harm to someone (in this case, someone who belongs to the ethnic group in question, or the joke teller, or the joke hearer), and the difficulty in this case is that "genuine harm" is hard to establish or prove. One therefore risks having to give up one's moral complaint, "and you shouldn't do that" (82). Instead, you should trust your sense of uneasiness and "hold on to that feeling, and continue to express the feeling in terms of moral condemnation" (82). If someone asks you to provide a moral-theoretical reason for your condemnation, ask them why they think you need one. Also, you don't have to prove that the joke is unfunny in order to express your moral disapproval. It can be both funny and morally objectionable. You should not allow yourself to be judged lacking in a "sense of humor" when what you are actually doing is expressing your uneasiness with the joke on moral grounds.

Ethnic jokes are only one of many types of jokes that enable us to raise and discuss the issue of moral disapproval. What is important to note here, however, is that Cohen's treatment of the whole issue of taste, morality, and propriety in joking arises out of his emphasis on the fact that joking is a form of intimacy. If so, this intimacy, in his view, should not be gotten on the cheap. It should be genuine, not based on fraudulence, avoidances, and asymmetries. The internal locus of the need for such intimacy is the same locus from which our moral uneasiness originates. In fact, our moral uneasiness is due to an implicit awareness that we are settling for a cheapened form of intimacy instead of holding out for the real thing.

I decided to test Cohen's view that you can find a joke morally objectionable without having to assert that the joke isn't funny by giving students in one of my classes the following joke:

A small manufacturing company in the Northwest, Anderson Nails, had been experiencing years of success and growth. Feeling the company was ready to try for the big time, the owner, Mr. Anderson, contracted a big

Madison Avenue advertising agency to help him promote his product. Aiming to get the greatest possible exposure, the agency booked a full minute at the beginning of the Super Bowl's halftime show. Anderson was pretty excited about this and invited all of his friends and relatives to his home for a big Super Bowl party. At the end of the first half, everybody drew closer to the TV, waiting to see the premiere of the commercial. It began with an aerial shot of the desert and zoomed in on a small walled city. As the camera slowly panned around the city, it became apparent that this was Jerusalem during the Roman occupation. A large hill on the horizon came into view, and as the camera drew closer, a number of crosses became visible. The focus settled on a naked man wearing a crown of thorns, then moved in for an extreme close-up of his bleeding hands and the nails that held them to the cross. Clearly visible were the words MANUFACTURED BY ANDERSON NAILS. A subtitle appeared on the screen bearing the words "Anderson Nails—The Expert's Choice." Anderson's guests were horrified. The party broke up before the end of the game. The next day he began to get phone calls from his oldest and most loyal customers, expressing their outrage and canceling their orders. By the end of the week, his sales were down to nothing. He called the president of the advertising agency to cancel his contract. When Anderson explained his situation, the ad man was surprised and offered to run a new campaign at no charge. The new campaign was slated to start in a few weeks' time. This time, Anderson nervously watched the commercial alone in the privacy of his office. It began the same way as before, with an aerial view of Jerusalem. The camera finally settled on two Roman soldiers drinking wine at a table near the marketplace. Hearing a disturbance nearby, they looked up from their drinks in time to see a naked man with bleeding hands and feet being pursued by a group of soldiers. The first soldier looked at his companion, smiled knowingly, and said, "I bet they didn't use Anderson Nails!"[2]

After they had read the joke, the students were to check one of four boxes relating to the joke's funniness (very, quite, somewhat, not funny) and one of four boxes relating to its offensiveness (not, somewhat, quite, very offensive). On half of the questionnaires, the funny question came first; on the other half, the offensive question came first. The results (involving a total of 31 students, 16 women, and 15 men) were as follows: Nine students (5 men, 4 women) found the joke *very* offensive; of these, 8 found it *not* funny, 1 found it *somewhat* funny. Four students (2 men, 2 women) found the joke *quite* offensive; of these, 2 found it *not* funny, 2 found it *somewhat* funny. Ten students (8 women, 2 men) found the joke *somewhat* offensive; of these, 4 found it *not* funny, 3 found it *somewhat* funny, and 1 found it *quite* funny. Finally, eight students (6 men, 2 women) found the joke *not* offensive; of these, 5 found it *somewhat* funny, 2 found it *quite* funny, and 1 found it *very* funny. Thus, better than three-fourths of the students (24) found the joke offensive at least to some degree, and 14 of these did not find any humor in the joke at all. Conversely, among the eight students who found the joke inoffensive, all considered it funny to at least some degree. The fact, however, that there were seven students who found the joke funny despite the fact that they also found it offensive makes Cohen's point that one can view a joke as offensive yet not have to declare that it is also unfunny.

Because I thought the joke was "very funny" the first time I read it, and continue to think so, I realized from the survey that I was in a distinct minority. In fact, in support of Cohen's point that jokes are a way of expressing intimacy, I very much wanted to learn the identities of the three students who felt the joke was inoffensive and either quite or very funny. After class, one male student *did* in fact identify himself as one of the students who thought the joke was both inoffensive and *very* funny. Did he sense that I felt the same way, perhaps because he suspected that a professor would not have distributed the joke if he, personally, considered it offensive? Was he aware that many of the other students were offended by the joke—noting, as I did, their body language—and was therefore reaching out to me as one who seemed to share his beliefs and feelings about the joke? I don't know. What I *do* know is that I greatly appreciated his gesture, as the experiment had left me feeling somewhat isolated and alone because of my genuine surprise that so many of the students in the class found the joke both offensive and not very funny.

Why, then, did the majority of the students find the joke both offensive and not particularly funny? In the course of a conversation with a woman in the class who, in my view, has a great sense of humor and who I thought would find the joke both inoffensive and funny, I learned instead that she found it offensive. Why? "Because I don't think we should make fun of someone else's agony." Her response prompted me to think about the survey results in the light of Cohen's emphasis on the "conditions" that lie behind or beneath the joke. As I reflected on why I thought the joke was "very funny," I noticed that the "condition" that was central in my mind was the assumption held by many if not most Americans that the advertising industry is often ignorant of or chooses to disregard the tastes and standards of much of the American public. What I was responding to was the utter obtuseness of the advertising man, his inability to understand that his ideas for advertising Anderson Nails would be utterly offensive to the manufacturer's primary customers. In fact, what makes this a particularly useful joke for testing the very issue of funny versus offensive is that offensiveness is an integral theme of the joke itself. But if the condition that made the joke "very funny" to me was the obtuseness of the Madison Avenue advertising agency, the condition that made the joke "very offensive" to her was that it invoked the crucifixion of Jesus, and this, as she put it, is "no laughing matter."

In one sense, therefore, this experiment supports Cohen's view that knowledge of the conditions that the joke assumes may make a significant difference in one's appreciation of a joke. I confess in this regard that I suspected that the students in my class were insufficiently aware of the way in which the advertising industry runs roughshod over our values, ideals, and tastes and that they therefore failed to see the humor in a joke that satirized the tastelessness of a major and very influential American industry. On the other hand, I had to acknowledge that I was insufficiently sensitive to the condition that the students—in a course, after all, in pastoral care—would be most sensitive to, namely, the agony of a dying man. Thus, my enjoyment of the joke may well come under the indictment to which Cohen alludes when he says, "But joking is almost always out of place when it is a kind of avoidance," and adds, "Telling a joke about death can be a way of dealing with death, even of grappling with it; but sometimes the only proper way to think about death is to try looking it straight in its morbid, mordant eye, and on those occasions telling a joke is exactly the wrong thing to do because it is a way of avoiding the real issue" (69).

In this regard, it would have been the height of perversity for me to have distributed the questionnaire during Holy Week. Was it wrong, though, to distribute the questionnaire at all? I do not think so, but this is the very question that Cohen encourages us to ask, and in asking it, not to take refuge in a moral theory that requires those who have moral objections to this sort of joke to demonstrate that genuine harm was done by my doing so. On the other hand, if Cohen worries that a person who has moral objections to a particular joke may have these objections dismissed by others because he or she cannot prove that genuine harm was done, I think that many of the students in my class would have invoked some moral theory to support their belief that harm *was* done by my distribution of the questionnaire. In fact, they might have made their own uneasiness with the joke the basis of such a moral theory; that is, these persons might have argued that the harm itself was that of making them feel uncomfortable, and more objective evidence of harm would be perceived as unnecessary or superfluous. Thus, it may be that Cohen does not give sufficient attention to the fact that some persons believe that they have an adequate moral theory for their objections to a particular joke when in fact this theory may not be adequate. It also seems to be the case that in his concern to defend the person who finds a particular joke offensive, he does not give as much attention to the question of whether the offended person has a right to judge the unoffended person negatively.

I mentioned above that I wanted to learn the identities of all three students who found this joke inoffensive and quite or very funny. This desire supports Cohen's view that joking is a form of intimacy. Given the context in which the experiment took place, however, this intimacy could not be shared, though the fact that one student *did* come up to me after class to tell me how much he enjoyed the joke was an expression of a felt need for intimacy, one that was probably exacerbated by the fact that he felt like he was one of a rather beleaguered minority in this case. Thus, this too supports Cohen's view that even as humor creates intimacy, a community of appreciation among those who have a shared sense of beliefs, dispositions, prejudices, and preferences and a shared response to something, so humor also enables us to identify those who are *not* like ourselves. What I find especially valuable in this regard is his admonition that the "unlaughing listener is, in the end, nothing worse than not like you. He is not less human, at least in any demonstrable regard" (26). Also, as was proven by my conversation with the woman who objected to the joke on the grounds that it isn't right to make fun of someone else's agony, it is not the case that those who did not find this joke funny necessarily lack a sense of humor. As we saw in the previous chapter, what each of us finds humorous is directly and intimately related to our own identity themes.

Absurdity in Jewish Humor

I will conclude my discussion of Cohen's book with his chapter "Jewish Jokes and Acceptance of Absurdity." This, the longest chapter in the book, begins with the observation that while death is perhaps the final absurdity, it is not the only one, and it is certainly not the only absurdity that jokes may embrace. He suggests that joking is viewed within the very traditions of Judaism as a legitimate response to such incomprehensibilities. The sanction for this view is both biblical and Talmudic. He cites several Jewish jokes that display "a crazy logic . . . an insane rationality, a logical rigor gone over the edge" (48). These jokes fall under the heading of Freud's third joke category, those that rebel against the demand that human society places on us to engage in clear, rational thinking. For example:

> A man is lying asleep in bed with his wife one night when she wakes him, saying, "Close the window; it's cold outside." He grunts, rolls over, and goes back to sleep. His wife nudges him. "Close the window; it's cold outside." He moans, pulls the blankets closer, and goes back to sleep. Now his wife kicks him firmly and pushes him with both hands. "Go on. Close the window; it's cold outside." Grumbling, he slides out of bed, shuffles to the window, and bangs down the open lower half. Glaring at his wife, he says, "So now it's warm outside?"

In other cases, the joke incorporates a genuine contradiction or even a palpable implausibility, as when a Jewish man in New York asks the cabbie to take him to the Palmer House in Chicago. As the cabbie, after two days of nonstop driving, drops the man off, two women slide into the backseat and ask him to take them to Flatbush Avenue, to which the cabbie responds, "Sorry, ladies, I don't go to Brooklyn."

Then there are jokes in which the "logic" is very keen, as in this contemporary version of the traditional beggar joke:

> A poor Jewish man stopped at the home of a rich Jewish man to ask for a handout. "I don't give away money," declared the rich man, "but I have a Gentile who mows my lawn and I pay him $20. You mow my lawn and I'll pay you $25." "Let the Gentile keep the job," says the poor Jew. "Just give me the $5."

Or consider this beggar joke in which the "logic" becomes clear once one realizes that both beggars are Jewish and are working together:

> Two beggars are sitting on a park bench in Mexico City. One is holding a cross and one a Star of David. Both are holding hats to collect contributions. People walk by, lift their noses at the man with the Star of David, and drop money in the hat held by the man with the cross. Soon the hat of the man with the cross is filled, and the hat of the man with the Star of David is still empty. A priest watches and then approaches the men. He turns to the man with the Star of David and says, "Young man, don't you realize that this is a Catholic country? You'll never get any contributions in this country holding the Star of David." The man with the Star of David turns to the man with the cross and says, "Moise, can you imagine? This guy is trying to tell us how to run our business!"

Cohen traces this appreciation for "logic" that operates within the conditions of absurdity to the Bible, and specifically to God's announcement to Abraham that his wife, Sarah, will give birth to a child despite the advanced age of both parents. This announcement causes Abraham to throw himself on his face and laugh. "Can a child be born to a man who is a hundred years old? Can Sarah, who is ninety years old, bear a child?" (Gen 17:17). Cohen asks, Why is Abraham laughing? And exactly what is he laughing at? Is he laughing at the idea that a child might be born to a couple whose combined age is 190 years? Does he think it is impossible that there could be such a birth? In Cohen's view, what prompts Abraham to laugh is not that he finds it *impossible*, but that he cannot *comprehend* it. His laughter is a response to the fact that he has been presented with a situation that is beyond his capacity to understand.

It is the same for Sarah. As Genesis 18:1–15 reports, the Lord approached Abraham again via the presence of three strange men. They asked the whereabouts of Sarah, and when he answered, "There, in the tent," one of the men replied, "I will surely return to you in due season, and your wife Sarah shall have a son." Sarah was listening at the entrance of the tent, which was behind him, and she laughed to herself, saying, "After I have grown old, and my husband is old, shall I have pleasure?" Then the Lord said to Abraham, "Why did Sarah laugh?" adding, "Is anything too wonderful for the LORD?" Sarah denied that she laughed, "for she was afraid," but the Lord replied, "Oh yes, you did laugh" (Gen 18:9–15).[3]

What interests Cohen here is that the Lord insists on the fact of Sarah's laughter: "It is not at all clear that God disapproves of Sarah's laughter. He demands persistently that she admit that she laughed, and therein she acknowledges that God knows her laughter" (53). To be sure, one *could* say that if Abraham and Sarah were persons of perfect faith, they would not have laughed at God's idea. Cohen, however, "would not say that. I prefer to say that what Sarah is being shown—and what we are shown in Sarah—is that the most nearly per-

fect human faith and understanding are consistent with laughter" (53–54). That
Isaac's name means "laughter" and that Sarah says on the occasion of Isaac's birth
that "God has brought laughter for me; everyone who hears will laugh with me"
(Gen 21:6) is, to Cohen, confirmation not only that laughter is an appropriate
response to the incomprehensible experiences in life, but also, and more importantly, that God is the very one who creates the conditions for the laughter. Even
the sparing of Isaac on Mt. Moriah may be understood as "God Himself direct-
ing that laughter be freed and let loose in the world" (55).

Cohen also cites a passage from the Talmud in which a debate among scholars as to whether a cooking oven of a particular kind is ritually clean is settled on
the basis not of a heavenly voice but on the principle that the majority rules.
What did God say in response to this? According to the prophet Elijah, who was
there when God got wind of it, "He laughed, saying, 'My sons have defeated Me,
My sons have defeated Me" (56–57). What interests Cohen in this case is that
God laughs when *he* suffers defeat at the hands of these learned scholars.

In a contemporary version of this Talmudic story, four rabbis had had a series
of theological arguments in which three were always in accord against the fourth.
One day, after losing yet another argument by a vote of three to one, the fourth
rabbi decided to appeal to a higher authority. "Oh, God," he cried, "I know in my
heart that I am right and they are wrong! Please give me a sign to prove it to
them!" Suddenly a storm cloud appeared. But the other rabbis were unimpressed,
noting that storm clouds often form on hot days, and this was an especially hot
day. The rabbi appealed to God for a bigger sign, and all of a sudden a bolt of
lightning slammed into a tree on a nearby hill. But the other rabbis were unimpressed, for lightning is known to strike trees. So the rabbi appealed to God a
third time, and this time the sky turned pitch black, the earth shook, and a deep,
booming voice intoned, "He is right!" The rabbi turned to the others and in a triumphant voice said, "Well?" "So," shrugged one of the other rabbis, "now it's
three to two."

But back to Isaac, the man whose name means "laughter." A recent article by
Joel Kaminsky (2000), a religion professor at Smith College, lends support to
Cohen's view that "the most nearly perfect human faith and understanding are
consistent with laughter." Kaminsky acknowledges that several scholars have
examined the character of Isaac and the narratives that surround him with an eye
toward uncovering elements of humor, but they have generally referred to various Greek genres such as comedy, satire, and irony to illuminate these stories. In
Kaminsky's view, these interpreters have overlooked the fact that Isaac is a kind
of ancient schlemiel, and thus anticipates the bumbling stupidity of the Three
Stooges and the slapstick antics of the Marx Brothers. In other words, this is an
example of Jewish humor employing what Cohen calls "the acceptance of
absurdity." Kaminsky mentions the laughing theme that we have already discussed and then moves to the story of Isaac and Ishmael, and specifically to the
ambiguity in Genesis 21:9, which says that Ishmael was "playing with" Isaac.
Does this mean that he was acting like Isaac, claiming his position? Or even

more sinisterly, that he molested him? Kaminsky acknowledges that we cannot be certain, and perhaps the author was being purposely ambiguous. What *is* clear is that Sarah objected to Ishmael's behavior and intervened on her own son's behalf. Thus, "it is not difficult to see in Isaac elements of the male who is dominated by the women in his life, first by his mother and later by his wife" (367)

Kaminsky next turns to the binding of Isaac story and sees humor in it as well. Because Isaac is capable of carrying wood, he is undoubtedly a teenager or young adult, and this is how he is portrayed in religious art. If so, maybe Isaac's question concerning the fact that there is no sacrificial animal and his silence after Abraham explains, "God himself will provide the lamb for a burnt offering, my son," are "less a sign of Isaac's innocence or consent than an indication that he is mentally deficient" (367). Kaminsky admits that this view may not be persuasive when this episode is taken alone, but when later episodes in Isaac's life are considered, evidence begins to accumulate in support of the view that he is "a bit of a bumbler and a dullard" (368).

The episode in which Rebekah first catches sight of her future husband, Isaac, is an especially strong case in point (Gen 24:61–67). Kaminsky points out that Isaac is forbidden to leave Israel and wonders if this is because both God and Abraham worry that he might have trouble finding his way back home again. So a servant is sent to Mesopotamia to find him a wife. Perhaps, also, Abraham believes that anyone who met Isaac before the engagement would never agree to marry him, the reverse condition of the marriage-broker jokes that Freud relates. In any case, when the caravan bearing Rebekah approaches, Isaac sees it from afar. He had gone out in the field that evening. But to do what? The Hebrew word for the activity in which he was engaged has been variously translated, "to think," "to meditate," "to pray," "to lament the dead," or "to take a stroll." But Kaminsky notes that there is a history of interpretation now reinforced by modern philological research that suggests a similar word in 1 Kings 18:27 (where Elijah mockingly asks the priests of Baal what their deity is up to at the moment) has to do with urination or defecation. Elijah implies, in other words, that their deity's absence is due to the call of nature. If this is also the meaning in Genesis 24:63, "one has here a hysterically funny and crude parody of a 'classic love scene'" (369).

But this is not all. When Rebekah sees the man in the fields who is to be her husband, she, in traditional translations, "alights," "dismounts" or "slips quickly from" her camel. (The phrase "She alighted her camel" was a matter of some amusement to boys of my generation who inferred that she smoked a popular brand of cigarette.) But here again, Kaminsky thinks the translations are being too decorous, as a more literal translation would be "She fell off of the camel," perhaps because her first sight of her future husband was not especially flattering.

There is more to Kaminsky's analysis of the Isaac character, such as the fact that Isaac is the only biblical character to bring his new wife into his mother's tent, suggesting, perhaps, some unresolved Oedipal issues (370), and that he was easily duped by Rebekah and Jacob, his younger son, in the famous blessing of "Esau" scene, a scene that "does not reveal Jacob's great acting ability, but Isaac's utter stupidity" (371). But this brief summary of Kaminsky's article is sufficient to raise the question of whether the laughter springing from God's intention to "bless" Abraham and Sarah with a male child continues to resound throughout the ensuing narratives. And once the question is raised, it is difficult to set it completely aside, for such is the power of humor. If Isaac is the "dimwitted" character that Kaminsky takes him to be, then Kaminsky's concluding observation is most pertinent:

> The tendency to upset human expectations in humorous fashion . . . has connections to the well documented biblical propensity to proclaim that God favors the underdog. The writers can thereby show how God brings God's plan to fruition even when all the odds are against success. Isaac's incompetence, far from interfering with God's unfolding plan, is itself part and parcel of this plan. . . . My contention is that because the promises made to Abraham appear to be in constant danger of coming to an abrupt end in the narratives surrounding Isaac, the authors of these narratives consistently use humor to help one continue to believe in God's promises. (374)

Thus, Kaminsky supports Cohen's view that "the most nearly perfect human faith and understanding are consistent with laughter," and that intimacy—shared feeling—is based on shared beliefs, dispositions, preferences, and so forth, which in this case include belief in the value of absurdity.

Intimacy Anxiety and the Moderating Effects of Humor

In chapter 1, I discussed Freud's theory that humor involves a savings in expenditure of painful emotions, costly inhibitions, and difficult thinking, and I related this theory to jokes that address death anxiety and humorous treatments of penis anxiety. I suggest that the biblical stories with which Cohen and Kaminsky are concerned address another form of anxiety, the anxiety that arises from the very intimacy that Cohen recognizes to be one of the great contributions of humor. The intimacy here, however, involves gender issues, especially in relation to conception and courtship, but also, as I will show, in relation to mothers and sons. In effect, the following consideration of the anxieties that these biblical stories address and seek to minimize through humor reflects the fact that, as noted at the beginning of this chapter, intimacy and isolation are linked together in Erik H. Erikson's life cycle schema, and that intimacy versus isolation anxieties are especially prominent among young adults. Hence, lurking behind the theme of intimacy is the spectre of isolation, and intimacy may therefore be the very cause of considerable anxiety. Furthermore, there are the anxieties that arise from too much intimacy or from the consequences of intimacy with the wrong partners. I will first take up the story of Abraham and Sarah with which Cohen is concerned, then consider the story of Jacob and Rebekah, the story that Kaminsky, who is more concerned with Jacob's father Isaac, does not explore.

The Conception of Isaac

Observe that the laughter in the story of Abraham and Sarah involves the conception of a child. This means that sexual intimacy between a man and a woman is necessarily involved. But this also raises an issue that has caused all sorts of anxiety for millions of humans down through the ages, the question of the identity of the father. Because the mother bears the child, the mother's identity is never in doubt. But the father's identity is not always self-evident. If a woman has had sexual relations with more than one man during the year preceding the child's birth, the answer to the question of the father's identity is a matter of conjecture, and the question itself is a highly emotional one. The following joke addresses this issue: "Honey, something's always bugged me about the children. I can't help noticing that out of our eight kids, Ben looks different from all the others. I know it's a terrible thing to ask, but does he have a different father?" "Yes, it's true. He does." "Please tell me. Who is Ben's father?" "You."

While this issue may not seem relevant to the story of Abraham and Sarah, there are features of this story that suggest it is, in fact, highly relevant. One is the fact of Abraham's advanced age. Abraham himself raises this issue when God tells him that he will father a child by Sarah: "Can a child be born to a man who is a hundred years old?" (Gen 17:17). This is a very good question, and one that leads Abraham to make a countersuggestion to God: "O that Ismael might live in your sight!" (17:18). That is, it would be easier all around if God would simply recognize Ishmael as Abraham's heir and as the son through whom the covenant would be established. Other features of the story that make this question highly relevant are the accounts of Sarah's residence in the house of King Abimelech (Gen 20:1–18) and the account of the visit of the three strangers (Gen 18:1–15), both of which occur in the interim between God's initial announcement that Sarah will conceive a son and the actual birth of Isaac.

I was first introduced to the idea that these stories surrounding the birth of Isaac concern the problem of "doubtful paternity" in a course on the psychology of religion taught by David Bakan at the University of Chicago in 1965. His view that Genesis 18:1–15 and 20:1–18 are concerned with doubts about Abraham's paternity of Isaac was presented in published form in his book *The Duality of Human Existence* (1966). Here, he first takes up the account of Sarah, whom Abraham had misrepresented as his sister (as he had previously done in the case of the Egyptian pharaoh), being taken into the house of King Abimelech. The story says that Abimelech was warned by God in a dream not to touch Sarah and that he subsequently returned her to Abraham, demanding to know why Abraham had not told him that she was his wife. Abraham defended his misrepresentation of Sarah by mentioning that she was, in fact, his half sister. Bakan then points out that Genesis 25:19 reads, "These are the descen-

dants of Isaac, Abraham's son: Abraham was the father of Isaac," and cites the
commentary on this text by Rashi, the rabbinical scholar. Bakan writes:

> The possibility of Abraham not being the biological father seems to have
> been enough on the mind of the distinguished commentator Rashi [an
> eleventh-century rabbi named Rabbi Shlomo ben Isaac], for him to deal
> with it and deny it. The proof is, according to Rashi, that the text reads,
> "And these are the generations of Isaac, Abraham's son; Abraham begot
> Isaac." Why does the Biblical text deviate from its usual pattern here? If
> these are the "generations of Isaac," why does the Biblical writer go back-
> ward to mention Abraham? And why is it necessary to say it twice?
> Rashi's commentary is: "Since the text wrote, 'Isaac, the son of Abraham,'
> it became necessary to state, 'Abraham begot Isaac'; for the scorners of the
> generation were saying, 'From Abimelech did Sarah conceive, since for
> many years she tarried with Abraham and did not conceive from him.'
> What did the Holy One Blessed Be He do? He formed the features of
> Isaac's face similar to Abraham, and there attested to everyone, 'Abraham
> begot Isaac.' And that is why it is written here, 'Isaac was the son of Abra-
> ham,' for there is testimony that 'Abraham begot Isaac.' " (213)

Bakan comments on Rashi's argument: "Needless to say, Rashi and his sources
in the *Midrash* had neither photographs nor testimonials. Having to add a facial
similarity between Abraham and Isaac would indicate that doubt was suggested
by the text" (213–14). He adds in a footnote, "That such doubt may even have
been on Paul's mind is suggested by, 'Neither because they are the seed of Abraham, are they called children; but, 'In Isaac shall thy seed be called' " (214). As
Rashi's own commentary indicates, the "doubts" surrounding Abraham's paternity of Isaac were raised by the fact that "for many years Sarah tarried with Abraham and did not conceive from him," yet she *did* conceive a child in the short
time that she was living in the house of King Abimelech. Such situational factors would have been the very evidence adduced in favor of one man being
judged the biological father over another man. Rashi seeks to undermine the
appeal to these situational factors by claiming other evidence that also would
have been advanced in cases of doubtful paternity, the facial resemblance
between one of the men and that of the child.

Bakan next takes up the story of the three visitors in Genesis 18:1–15, pointing out that this text also "has difficulties." The text, which involves three visitors
coming to Abraham and Sarah to announce what God has already told them, is
evidently the work of more than one writer. Bakan points out: "This chapter
begins with three angels. Then the next chapter begins with only two angels, and
there is no indication of what happened to the third angel" (214). He continues:

> The ninth verse is, "And they said unto him, Where is Sarah thy wife?
> And he said, Behold in the tent." According to Biblical scholars, the next

six verses, verses 10 through 15, are a substitution by the J2 author for something that had been put there earlier by the J1 author. These six verses are the critical ones in connection with the birth of Isaac, and one can only speculate that perhaps what is now only hinted at in the text might have been more explicit in the earlier version. (214)

Bakan notes that verse 10, in which the visitor tells Abraham that he will return in due season and Sarah will have a son, is especially problematic. While the usual translation of the second part of this verse is that Sarah, standing behind him, overheard what he told Abraham, it could just as well be translated to suggest that the angel was in the tent with Sarah. In fact, "in one commentary, *Sifte Hakhamin*, it is explicitly suggested that the angel was in the tent and Abraham was outside" (215). In other words, the suspicion that the angel who did not join the other two on their journey to Sodom was implicated in the conception of Isaac is raised by the very ambiguity of this verse, and it is enough that this suspicion is raised to warrant the conclusion that the text is addressing the anxiety that hovers around the question of the true identity of the biological father.

I suggest that these biblical texts surrounding the conception of Isaac were intended to be humorous and that humor is used here to address men's anxieties relating to the paternity of the children that their wives have conceived. By making Abraham a very old man, these stories make a sort of joke of a situation that otherwise would have engendered painful emotions. Here is a contemporary joke that has a similar purpose:

A ninety-year-old man went to his doctor and said, "Doctor, my wife, who is eighteen, is expecting a baby." The doctor said, "Let me tell you a story. A man went hunting, but instead of his gun, he picked up an umbrella by mistake. And when a bear suddenly charged at him, he pointed his umbrella at the bear, shot at it, and killed it on the spot." "Impossible. Somebody else must have shot that bear." "Exactly my point."

Here is another:

This old guy goes to the doctor for a checkup. Doctor: You're in great shape for a sixty-year-old. Guy: Who says I'm sixty years old? Doctor: You're not sixty? How old are you? Guy: I turn eighty next month. Doctor: Gosh, eighty! Do you mind if I ask you at what age your father died? Guy: Who says my father is dead? Doctor: He's not dead? Guy: Nope, he'll be 104 this year. Doctor: With such a good family medical history, your grandfather must have been pretty old when he died. Guy: Who says my grandfather's dead? Doctor: He's not dead? Guy: Nope, he'll be 129 this year, and he's getting married next week. Doctor: Gee whiz! Why at his age would he want to get married? Guy: Who says he wants to?

The first joke addresses the anxiety of doubtful paternity, while the second one concerns the anxiety of having fathered a child out of wedlock. By suggesting that very old men are confronted with these anxieties, the jokes minimize the psychological pain involved. Much the same is occurring in the story of Abraham. A situation that would be emotionally devastating were the man much younger is given a humorous twist by presenting him as a ninety-nine-year-old man. In the two contemporary jokes, age is the basis for the doctors' incredulity—the incredulity that often occurs when the principals in cases of doubtful parentage "explain" what really happened—and a similar incredulity is at the heart of the Abraham story.

The Rebekah-Jacob Relationship
If conception is a matter of great anxiety in the story of Abraham and Sarah, courtship is a matter of considerable anxiety in the case of Isaac and Rebekah. As Kaminsky suggests, the first meeting between Rebekah and Isaac is not an auspicious one. As a prospective bridegroom, Isaac hardly puts his best foot forward, and Rebekah, in tumbling off her camel, doesn't come off very well herself. Humor is therefore employed here to address the anxieties that accompany the courtship ritual, anxieties that may well have been heightened by the fact that marriages were arranged and that, in this case, the servant played the role of the marriage broker.

I suggest, however, that a whole other set of anxieties was being played out in the episode involving Jacob's acquisition of the birthright that rightfully belonged to his brother, Esau. These are anxieties involving the relationship between Rebekah and Jacob, anxieties generated by the fact that Jacob had both the good and the bad luck to be his mother's favored son. While Kaminsky discusses the fact that father Isaac was "passively manipulated by Rebekah," he does not explore in any detail the fact that son Jacob also was manipulated by her, and far more actively. I suggest that the anxiety that hovers around this story is that generated by the excessive intimacy that a mother expects from her son as her reward for having chosen him as her favorite.

Rebekah is the prototype of that famous stock character in Jewish humor, the "Jewish mother." She manipulates Jacob into securing the birthright that belongs to Esau. Then when Esau reacts as anyone would predict that a hunter would react ("I'm gonna kill that guy"), she advises Jacob to stay with her brother, Laban, until Esau cools off and "forgets what you have done to him." ("And when will that be?" a less compliant Jacob surely would have asked, a note of sarcasm in his voice.) Then she will "fetch" Jacob, for "Why should I lose both of you in one day?" (Gen 27:45). She conveniently overlooks the fact that her own manipulations produced this unhappy outcome in the first place. Yet she expects Jacob, who has benefited from her manipulations, to feel sorry for her now because she is in danger of losing both of her boys simultaneously. No mother should be required to suffer so! (Note the tone of sarcasm in *my* voice.)

Immediately after tricking her husband into bestowing the birthright on Jacob, Rebekah goes to him to complain about the Hittite women, saying, "I am weary of my life because of the Hittite women. If Jacob marries one of the Hittite women such as these, one of the women of the land, what good will my life be to me?" (Gen 27:46). Since Esau had married a Hittite woman (Gen 26:34), Rebekah seems determined that her younger son will marry one of her own kind. So Isaac charges Jacob not to marry one of these "women of the land" but to go to his mother's ancestral home and marry one of the daughters of her brother. Thus, Isaac, perhaps to placate Rebekah, reinforces her plan for Jacob to go to her brother's home until Esau, cheated of his birthright, "forgets" what Jacob has done to him, and to choose one of his maternal uncle's daughters for his wife. Thus, with Isaac, as with Jacob, Rebekah plays on his sympathies for this poor, seemingly defenseless woman.

If Rebekah is the first and prototypical "Jewish mother," in his *Great Jewish Joke Book* (2002), Allen King introduces us to several of her successors. Here's one:

A young Jewish man excitedly told his mother that he'd fallen in love and was going to get married. He said, "And just for fun, Ma, I'm going to bring over three women and you try and guess which one I'm going to marry." The mother agreed. The next day, he brought three beautiful women into the house and sat them down on the couch. They chatted with each other and his mother for a while. Finally, the man said, "OK, Ma. Guess which one I'm going to marry." She immediately replied, "The redhead in the middle." "That's amazing, Ma! You're right. How did you know?" "I don't like her."

Here is another one:

A young Jewish man calls his mother and says, "Mom, I'm bringing home a wonderful woman I want to marry. She's a Native American and her name is Shooting Star." "How nice," says his mother. "I have an Indian name too," he says. "It's Running Deer, and I want you to call me that from now on." "How nice," says his mother. "You should have an Indian name too, Mom," he says. "I already do," says his mother. "You should call me Sitting Shiva."

Here's a third:

Three Jewish mothers were talking rather competitively about how much their sons love them. The first one said, "My son loves me so much, he spent a hundred dollars on flowers he sent me the other day." The second one said, "My son loves me so much, he paid for my trip to Europe last month." The third one said, "My son loves me most. He goes to a therapist twice a week, paying five hundred dollars a visit, and all he talks about is me!"

Then there's this question: "Why don't Jewish mothers drink?" Answer: "Because alcohol would interfere with their suffering."

The Bad-enough Mother

Having mentioned that Rebekah is the first "Jewish mother," I would like to expand on this point by noting that her manipulations are not unique to Jewish mothers. I suggest, instead, that we simply view her as a biblical example of what I would call the "bad-enough mother." This is a play on British psychoanalyst D. W. Winnicott's concept of the "good-enough mother" as presented in his essay "Transitional Objects and Transitional Phenomena" (1991). He says that the good-enough mother "is one who makes active adaptation to the infant's needs, an active adaptation that gradually lessens, according to the infant's growing ability to account for failure of adaptation and to tolerate the results of frustration" (10). In other words, the good-enough mother "starts off with an almost complete adaptation to her infant's needs, and as time proceeds she adapts less and less completely, gradually, according to the infant's growing ability to deal with her failure" (10). Winnicott believes that the frustration the son experiences from his "good-enough mother" will condition him for the tolerance of frustrations in life. Winnicott is entitled to his opinion of what makes a "good-enough mother," but a mother who becomes less actively adaptive as time goes on isn't *my* idea of a "good-enough mother." This, however, is beside the point, as I am concerned here with the "bad-enough mother." I wish I could provide an equally pithy description of the "bad-enough mother," but this is impossible, as there is something about her that defies easy description. Perhaps this is why the writers of Genesis needed to resort to the narrative form via their stories of Rebekah, and why the "Jewish mother" joking tradition has followed suit.

In any event, as I began thinking and reminiscing about the "bad-enough mother," I ran across the following poem by Paul Dehn (1912–1976) in *The Oxford Book of Comic Verse* (Gross, 1994, 360–61). Because it was the inspiration for several poems of my own, I reproduce his poem here in full:

ALTERNATIVE ENDINGS TO AN UNWRITTEN BALLAD

I stole through the dungeons, while everyone slept,
Till I came to the cage where the Monster was kept.
There, locked in the arms of a Giant Baboon
Rigid and smiling, lay . . . Mrs. RAVOON!

I climbed the clock-tower in the first morning sun
And 'twas midday at least ere my journey was done;
But the clock never sounded the last stroke of noon,
For there, from the clapper, swung Mrs. RAVOON.

I hauled in the line, and I took my first look
At the half-eaten horror that hung from the hook.
I had dragged from the depths of the limpid lagoon
The luminous body of Mrs. RAVOON.

I fled in the storm, through lightning and thunder,
And there, as a flash split the darkness asunder,
Chewing a rat's-tail and mumbling a rune,
Mad in the moat squatted Mrs. RAVOON.

I stood by the waters so green and so thick,
And I stirred at the scum with my old, withered stick;
When there rose through the ooze, like a monstrous balloon,
The bloated cadaver of Mrs. RAVOON.

Facing the fens, I looked back from the shore
Where all had been empty a moment before;
And there, by the light of the Lincolnshire moon,
Immense on the marshes, stood . . . Mrs. RAVOON!

It occurred to me that whether Dehn knew it or not, he had written six alternative endings to an unwritten ballad about the "bad-enough mother." So since the "bad-enough mother" concept was on my mind at the time, I decided to write my own ballad about Mrs. RAVOON. The approach I took was inspired by Sigmund Freud's essay on Shakespeare's *The Merchant of Venice*, "The Theme of the Three Caskets" (1913/1997). Freud concludes that the caskets in Shakespeare's play may be interpreted allegorically as "the three forms taken on by the mother as life proceeds: the mother herself, *the beloved who is chosen after her pattern,* and finally the Mother Earth who receives him [her son] again" (121, my emphasis). Of the three, it seemed that the second is especially destined to create intimacy anxiety in the heart of any son, so I wrote the following poem to illustrate the power of the "bad-enough mother" to do mischief and sow confusion.

A LETTER TO MY FUTURE BRIDE

I was sleeping quite soundly and dreaming of you,
And pledging, my darling, I'd always be true,
When I suddenly spied by the light of the moon,
Stretched out by my side lay . . . Mrs. RAVOON!

"How could you get in here?" I asked with a start,
As I felt the mad beating of my horrified heart.
For aghast, I beheld her, and started to swoon,
For 'twas my old mother, she's . . . Mrs. RAVOON!

"Oh, Mother, how could you?" I asked with dismay,
"You disrupted my dream of my blest wedding day!"
She answered, "Oh, Willy, what a tired old tune.
You don't know the power of . . . Mrs. RAVOON!

She left and I vowed my dream to resume,
But I felt all around me a dire sense of doom.
So I leapt from my bed—tripping o'er the spittoon—
And dashed off in search of . . . Mrs. RAVOON!

I thought that writing this poem about the "bad-enough mother" would be
sufficiently cathartic that I could put the whole issue behind me and move on to
more edifying topics. But the story of Rebekah and Jacob continued to haunt
me, and as I ruminated about it, I struck upon the idea that there is a Mrs.
RAVOON subtext to every biblical story in which a man desires a woman. So I
decided to rewrite several biblical narratives that become male "texts of terror"
once this subtext is recognized.[4]

ADAM'S MISTAKE

Naming the birds and the beasts was a chore,
So I lay down to rest and proceeded to snore.
Awakening I saw what appeared a baboon.
Not so, 'twas a woman . . . Mrs. RAVOON!

DAVID'S MISJUDGMENT

I walked out on my terrace and peered down below,
And my eyes lit upon a most wonderful show.
A woman was bathing and crooning a tune.
"Bathsheba," I cried! No, 'twas . . . Mrs. RAVOON!

HOSEA'S ERROR

I wandered through town, unhappy and glum,
For Jezreel, the eldest, was missing his Mum.
Then a surreal shape loomed over the dune.
"Is it Gomer?" I cried. Nope, 'twas . . . Mrs. RAVOON!

JOHN THE BAPTIST'S REVENGE

Amid cheering and clapping while the veiled woman danced,
Herod beckoned her toward him and said, "I'm entranced.
But please, little butterfly, shed your cocoon."
She did, and he saw. 'Twas . . . Mrs. RAVOON!

JESUS' CONFUSION

I stood in the garden 'mid roses and such,
When from out of the haze came a womanly touch.
"Oh, Mary, sweet Mary," I proceeded to croon,
But my senses deceived me. 'Twas . . . Mrs. RAVOON!

If one endorses the theory for reading biblical texts presented here—that there is a "bad-enough mother" subtext to every biblical story in which a man desires a woman—then the quintessential male "texts of terror" are chapters 4 and 7 of Song of Solomon. These are the chapters in which a young man describes his flawlessly beautiful queenly maiden in language certain to make much younger boys grin and snicker, or even declare their need to puke. On the other hand, their terror is neutralized if one adopts the same device that the Abraham and Sarah story employs, that of adding several decades to the man's age. Then the desire of a man for a woman is no longer cause for terror but grounds for humor. This insight came to me when I was reading *The Norton Book of Light Verse* (Baker 1986) and I came across the following poem by James B. Naylor (1860–1945; 164).

AUTHORSHIP

King David and King Solomon
Led merry, merry lives,
With many, many lady friends
And many, many wives;
But when old age crept over them,
With many, many qualms,
King Solomon wrote the Proverbs
And King David wrote the Psalms.

I grudgingly admitted to myself that Naylor's poem was clever, but because I have been struggling of late with the fact that old age also is creeping over me, I set to work on a poem of dissent. Between the two kings, I felt that my best case would be Solomon, whose very name is synonymous with wisdom, the virtue that Erik H. Erikson has correctly assigned to those who have reached the "old age" stage of the cycle of life (1964, 132–34). Here is my poem:

THE CANONICAL KING

Solomon wrote his Proverbs
As a young precocious sage,
Then penned Ecclesiastes
In cynical middle age.

> But old age brought him wisdom
> Which inspired Songs on Sex.
> And this concludes my lecture
> On the works of Solomon Rex.

If you think of the author of "Song of Solomon" as an old man, the chapters in which a man desires a woman are no longer cause for anxiety. True, his attempt to flatter his beloved with such euphemisms as this—"Your teeth are like a flock of shorn ewes that have come up from the washing, all of which bear twins, and not one among them is bereaved" (4:2)—may lead her to wonder if he has not gotten a little balmy in his old age—but his words no longer reflect or engender anxiety, and the laughter they provoke is no longer nervous but simple and pure.

"A Guy Goes into a Bar" Jokes

As we have seen, Cohen emphasizes that joke telling is an expression of the need for intimacy. He underscores this point by mentioning in footnotes the names of the persons who introduced him to the jokes that he includes in his book. More than thirty persons are named, and in many cases, the context in which he heard the joke from the other person and the name of the person from whom this person heard it also are indicated. Clearly Cohen is intent on showing that jokes and joke telling are about the creation of intimacy, a sense of community.

In his review of the book, Adam Phillips notes Cohen's contention that "a deep satisfaction in successful joke transactions is the sense held mutually by teller and hearer that they are joined in feeling." Phillips continues, "And to be joined in feeling is different from being joined in belief, or joined in business (the consequences, for one thing, are less predictable). If a joke, when it's successful, is a transaction—an action performed, and a deal done—it may be, by the same token, a communal act—the closest some of us ever get to a so-called sense of community" (2001, 350).

Cohen's approach to the contribution of humor to the need for intimacy focuses on the "joke transaction" itself. This explains, in large part, why he is concerned with issues of taste and propriety, for these issues need to be taken into account if one wants a joke transaction to be "successful." What he does not address, however, is the fact that there are jokes in which the need for intimacy, an intimacy that does not engender anxiety, is the joke's own implied theme. Jokes whose locus is a bar or local tavern are excellent examples. The popular TV show *Cheers* played on this association of the local tavern with the need for intimacy, as *Cheers* was represented as the place where "everybody knows your name."

It is not surprising that Cohen, a Jewish man, did not include jokes about taverns or drinking buddies in his book, for as Christie Davies points out in his chapter "Ethnic Jokes about Alcohol: A Study of the Humor of Ambivalence" in *Jokes and Their Relation to Society* (1998), as far as alcohol consumption is concerned, "In the case of Jews there is very little to tell jokes about. The Jews are in general moderate drinkers who have built alcohol into their way of life in a careful and controlled fashion such that there are definite social rules about when, where and how such alcohol is consumed. . . . Moderation is not the stuff of which ethnic jokes are made and there are very few jokes about drunken Jews, and practically none about Jews who are anti-alcohol" (120–21). The few jokes about drunken Jews that exist are rather forced and artificial and belong, in Davies' view, to the category of "pseudo-ethnic jokes." Ethnic groups that *are* prominently identified with alcohol consumption in jokes are the Irish, Australians, and Finns, while the Scots are represented in a very ambivalent way as either heavy drinkers or teetotalers, and nothing in between.

Davies suggests that the association of the Irish with heavy drinking may be traced to economic conditions in the nineteenth century following the potato famines of the 1840s. Previously, young men could earn a decent living for themselves and their families with a small plot of ground if they planted potatoes. This meant that a man who had several sons could subdivide his farm and give each a share. After the famines, it became customary for fathers to bequeath the eldest son the farm, while the younger sons received nothing. With few prospects, the younger sons would delay or even forgo any thoughts of marriage. The eldest sons also would delay marriage because their inheritances depended on their fathers' deaths. Davies also notes that the Roman Catholic Church forbade premarital sex, leading the Irish birthrate to become one of the lowest in Europe. Thus, a bachelor community developed, and its setting was the local tavern.

It is not surprising, therefore, that this particular joking tradition emphasizes the need for intimacy among males. There are jokes about men meeting "beautiful" women in bars, but these jokes do not reflect the same longing for intimacy reflected in jokes about two men meeting in a tavern or bar. Instead, these jokes about meeting a beautiful woman usually involve witty repartee, usually in relation to negotiations over sexual favors. Here's a typical example:

A guy goes into a bar and sits down on a stool next to a beautiful woman. After a couple of minutes pass, he turns to her and asks, "Would you be willing to go to bed with me for a million dollars?" She hesitates for a few seconds and then says, "Yes, for a million dollars I sure would." The man then asks, "Would you go to bed with me for a dollar?" The woman gets angry and says, "Just what kind of woman do you think I am?" "Well," the man says, "we've already established that. All we're doing now is haggling over the price."

Here's an example of a related theme, the inability of the male to consummate his sexual desires:

A guy goes into a bar that he has frequented daily for the last sixty years. It's his ninetieth birthday, so the bartender and his friends decide to surprise him. They wheel in a big birthday cake, and out pops a beautiful young woman who says, "Hi, I can give you some super sex!" And the old man says, "Well, I guess I'll take the soup."

While this joke uses age as the explanation for the man's resigned response, this joke may be traced back to the fact that the community found in local taverns in Ireland was a bachelor community.

The idea that drinking together in a local tavern is a convivial communal act is not, of course, unique to the Irish, but jokes about Irishmen and alcohol typically involve two or more Irishmen getting drunk together. Here's an example:

Irish immigrants Patrick and Michael were staggering home one night after a convivial session at a Mawbanna pub. Taking a shortcut across a farm, they passed a well. Pat fell in. Mike ran to the farmhouse to get a rope. With great difficulty he began hauling Pat up. Pat had almost reached the top when Mike called out, "Hold tight, my brave boy, whilst I shpit on me hands."

In contrast, here is a joke involving a Swede and a Finn:

A Swede and a Finn got together to have a drinking night. All they had was Schnapps and cucumbers. After having sat there drinking for three hours, the Swede looked up at the Finn and said, "Skol" [cheers]. Then the Finn said, "Are we here to talk, or are we here to drink?"

The following joke about an Irishman who is drinking in memory of a dear friend also reflects the theme of intimacy:

Fogarty began to drop in at Barney's bar regularly, and his order was always the same—two martinis. After several weeks of this, Barney asked him why he didn't order a double instead. "It's a sentimental thing," said Fogarty. "A very dear friend of mine died a few weeks ago, and before his death he asked that when I drink I have one for him too." A week later Fogarty came in and ordered one martini. "What about your dead buddy? Why only one martini today?" "This is my buddy's drink," came the reply. "I'm on the wagon."

In another version of the same joke, the Irishman orders three pints of beer because he and his two brothers, one of whom emigrated to America, the other to Australia, promised that they would drink this way in remembrance of the days they drank together. When he ordered two drinks instead of the usual three, the bartender assumed the death of one of his brothers and offered his condolences. "I don't want to intrude on your grief, but I wanted to express my sympathy over your great loss." The Irishman looked confused for a moment, then a light dawned, and he laughed. "Oh, no," he said, "me brothers are fine. I've just quit drinking!"

Then there's this joke about an Irishman who meets another Irishman with a remarkably similar background:

> A guy goes into a bar and stumbles up to the only other patron there and asks if he can buy him a drink. "Why, of course," comes the reply. The first man then asks, "Where are you from?" "I'm from Ireland," replies the second man. The first man responds, "You don't say. I'm from Ireland too! Let's have another round to Ireland." "Of course," replies the second man. Curious, the first man then asks, "Where in Ireland are you from?" "Dublin," comes the reply. "I can't believe it," says the first man. "I'm from Dublin too! Let's have another drink to Dublin." "Of course," replies the second man. Curiosity again strikes, and the first man asks, "What school did you go to?" "Saint Mary's," replies the second man. I graduated in 'sixty-two." "This is unbelievable," the first man says. "I went to Saint Mary's and I graduated in 'sixty-two also!" At about that time, in comes one of the regulars and sits down at the bar. "What's been going on?" he asks the bartender. "Nothing much," replies the bartender, "but the O'Malley twins are drunk again."

If jokes about Irishmen in bars concern the theme of intimacy, the theme itself is not limited to Irish jokes. In *A Guy Goes into a Bar . . .* (2000), Albert Tapper and Peter Press have assembled 161 jokes, and only a few of these jokes have an ethnic reference (I counted 10). Most simply begin with the phrase, "A guy goes into a bar . . ." Most often, he comes in alone, though occasionally he is accompanied by a pet (a dog, a parrot, an alligator, etc.). If he is accompanied by his wife, this usually means that she has come to find out why he spends so much time there. For example:

> An angry wife was complaining about her husband spending all his time at the pub, so one night he took her along. "What'll ya have?" he asked. "Oh, I don't know. The same as you, I suppose," she replied. So the husband ordered a couple of Jack Daniel's and threw his down in one go. His wife watched him, then took a sip from her glass and immediately spit it out. "Yuck, it's nasty poison!" she sputtered. "I don't know how you can drink this stuff!" "Well, there you go," cried the husband. "And you think I'm out enjoying myself every night!"

The following joke suggests that wives accompany their husbands to the bar very infrequently and only on special occasions:

> On New Year's Eve all the wives of the regular patrons of the bar suggested that at the stroke of midnight every husband should stand next to the one person who has made his life worth living. Well, it was kind of embarrassing. The bartender was almost crushed to death.

The idea that the husband is out drinking while his longsuffering wife is sitting home alone is a common theme. The following joke about six men who have spent the evening together is illustrative:

> Six men who were feeling no pain staggered out of the bar and headed down the street at about one in the morning. Laughing and singing loudly, they walked up to a two-story home. One of them managed to make it to the door and pounded on the doorbell insistently. A light came on in an upstairs window. The spokesman for the group yelled up, "Is this where Mr. John Smith lives?" "Yes, it is. What do you want?" "Are you Mrs. Smith?" "I am Mrs. Smith. What do you want?" "Could you come down here and pick out Mr. Smith so the rest of us can go home?"

A variation is this joke about a Norwegian who is returning home after an evening in the bar:

> Ole was staggering home from the tavern one night, weaving from side to side. The Lutheran minister saw him and in a Good Samaritan impulse, offered to guide Ole to his home. As they approached the house, Ole suggested that the minister come inside for a moment: "I vant Lena to see who I've been out vith."

But not all wives are sitting around, staring at the ceiling, while their husbands are out enjoying the company of other men. On the contrary, some are entertaining other men. Typically, the husband staggers home and suspects that something has been going on but is too confused to figure it out. A related joke, and one with many variants, concerns a guy who has discovered his wife in a compromised situation and needs a few stiff drinks to calm down:

> A guy goes into a bar and orders a triple Scotch whiskey. The bartender pours him the drink and says, "That's quite a heavy drink. What's wrong?" After downing his drink, the guy says, "I got home and found my wife in bed with my best friend." "Wow," says the bartender, "No wonder you needed a stiff drink. The second triple is on the house." As the man downs his second triple Scotch, the bartender asks him, "What did you do?" The guy says, "I walked over to my wife, looked her straight in the eye, and told her that we were through and to get the hell out." The bartender says, "That makes sense, but what about your best friend?" "Oh, I walked over to him, looked him straight in the eye, and said, 'Bad dog!'"

This joke, with its implication of sodomy, would almost certainly fall under the heading of a morally objectionable joke despite the fact that the men to whom I have related it find it enormously funny. Perhaps this is because it not only plays on the "a dog is a man's best friend" cliché but also parodies the recommended method for housebreaking a dog ("Bad dog"). It places discovering the dog in bed with one's wife on the same moral scale as discovering that the dog has soiled the carpet.

Finally, here is a joke in which the woman with whom the "guy" has an encounter at the bar is all too reminiscent of the wife he left at home:

> A guy goes into a bar and begins to get seriously loaded, and after staring for some time at the only woman seated at the bar, he walks over to her and kisses her. She jumps up and slaps him silly. He immediately apologizes and explains, "I'm sorry. I thought you were my wife. You look exactly like her." "Why, you worthless, insufferable, wretched, no-good drunk!" "Funny," he mutters, "you even sound like her."

For every joke about a man being confronted with his wife's displeasure when he returns home from an evening at the local tavern, there is another joke about a man complaining about his marriage to a drinking buddy or the bartender. The following joke is typical:

> A guy goes into a bar and says, "Bartender, give me a drink, I'm celebrating my fifth wedding anniversary." The bartender comes over and says, "Sure, kid, the drink is free. What are you going to do to celebrate?" He says, "Well, I'm going to take my wife to Europe." The bartender says, "You're going to take your wife to Europe for your fifth anniversary? That's really nice. What are you going to do for your tenth?" "Oh, I'm going to go and get her."

Or this one:

> A guy goes into a bar. "Pour me a stiff one, Eddie. I just had another fight with the little woman." "Oh, yeah?" says Eddie. "And how did this one end?" "Well, when it was over, she came to me on her hands and knees." "Really? Now that's a switch! What did she say?" "She said, 'Come out from under the bed, you gutless weasel!' "

If the wife jokes play on the theme of the absence of intimacy in the "guy's" marriage, the interaction that occurs in the bar itself reflects a "guy's" idea of what makes for genuine intimacy. Some might argue that the maturity level of his idea of intimacy is roughly equivalent to that of schoolboys, but if this is so, it may reflect men's nostalgia for what psychiatrist Harry Stack Sullivan (1953) called the "chumship" period of preadolescence in which a boy experiences strong emotional feelings toward another boy and views girls as a threat to this relationship (43–44).

In "a guy goes into a bar" jokes, the attempt to gain the attention of others is often a preliminary means to experiencing intimacy. One way to gain others' attention is to offer to buy drinks for everyone. The following joke, however, reveals the ambivalences involved in this magnanimous if grandiose gesture:

> A guy goes into a bar and shouts, "When I drink, everybody drinks!" He gets a cheer from everybody in the bar. Feeling pretty happy, he shouts out, "When I drink again, everybody drinks again!" Again he gets a cheer, and this one is louder. But now reality sets in. His funds are limited. After all, he's an ordinary working guy, so after finishing his second drink, he pulls out his wallet and shouts, "When I pay, everybody pays!"

Another way to gain attention is to enter the bar with an animal or bird in tow and to use the creature to engage someone else in a friendly wager. Typically, the animal or bird has a special skill—it can talk, dance, or play the piano—and its owner exploits its talents in order to get a free drink or pick up some easy money. Here's one about a guy who has two animals:

> A guy goes into a bar smelling and looking like he hasn't had a bath in a month. He orders a drink, but the bartender refuses. "I don't think you can pay for it." The guy says, "You're right. I haven't got any money, but if I show you something you've never witnessed before, will you give me a drink?" The bartender agrees. So he reaches into his coat pocket and pulls out a hamster. He puts the hamster on the bar and it runs to the end of the bar, down the bar, across the room, up the piano, and onto the keyboard and begins playing Gershwin. The bartender says, "You're right. I've never seen anything like that before. I'm impressed. Here's your drink." The guy downs the drink and asks for another, suggesting the same deal as before. The bartender agrees. He reaches into his coat and this time pulls out a frog. He puts the frog on the bar and the frog begins to sing. He has a marvelous voice and great pitch. A stranger from the other end of the bar runs over to the guy and offers him $300 for the frog. "It's a deal," the guy says, and he takes the $300 and gives the stranger the frog. The stranger runs out of the bar. The bartender says to him, "Are you some kind of nut? You sold a singing frog for $300? He's got to be worth millions. You must be crazy." "Don't worry," the guy replies, "the hamster is also a ventriloquist."

There is another way, however, in which patrons gain attention, and this one is more commensurate with what we normally view as expressive of the need for intimacy. It is certainly closer to Cohen's understanding of intimacy as the sharing of feelings. In these jokes, the guy who goes into the bar reveals through his body language that he is depressed, unhappy, weighed down by personal cares, and so forth. Here's a typical example:

A guy goes into a bar, orders a drink, and stares at it for a half hour without moving. A big truck driver finally walks up to him, takes the guy's drink, and guzzles it down in one swig. The poor man starts crying. The truck driver says, "Come on, man, I was just joking. Here, I'll buy you another drink. I can't stand seeing a man cry." "No, it's not that. This day is the worst of my life. First, I fall asleep and get to the office late. My boss is outraged and he fires me. When I leave the building to go to my car, I find out it was stolen. I get a cab to return home, and when I get out, I remember I left my wallet and credit cards in my car. I enter my house and find my wife in bed with the gardener. I leave home and come to this bar. And while I'm thinking about putting an end to my life, you show up and drink my poison. . . . "

Here's another example of a man who appears depressed:

A guy goes into a bar and sees a friend at a table drinking by himself. Approaching the friend, he comments, "You look terrible; what's the problem?" My mother died in June," he says, "and left me $10,000." "Gee, that's tough," he replies. "Then in July," the friend continues, "my father died, leaving me $50,000." "Wow, two parents gone in two months; no wonder you're depressed." "And last month my aunt died and left me $15,000." "Three close family members lost in three months? How sad." "Then this month," continues the friend, "nothing!"

The expectation that the bartender will recognize that the patron is in an unhappy mood and is looking for sympathy is reflected in this one: "A horse goes into a bar. The bartender looks at him and says, 'Why the long face?'" (See page 6.) And finally, here's a somewhat related joke about a bartender who sets the terms on which he will have a conversation with a patron:

A guy goes into a bar, approaches the bartender, and says, "I've been working on a top-secret project on molecular genetics for the past five years, and I've just got to talk to someone about it." The bartender says, "Wait a minute. Before we talk about that, you answer a few questions. When a deer defecates, why does it come out like little pellets?" The guy doesn't know. The bartender then asks, "Why is it that when a dog poops, it lands on the ground and looks like a coiled rope?" The guy again says, "I don't have any idea." The bartender then says, "You don't know crap, and you want to talk about molecular genetics?"

This joke may express the unacknowledged feelings of a friend who is challenged with being a supportive listener when the issue at stake is one that he knows little or nothing about.

And this brings me to my final comment concerning the "a guy goes into a bar" type of joke: As Davies points out, in the late nineteenth and early twentieth centuries, temperance societies were formed in America and in many parts of northern Europe which sought to restrict the sale and consumption of alcohol or even to ban it altogether. Legal controls were introduced in many countries, and in the United States and parts of Canada and Scandinavia, there were attempts to impose total prohibition. Disagreements about the control of alcohol set class against class, rural areas against cities, women against men, religious denomination against religious denomination, and in the United States, ethnic group against ethnic group (103). While it is certainly not my purpose here to extol the virtues of the local tavern or to dismiss the fact that alcohol addiction destroys human life and ruins families, one can, nonetheless, note that implicit in "a guy goes into a bar" jokes is a need and longing for intimacy, especially among men, an intimacy that they may not experience in their workplaces, their churches, or even their family lives.

I believe these jokes can provide useful commentary on how the churches, perhaps inevitably, fail especially to meet the emotional needs of men. Yet maybe the churches can take a lesson from these jokes, however trivial they may seem, and make an effort to address the needs that the local tavern is perceived to meet in this joking tradition. The point of these jokes is not that alcohol itself will meet one's needs for intimacy, for the jokes emphasize the importance of drinking in company with others. Thus, it is not alcohol as such, but the communal ethos of the tavern that these jokes extol and value. This brief joke makes this very point: "A guy goes into a bar on the moon complaining, 'The drinks are okay, but there is no atmosphere.'" Cohen's book on jokes suggests that the "atmosphere" desired is one that promotes a sense of intimacy, one in which shared beliefs, dispositions, and preferences evolve into shared feelings among one another.

While "a guy goes into a bar" jokes imply that women are usually antithetical to this communal ethos, this is not always the case. In the course of reading William James's talks to students at various women's colleges, I ran across the following reference to Norwegian women:

Fifteen years ago the Norwegian women were even more than the women of other lands votaries of the old-fashioned ideal of feminity, the "domestic angel," the "gentle and refining influence" sort of thing. Now these sedentary fireside tabby cats of Norway have been trained, they say, by the snow-shoes into lithe and audacious creatures for whom no night is too dark or height too giddy; and who are not only saying good-bye to the traditional feminine pallor and delicacy of constitution, but actually taking the lead in every educational and social reform. (James 1992, 827–28)

I doubt that either the sedentary or the reformist woman would be particularly welcome in the tavern that these jokes imagine, but there is another type of Norwegian woman who would fit right in. I wrote the following poem a couple of years ago on St. Valentine's Day in honor of her:

A NORDIC LOVE SONG

Thor Engval

Your Boston ladies of muscle flabby
Can't hold a candle to my Viking tabby.
O'er rocks and rills my Lena leaps.
By golly, she's built like your off-road Jeeps!

While Bostonians chat over tea and crumpet,
My Lena belts a ballad on her father's trumpet.
And Grieg couldn't match her melodious snore
When she sprawls exhausted on the barroom floor.

For a guy like Thor, Lena is more than good-enough.

Conclusion

An old article titled "The Absence of Humor in Jesus" (1908) by Henry F. Harris makes the case that Jesus did not exhibit or express humor. One of the reasons Harris offers for this view is that Jesus was Jewish and the Jewish spiritual temper, which grows out of a history that has been predominantly tragic, "does not readily combine with humor" (460). Another reason is that because Jesus was fully human, he was as much "feminine" as "masculine," and "no doctrine of current psychology seems more generally conceded than that women, broadly considered without reference to special exceptions, are defective in the sense of humor" (462). A third reason concerns the type of man Jesus was. Here, Harris emphasizes that Jesus was a "primitive" type of man, that is, he was simple and elemental and thus far removed from the dilettante who engages in subtleties of wit and clever, even casuistic wordplay (464). And finally, Harris notes that humor gives disproportionate attention to some things to the neglect of other things, often engaging in exaggeration, and it is the very nature of the divine that it views all things in their rightful proportionality. Thus, to claim that Jesus was humorous, as some "popular preaching" has been prone to do, is to challenge his divinity. And this, Harris could add but doesn't, is no laughing matter.

Harris's argument that Jews do not exhibit much humor because their history has been predominantly tragic is, of course, rather easy to challenge, as one could just as well argue that a predominantly tragic history would foster a humorous attitude toward life in this world. As we have seen, this is precisely the argument that Ted Cohen makes. Similarly, Harris's argument that women as a group lack a sense of humor is easy to dispute. If this were so, why is it that women laugh more than men do? (Provine 2000, 28–29). More difficult to challenge, however, are the arguments related to what type of man Jesus was and to what characterizes divinity. The former presumes a knowledge of Jesus' personality that is not very easy to come by, and the latter assumes a knowledge of what makes for divinity that only those with doctorates in systematic theology could claim to possess. But the more one thinks about these arguments, the more it seems that Harris is himself caught in a contradiction. If Jesus was a wholly serious man, would this not suggest that, humanly speaking, he lacked "proportionality" and was therefore deficient in what Harris himself has taken to be a primary characteristic of divinity? Harris's own criterion of proportionality as a divine characteristic would suggest that Jesus was both humorous and serious. In fact, his seriousness would have been reinforced by his capacity for humor. I suggest, therefore, that Jesus may well have been at his most humorous when he was with his disciples, sharing some intimate moments together.[5]

One such occasion was the time he and his disciples were eating and drinking together after he had spoken to a crowd about sin:

> Then he called the crowd again and said to them, "Listen to me, all of you, and understand: there is nothing outside a person that by going in can defile, but the things that come out are what defile."
>
> When he had left the crowd and entered the house, his disciples asked him about the parable. He said to them, "Then do you also fail to understand? Do you not see that whatever goes into a person from outside cannot defile, since it enters, not the heart but the stomach, and goes out into the sewer?" (Thus he declared all foods clean.) And he said, "It is what comes out of a person that defiles. For it is from within, from the human heart, that evil intentions come: fornication, theft, murder, adultery, avarice, wickedness, deceit, licentiousness, envy, slander, pride, folly. All these evil things come from within, and they defile a person." (Mark 7:14–23)

Given Mark's list of twelve evil intentions, we may assume that his rendition of the scene is much more formal than it actually was. To capture its more informal and intimate tenor, a parody of Henry Wadsworth Longfellow's "Hiawatha" proves inspirational. It seems that Hiawatha had a pair of magic mittens that enabled him to crush large boulders into hand-size rocks, which he flung at Mudjekeewis, the "Immortal Father," in an attempt to kill him. In Longfellow's version, the attempt did not succeed, but in the parody, "The Modern Hiawatha," by George A. Strong (in Gardner 2001, 91–92), he was more successful. This parody also appears in *The Norton Book of Light Verse* (Baker, 1986, 67–68) as written by an anonymous poet under the title "What Hiawatha Probably Did."

WHAT HIAWATHA PROBABLY DID

He slew the noble Mudjekeewis
With his skin he made him mittens;
Made them with the fur-side inside;
Made them with the skin-side outside;
He, to keep the warm side inside,
Put the cold side, skin-side, outside;
He, to keep the cold side outside,
Put the warm side, fur-side, inside:—
That's why he put the cold side outside,
Why he put the warm side inside,
Why he turned them inside outside.

I found myself imagining that Jesus' explanation of the parable to his puzzled disciples went something like this:

WHAT JESUS PROBABLY SAID

Sin works from the inside-outside,
And not, my friends, from outside-inside.
For outside-inside ends up outside,
While inside-outside just stays inside,
And this is sin's unhappy downside.
But that's why I came thereside-hereside,
To turn this matter rightside-upside,
And make the Devil take the hindside.
So now, if this be on the clear-side,
It's time, my friends, to bottoms-upside.

My point here is that given the intimacy that Jesus shared with his close companions, they also must have been, on many occasions, a "joking community."[6] This makes the palpable tension of the Last Supper seem all the more anomalous. Yet even here, some find humor in the fact that when Jesus says one of them will betray him, one after another of them asks, "Surely not I, Lord?" (Matt 26:22). Which is also to say that there are occasions when the time to weep and the time to laugh (Eccles 3:4) are one and the same.

Motoring through the Bible Belt

"Grow Up, You Hairy Heads!"

[Elisha] went up from there to Bethel; and while he was going up on the way, some small boys came out of the city and jeered at him, saying, "Go away, baldhead! Go away, baldhead!" When he turned around and saw

them, he cursed them in the name of the LORD. Then two she-bears came out of the woods and mauled forty-two of the boys. From there he went on to Mount Carmel, and then returned to Samaria.
    2 Kings 2:23–25

Small boys jeered
At Elisha's pate.
And two she-bears
The forty-two ate.
    Burma-Shave

4. Humor as Soul Maintenance

In his review of Cohen's *Jokes: Philosophical Thoughts on Joking Matters (1999)*, Noel Carroll quotes what he calls Cohen's "eloquent" comment on "the metaphysical significance of joking" (Carroll 2000, 440). The quotation reads, "That we do it [i.e., joking] *together* is the satisfaction of a deep human longing, the realization of a desperate hope. It is the hope that we are enough like one another to sense one another, to be able to live together" (Cohen 1999, 29). Carroll adds, "This, it seems to me, is the soul of Cohen's book—in more senses than one" (440). Perhaps the book has a soul because humor itself is soulful.

This chapter is devoted to the fourth gift of humor, that of soul maintenance. To set the stage for this discussion of humor as soul maintenance, I want to introduce a model of the person that I developed several years ago (Capps 1994), one that suggests that our personhood is comprised of three elements or dimensions: the self, the spirit, and the soul.

The Model of the Person

First, let's review some dictionary definitions of the three major terms of the model: *Self* is primarily defined as "the identity, character, etc. of any person or thing" and "one's own person as distinct from all others." This is what Holland's approach to humor is about, as he is concerned with the identity themes of an individual and with how humor enables one to identify and gain insight into these themes.

Spirit has many dictionary meanings (there were ten in the dictionary I consulted), but the ones that relate to the model of the person presented here are "disposition; mood (e.g., high *spirits*)," "real meaning; true intention (the *spirit* of the law)," and "a pervading animating principle or characteristic quality (the *spirit* of the times)." The sense one gets when reading the dictionary definitions of *spirit* is that there is something ineffable or inexpressible about it.

Soul also has several meanings, and some of these meanings use the word *spirit* or *spiritual*, for example, "an entity without material reality, regarded as the spiritual part of a person," or "spiritual or emotional warmth, force, etc." But the definition that comes closest to what the model understands by "soul" is this one: "vital or essential part, quality, etc."

One thing that we learn from these definitions is that spirit and soul have considerable overlap, and therefore it may not be easy to distinguish them, whereas self seems to be of a rather different order, and its relation to both spirit and soul is less evident than the relationship of spirit and soul to one another. Therefore, I will begin with spirit and soul and discuss their relationship to one another.

Spirit and Soul

In *Re-Visioning Psychology* (1975), James Hillman discusses the tendency of humanistic psychology (especially Abraham Maslow) to deny the soul and its afflictions. Following this discussion, he offers a brief excursus on the differences between spirit and soul. In his view, soul and spirit need to be differentiated because in Christianity, soul has become identified with spirit, to the soul's own detriment: "Already in the early vocabulary used by Paul, pneuma or spirit has begun to replace psyche or soul. The New Testament scarcely mentions soul phenomena such as dreams, but stresses spirit phenomena such as miracles, speaking in tongues, prophecy, and visions" (68).

The images ascribed to spirit blaze with light: "Spirit is fast, and it quickens what it touches. Its direction is vertical, and ascending" (68). Although there are many spirits, and many kinds of spirit, the notion of spirit has come to be associated with "the sublimations of higher and abstract disciplines, the intellectual mind, refinements, and purifications" (68). Thus the philosophers have tended to view spirit as their province and have kept soul out of their works or assigned it a lower place: "Descartes confined soul to the pineal gland, a little enclave between the opposing powers of internal mind and external space. More recently, Santayana has put soul down in the realm of matter and considered it an antimetaphysical principle. . . . The spiritual point of view always posits itself as superior, and operates particularly well in a fantasy of transcendence among ultimates and absolutes" (68).

In contrast to images of spirit, soul images are connected with the night world, the realm of the dead, and the moon: "We still catch our soul's most essential nature in death experiences, in dreams of the night, and in the images of 'lunacy'" (68). Unlike spirit, which extracts meanings (insights) and puts them into action, soul sticks to the realm of experience and to reflections within experience: "It moves indirectly in circular reasonings, where retreats are as important as advances, preferring labyrinths and corners, giving a metaphorical sense to life through such words as *close, near, slow,* and *deep.* Soul involves us in the pack and welter of phenomena and the flow of impressions. It is the 'patient' part of us. Soul is vulnerable and suffers; it is passive and remembers" (69). Whereas spirit says to look up, gain distance, attend to the beyond and above, and travels by means of *a via negativa*—"not this, not that"—for "strait is the gate and only first things and last things will do," soul replies, "But this too may have a place—who knows?" So "the cooking vessel of the soul takes in everything, everything can become soul; and by taking into its imagination any and all events, psychic space grows" (69).

Hillman elaborates these differences between spirit and soul in his article "Peaks and Vales" (1979). Here again he attributes the loss of soul to Christianity, which, beginning with Paul, substituted spirit for soul. He observes that at the Council of Constantinople in 869, "the soul lost its dominion. At this council, the idea of human nature as devolving from a tripartite cosmos of spirit, soul and body was reduced to a dualism of spirit (or mind) and body (or matter)" (54). Yet this council only made official "a long process beginning with Paul, the Saint, of substituting and disguising, and forever after confusing, soul with spirit" (54).

A key figure in this development was Tertullian, who contended that the soul may be identified with a kind of "natural" Christianity, or Christianity in its most unreflective and least elevated form. Christians who aspire to a higher level of faith and commitment to God will cultivate the spiritual life and not be satisfied with soul religion. When the Council of Nicea in 787 deprived images of their inherent authenticity, soul was associated with images and image worship—with an unreflective, natural Christianity that spiritual Christians might tolerate in others, and even themselves have recourse to in moments of fear and dread, but recognize as base and immature.

In his essay, Hillman continues his critique of Maslow's notion of the "peak experience." He commends Maslow for bringing pneuma back into psychology but points out that in doing so, he also reintroduced the old confusion of pneuma with psyche (or soul). Peak experiences concern the spirit and its elevation, and "the peak experience is a way of describing pneumatic experience." The one who seeks the peak experience "is in search of spirit." But the peak experience has nothing to do with the psyche or soul; for soul is identified, metaphorically, with the vales of life, and in the usual religious language of our culture, the vale is a depressed emotional place—the vale of tears, the lonesome valley, and the valley of the shadow of death. The first definition of *valley* in the *Oxford English Dictionary* is "a long depression or hollow," and other meanings of the words *vale* and *valley* refer to "such sad things as the decline of years and old age, the world regarded as a place of troubles, sorrow, and weeping, and the world regarded as the scene of the moral, the earthly, the lowly." As Keats suggests in a letter, "Call the world, if you please, the vale of soul-making" (cited in Hillman 1979, 58).

Hillman points out that in mythology the valleys are the places where the nymphs hold sway, and nymphs are personifications of the wisps of clouds of mist clinging to valleys, mountains, and water sources. Thus, "nymphs veil our vision, keep us shortsighted, myopic, caught—no long range distancing, no projections or prophecies as from a peak" (58). The desire for spiritual transcendence is strong in us, especially when, in the vigor of youth, we leave the low and mundane valleys of our childhood and aspire to transcend the limitations of our lives and to breathe the spirit of limitlessness.

Hillman cautions, however, that the valley world of the soul is steeped in history, whereas in the peak experience of the spirit, history is that which can be overcome, the debris over which we climb in our ascent, and must therefore be denied: "Thus, from the spirit point of view, it can make no difference if our teacher be a Zaddik from a Polish shetl, an Indian from under a Mexican cactus, or a Japanese master in the gardens of stones; these differences are but conditionings of history, personalistic hangups. The spirit is impersonal, rooted not in local soul, but timeless" (62). Spirit ascends the mountain, thinking that it can leave soul behind and believing that it will not pay a price for having done so. But "from the viewpoint of soul and life in the vale, going up the mountain feels like a desertion. . . . Its viewpoint appears in the long hollow depression of the valley, the inner and closed objection that accompanies the exaltation of ascension" (62). Thus, "the soul feels left behind, and we see this soul reacting with resentments. Spiritual teachings warn the initiate so often about introspective broodings, about jealously, spite, and pettiness, about attachments to sensations and memories. These cautions present an accurate phenomenology of how the soul feels when the spirit bids farewell" (62).

So the soul develops its pathologies. These are the depressions and objections that come with spirit's rejections, and the resentment created by spirit's attempt to run roughshod over the soul's local history, resentments that emerge in what pschotherapy terms our "complexes." In mythological terms, the Appollonian spirit, with its desire to make us feel free and open and responsive to our higher aspirations, has to come to terms with old Saturn, who is imprisoned in paranoid systems of judgment, defensive maneuvers, and melancholic conclusions (72). If, as the name implies, the spiritual disciplines are disciplines of the transcendent spirit, then it is the task of psychotherapy, as *its* name implies (*psycho-therapy*), to concern itself with the residues of the spiritual ascent: with soul's depressions, resentments, paranoias, and melancholias.

However, if this contrast between spirit and soul appears to imply that soul is nothing but pathology, this would be the wrong conclusion to draw. As Hillman also points out, soul is "a wondrous quality in daily life," an appreciation for things and experiences that spirit considers mere local trivia. Also, whereas spirit assumes a position of humility as it confronts the inevitable limits of self and life, soul goes in for the humorous: "Humility and humor are two ways of coming down to *humus,* to the human condition. Humility would have us bow down to the world and pay our due to its reality. Render unto Caesar. Humor brings us down with a pratfall. Heavy meaningful reality becomes suspect, seen through, the world laughable—paranoia dissolved" (64). To illustrate the soul's preference for the humorous, Hillman cites a letter written by the fourteenth Dalai Lama of Tibet. This venerable master of the spirit uses the peaks and valleys metaphor to distinguish spirit and soul; he describes soul as "communal," as loving to hum in unison. But, says the Dalai Lama, soul is not enough, for "the creative soul craves spirit," and "the most beautiful monks one day bid farewell to their comrades to make their solitary journey toward the peaks, there to mate with the cosmos" (59). Meanwhile, the less "creative" or "aspiring" souls are content to pass the day sustained by the common ordinary amusements of daily life. Western visitors to Tibet have observed that these folks may spend the better part of the day recounting an amusing event, such as an accidental pratfall by one of their number who failed to notice a stone that lay—or was placed—in the path where he was walking. This too is soul, and it manifests itself not in songs of ascent, but in low laughter rising from the gut.

The Soul and Human Anatomy

Employing Hillman's distinction between spirit and soul, and his use of spatial imagery—peaks and vales—to express it, we can see how this spirit/soul split is embodied. In a sense, his spatial imagery for spirit and soul—peaks and vales— externalizes a conflict that we actually experience in our bodies, and this spatial imagery is transposable into the inner landscape of the human body, thus "anatomizing" it. This means reasserting the ancient tradition that the soul is "located," as it were, in the digestive system—the lower body—and, more precisely, in the central organ of the digestive system, the liver; and claiming that the spirit has its location in the higher blood vascular system, and, more specifically, in *its* central organ, the heart.

Throughout human history, our premodern predecessors have been vexed and perplexed by the question of the soul's location in our bodies: If you and I have a soul, where is it located? While we moderns may consider this a meaningless question, usually by asserting that the soul is not an entity but a way of talking about what transpires between us (as "soul mates"), we ought not dismiss this question quite so easily. According to Morris Jastrow Jr. (1912) and Richard Selzer (1974), the ancients believed the soul is located in the liver. The liver was regarded as the center of vitality, the source of all mental and emotional activity, "nay, the seat of the soul itself" (Selzer 1974, 64). It was also considered the organ through which the gods spoke, a belief that supported divination practices, for priests would slit open the belly of a sheep or goat and read the markings on the animal's liver. Selzer points out, however, that with "the separation of medicine from the apron strings of religion and the rise of anatomy as a study in itself, the liver was toppled from its central role and the heart was elevated" (65). Evidently, anatomical research demonstrated that it was not the size or marking of an organ but its essential function that counted, and on this measure, the heart came to be viewed as the true center of human vitality. After all, the heart is the organ that pumps blood—the life-giving fluid—throughout the body.

In Selzer's view, Christianity became a religion of the heart, and moreover, it transformed earlier barbaric heart rituals into a more spiritualized form. If the ancient warrior cut out the heart of his enemy and ate it with gusto, believing that to devour the slain enemy's heart was to take upon oneself the strength, valor, and skill of the vanquished, the early Christians engaged in the more civilized, and spiritualized, practice of *adoring* the heart of a saint: "It was not the livers or brains or entrails of saints that were lifted from the body in sublimest autopsy, it was the heart, thus snipped and cradled into worshipful psalms, then soaked in wine and herbs and set into silver reliquaries for the veneration" (63). This veneration of the heart also was supported by the Greek philosophical tradition, for as Selzer points out, it was Plato who "placed the higher emotions, such as courage, squarely above the diaphragm, and situated the baser appetites below, especially in the liver, where they squat like furry beasts even today, as is indicated in the term 'lily-livered,' or 'choleric,' or worse, 'bilious' " (65–66).

Although Selzer's history of the heart's triumph at the liver's expense as the seat of human vitality is rather sketchy, it supports Hillman's distinction between spirit and soul. If Christianity became the religion of spirit (pneuma), it did so in part by giving special prominence to the heart, displacing the liver as the locus of that which is divine in us. Also, Selzer's account of the heart's triumph over the liver supports Hillman's spatial imagery. Heart becomes associated with peaks, whereas liver has its place in the vales below. As Hillman himself points out: "Sometimes going up the mountain one seeks escape from the underworld, and so the Gods appear from below bringing all sorts of physiological disorders. They will be heard, if only through intestinal rumblings and their fire burning in the bladder" (Hillman 1979, 71).

Selzer's account of the triumph of the heart also may explain why Christians did not have much use for soul language. If, as Hillman argues, Christianity quickly became a religion of spirit, we may assume that for Christians, the soul continued to be identified with the liver, and for this reason alone it would need to be devalued. Spirit was central to its universalizing tendency, and therefore it is not surprising that Hillman would associate the origins of its emphasis on spirit with Paul. As Jastrow points out, the ancient Hebrews held that the liver is the seat of the soul, and he cites various biblical verses to support this (Job 16:13; Lam 2:11; Prov 7:23). He also notes that the Talmud refers to medical remedies that employ the liver of a dog or the gall of a fish: "Both remedies are clearly based on the supposition that the liver as the seat of life or of the soul is capable of restoring the intellect and sight, which are manifestations of soul life" (150).

The Self and Identity

I will return to the idea that the soul is located in the liver, but I want to comment now on the third term of our model of the person, the self. If the self has to do with our "identity," then according to the dictionary, identity is "the state or fact of being the same." This definition squares well with Erik H. Erikson's view that identity refers to an individual's "inner sameness and continuity" (Erikson 1959, 94). Thus, for a person undergoing an "identity crisis," this inner sameness and continuity is being threatened or cast into doubt. While "identity crisis" applies to an acute condition, examples of more chronic cases are persons suffering from multiple personality disorder (for identity assumes a selfsameness) and persons suffering from amnesia or dementia (where the sense of self-continuity is absent or lost). Thus, selfhood is based on the perception that one is the selfsame individual whom one has been and will be in the future, and that this selfsameness persists over time and space. Erikson calls this in his later writings the "sense of 'I' " (Erikson 1968, 1981).

Thus, to return to our anatomical framework with its emphasis on the person as *embodied*: If the spirit is associated with the heart and one's aspirations toward the "beyond and the above," and the soul is linked to the liver and one's rootedness in the local, circumscribed realities in which we live our daily lives, the self is associated with the brain and specifically with its memory function that enables us to maintain a sense or awareness of ourselves as being the selfsame person over the course of a lifetime, despite changes in physical appearance due to aging and the changes in physical location that result from the very aspirations of spirit that impel us out of the vales of our childhood and early youth. It is noteworthy in this regard that when individuals are asked to identify the physical locus of their sense of self, they tend to suggest that it feels as though it is behind the eyes. This makes intuitive sense, for it is largely by means of our eyes that we experience the world itself as continuous, as the selfsame world that greets us in the morning after we have taken leave of it the evening before.

The Soul and Self-regeneration

The drawing on page 110 shows, through the connecting line, that there needs to be a harmony between self, spirit, and soul for one to experience oneself as a whole person. All three make their claims on the individual person, and if any one of them is ignored, one's well-being will be diminished or harmed. Stress often is caused by the absence of harmony between these three domains, as when spirit is allowed to exert greater influence than the soul on the self, or vice versa. The self, as the locus of consciousness, bears primary responsibility for regulating the relationships among the three. In addition, spirit and soul make their own unique contributions to the self. Because spirit is associated with the beyond and above—with aspirations—it contributes to the *enlargement* of the self. It is the primary force behind the tendency of self to expand itself, to incor-

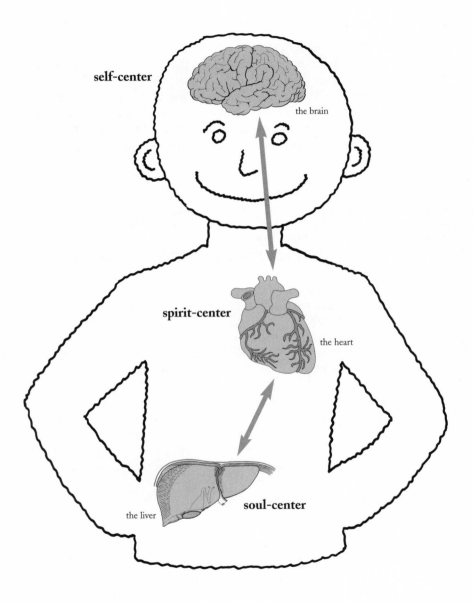

Model of the Person

porate into itself new horizons of meaning and significance. The spirit challenges the self to resist the inclination to become narrow, insular, turned in on itself. When the self is infused with spirit, it broadens itself and takes in more of life and the world. And this is why spirit is appropriately viewed as having its locus in the heart, as we think of the heart as capable of being "enlarged," as more copious and expansive.

What soul contributes to the self are powers of *regeneration,* especially the regeneration that comes from returning to its central concerns, its formative influences, its grounding in time and place. Thus, through its association with the liver, the soul may be understood as the regenerative agent within the human self. Through direct observation, the ancient Greeks recognized that the liver is self-regenerative, the only organ of the body that has the capacity to regenerate itself. Selzer describes its self-regenerative powers, citing the case of Prometheus: "Remember Prometheus? That poor devil who was chained to a rock, and had his liver pecked out each day by a vulture? Well, he was a classical example of the regeneration of tissue, for every night his liver grew back to the ready for the dreaded diurnal feast" (76). Likewise,

> So will yours grow back, regenerate, reappear, regain all of its old efficiency and know how. All it requires is quitting the booze, now and then. The ever-grateful, forgiving liver will respond joyously with a multitude of mitoses and cell divisions that will replace the sick tissues with spanking new nodules and lobules of functioning cells. This rejuvenation is carried on with the speed and alacrity of a starfish growing a new ray away from the stump of the old. (76–77)

When we associate the self-regenerative nature of the liver with the soul, as the ancients did, we can readily appreciate the soul's beneficent nature. The self-regenerative nature of the liver calls attention not to the soul's bitterness, but to its capacity to forgive, especially its forgiveness of the spirit's grandiosity, its visions of limitlessness, its callous denial of the "debris" over which it climbs in its dreams of transcendence.

A dramatic example of the liver's capacity for self-regeneration is one of the earliest attempts, carried out several years ago, to transplant a baboon's liver to a human. At the news conference following the recipient's death seventy-one days after the transplant operation, the medical team acknowledged that their "almost pathological fear of [organ] rejection" may have contributed to the patient's death. Organ rejection, which "had been seen in a virulent form in every other case ever done," led them to order far more diagnostic testing than customary, and one such test precipitated a serious reaction that may have contributed to the patient's death (quoted in the *New York Times,* September 9, 1992, A13). As it turned out, the medical team need not have worried, for the liver, unlike the heart in heart transplants, quickly adapted itself to the recipient's body: "Within a month of the transplant operation, the baboon liver had tripled in size on its own to meet the metabolic needs of the recipient." According to the pathologist who performed the autopsy, "It adjusted nicely for a man of his size and weight." Observing that "the liver is an unusual organ because it has the capacity to regenerate," he marveled, "No one knows why the liver grew and why it stopped when it did" (13).

If we moderns have difficulty believing that the soul is literally located in the liver, the fact that the liver is self-regenerative may at least support belief that the liver is an apt *metaphor* for the soul. For what the liver tells us—what its markings, in a sense, show us—is that we can try to kill the liver, yet it always has a way of coming back, of renewing itself. For the one who—whether the host self or an external enemy—has tried to kill it, this is an ambiguous prospect, for the soul may forgive, but it also may avenge itself and do so through its capacity to regenerate itself.

Soul Maintenance and the Fear of Failure

How are humor and the model of the person presented here relevant to one another? I have intimated an answer to this question in noting Hillman's association of humor to the soul. A point that Noel Carroll makes in his review of Cohen's book, however, enables us to present a more complex picture of humor's relevance to the model. Carroll points out that, for Cohen, "there is a recurring pattern in successful joke transactions: many jokes presuppose beliefs, knowledge, and/or feelings, shared by the teller and the listener, and when the listener activates these, thereby completing the design of the joke, a sense of intimacy is achieved" (442). He does not dispute Cohen's point here, but he cites the case of the professional comedian who has been commissioned to entertain some group of which he is not a member. Despite the fact that he is not a member of the group, his routine may succeed with them because he has found someone to write jokes appropriate for that group and is able to deliver these jokes effectively even if he does not understand all of the content of the jokes. To illustrate, Carroll cites Bob Hope's routines on USO tours in which he would incorporate humorous references to local characters, such as Sgt. Soandso. These were persons he did not know or have personal feelings about, yet he could work them into his jokes (442–43).

In the terms of my model, the professional comedian represents a *universalizing* tendency in humor, and this is associated with the spirit. It may have its origins in the comedian's identification with a particular ethnic group, yet in the course of his professional career, this association of humor with his own ethnic group gets attenuated, and his humor becomes more and more national, even international or global, in character. If this is true of the comedian, it is also true of humor itself, and these localistic versus universalistic tendencies of humor create a tension within humor itself. In effect, Cohen's book advocates the more localistic tendency of humor, and this means for him that ethnic humor is important, so important, in fact, that we should not subject it to a heavy barrage of moral theory. In the terms of the model of the person presented here, such theory reflects the universalizing tendencies of the spirit. In Freud's economical theory of humor, such tendencies lead to costly inhibitions. The purpose of this chapter, therefore, is to make a case for the more local or particularistic forms of humor, on the grounds that these forms of humor are especially good for the soul, and it is the soul, not the spirit, that is under threat in contemporary society.[1]

But how, precisely, is humor good for the soul? I suggest that ethnic humor is an especially valuable type of humor for soul maintenance, as it enables us to neutralize or relativize our anxieties about failure. (If previous chapters focused on Erik H. Erikson's life cycle theme of identity versus identity confusion and intimacy versus isolation, this one concerns the life cycle theme of industry versus inferiority, which he ascribes to the later childhood or preadolescent years.) The association between the soul and ethnic humor makes sense in light of the forgoing comparison of the soul and the spirit, for whereas the spirit is associated with the universal, the soul is linked to the local and particular. The spirit expresses itself in the desire to go off to college, to acquire an education that enables one to work in the corporate world of, say, international finance. The soul, on the other hand, expresses itself in one's homesickness and resulting depression during one's freshman year in college, in a longing for Mom's home cooking, for the familiar hangouts of one's hometown or neighborhood, and for one's high school friends. If one left a special boyfriend or girlfriend behind, a person who had not yet graduated from high school, the spirit-soul tensions are felt in the sense that one has outgrown this person versus the sense that this person makes one feel connected, safe, and secure. If the aspirations of the spirit present us with challenges, they also confront us with the prospect of failure. At times in which the anxiety of failure is especially acute and insistent, we think of home, the place where we grew up, and tell ourselves that there would be no shame in going back there, in reclaiming our bedroom and attending a local community college, or working in our parents' bakery or dry-cleaning business.

I suggest that ethnic humor, or at least certain kinds of ethnic humor (which I will define more precisely later), enable us to express this spirit-soul tension, especially as it manifests itself in failure anxieties. As we have already seen in our discussion of Hillman's essay "Peaks and Vales," humor is associated with soul in the same way that humility is associated with spirit. As he points out, humility is the downside of the spirit's ascent, a way of coming to terms with the fact that we cannot always have what we want, for there are others competing for the same prizes and rewards. Nor do we always reach the goals we set for ourselves. Sometimes we simply fall short of our goals; other times we suffer inglorious defeat. Humiliation and humility share the same Latin root word—*humiliatus*— and humiliation often has been the method employed to teach us humility. As Hillman notes, humor comes to our rescue in times such as these. By exaggerating the fall—for comic effect—"heavy meaningful reality becomes suspect, seen through, the world laughable—paranoia dissolved" (64). As Freud puts it in his essay on humor: "Look here! This is all that this seemingly dangerous world amounts to. Child's play—the very thing to jest about!" (Freud, 1927/1963, 268).

Despite the fact that Cohen makes a persuasive case for ethnic humor, a type of humor that helps to create a sense of shared intimacy, my emphasis here on this type of humor may require some justifications, for no one can seriously question the fact that a great deal of ethnic humor is offensive and degrading. This does not, however, mean that we should condemn all ethnic humor. Instead, it means that we should make an effort to become more knowledgeable about ethnic humor so that we can make more informed judgments about what is and is not acceptable ethnic humor. This need not result in the formulation of a moral theory per se (Cohen's caveat against such theories still holds), but it may provide justification for one's "uneasiness," or absence of uneasiness, when hearing or reading an ethnic joke. Mahadev L. Apte, an anthropology professor at Duke University, is especially helpful in this regard. In his chapter on ethnic humor in *Humor and Laughter: An Anthropological Approach* (1985), he notes that " stereotypes are crucial to ethnic humor and its appreciation. Because they are widely accepted by members of individual cultures, they constitute a shared set of assumptions necessary for ethnic humor" (114). Thus, "a basic assumption in ethnic humor is that it should be based on traits that are considered to be the consequence of ethnicity" (114).

This means that jokes based on stereotyped images of occupational groups, such as lawyers, physicians, secretaries, construction workers, and waiters, cannot be considered ethnic humor. If, however, an individual's social identity is based on ascribed status, and his or her occupational status results from it, then humor based on that identity constitutes ethnic humor. Apte points out, for example, that many proverbs in various South Asian languages making fun of goldsmiths, tailors, and barbers can be said to constitute ethnic humor because, in the context of Hindu society, these target groups are hereditary occupational caste groups, and the profession constitutes an integral part of members' ascribed status: "A son of a barber is identified as a member of the barber caste, though he may pursue another profession, and certain stereotypic images are associated with him, irrespective of his occupation" (115). A joke about a rabbi also would constitute ethnic humor, as all rabbis are Jewish. Cohen's suggestion that many psychiatrists also are Jewish implies that in certain cases, a psychiatrist joke may be an ethnic joke. As we saw in chapter 3, he suggests that the joke about the psychiatrist questioning the distraught patient's idea of a wholesome breakfast has an implicit ethnic theme. The psychiatrist is acting like the proverbial Jewish mother.

Apte points out that in Western society, certain occupations and professions are associated with ethnic groups. In addition to the association noted between psychiatrists and Jews, there are jokes about African-American athletes, Italian opera singers, French waiters, etc. (Incidentally, Apte includes racial jokes in his discussion of ethnic humor; the very term *African-American* may itself be an eth-

nic appellation, one that many members of this group prefer to such racial appel-
lations as *Negro* or *black*.)

In his analysis of ethnic humor, Apte first takes up the issue of its forms and
types, explaining that the most common forms are jokes, riddle-jokes, and
proverbs. Of the many variations of ethnic jokes, the most common is one that
"identifies an individual as a member of a specific ethnic group and portrays that
individual in a disparaging light. Usually the portrayal involves developing an
incongruity between verbal comments and actions or exaggerating a personality
trait or behavior that is stereotypically associated with the group. Most often
such jokes give the impression that a person of the target ethnic group is stupid,
ignorant, or unclean" (115). Another type of ethnic joke involves the "cross-cul-
tural" listing of slurs, "so that many ethnic groups are simultaneously targeted.
Individuals from different groups face a common situation and respond to it in
keeping with popular stereotypes involving their respective behavior, action, ver-
balization, or carrying out of a task" (116). He cites the following joke:

> An American, an Englishman, a Frenchman, and a German managed to
> survive a shipwreck on an island. After a few months, the German had
> organized the natives into an army, the American had built a plant using
> native labor, the Frenchman had opened a brothel, and the Englishman
> was sitting on the beach waiting to be introduced.

Or consider this contrast between heaven and hell: Heaven is where the police
are British, the mechanics are German, the cooks are French, the lovers are Italian, and the whole thing is organized by the Swiss; and hell is where the police
are German, the cooks are British, the mechanics are French, the lovers are
Swiss, and the whole thing is organized by the Italians.

Competition and one-upmanship are key elements in yet another type of
ethnic joke in which two or three individuals of different ethnic groups compete
with and try to outsmart each other. Winning often means coming up with the
most clever answer in verbal repartee. A variant form of this type is that the
members of two ethnic groups compete successfully while a third falls short:

> A German, an Italian, and a Norwegian were trying to get into the sta-
> dium at the World Olympics in Montreal, but the seats were all sold out.
> The enterprising German stripped down to his shorts and undershirt,
> picked up a cane fishing pole in a nearby alley, and marched right in, stat-
> ing boldly, "Heinrich Schneider, Germany, pole vault." Noting the suc-
> cessful ploy, the Italian took off his outer garments, grabbed a large round
> stone, then just as boldly strode through the gate, announcing, "Pasquale
> Galento, Italy, shot put." Not to be outdone, the Norwegian took off all
> but his BVDs and went into a nearby hardware store where he purchased
> some barbed wire. As he approached the gate, the Norwegian spoke out
> confidently, "Hjalmar Olson, Norway, fencing."

Apte also discusses the techniques used in ethnic humor, noting that imitation and exaggeration are among the most widely used. Imitations include body movements and gestures and language considered characteristic of the target groups. Foreign language imitations constitute major stimuli in ethnic humor.

Finally, Apte considers theoretical approaches to ethnic humor. The primary objective of most textual analyses of this type of humor is to discover from its contents "the underlying stereotypes, and the covert attitudes, beliefs, and motives, regarding the targeted ethnic groups" (121). Many of these studies attempt to identify the esoteric-exoteric factor in the joke lore. The esoteric factor is what one group thinks of itself and what it supposes others think of it, while the exoteric factor is what one group thinks of another and what it supposes the other group thinks the first group thinks. This esoteric-exoteric distinction has been equated in some of the research literature with "in-group" versus "out-group" humor, and it is generally assumed that in-group humor by and large reflects a group's positive image of itself, while out-group humor reflects a group's negative image. While some have argued that this is not always the case, that in-group humor is just as likely to be self-derogatory, Apte contends that little evidence has been offered in support of this argument. Appearances in this regard can be deceiving. For example, joke tellers and hearers may feel free to tell jokes that make fun of their own ethnic group because they themselves believe that they have transcended the stereotypes in question. As Apte points out, "people who tell jokes derogatory of the ethnic group to which they belong are likely to dissociate themselves from the underlying stereotype, believing in intracultural diversity and in the existence of several subethnic groups differentiated on the basis of generation, occupation, degree of religious orthodoxy, immigrant status, education, and overall socioeconomic status" (131). In effect, such dissociation is a manifestation of "spirit." One can make fun of one's own ethnic group because one believes one has, to some degree, transcended it (what I have called spirit's contribution to self-enlargement).

Apte also questions the argument that "if ethnic humor is based on a specific trait uniquely attributed to a particular group, its faithfulness to objective reality may more easily be verified" (131). The problem with this argument is that "humor results from a creative process that uses exaggeration—distortion—as one of its major techniques. Therefore the portrayal of individuals, groups, actions, personality traits, and physical features is rarely, if ever, faithful to objective reality" (131). Thus, the presence of such exaggeration, together with the fact that prejudice and negative attitudes seem universally to play a major role in ethnic humor, means that the degree of incongruity between an ethnic group and the humor associated with it is very high. It makes little sense, then, to try to ascertain whether a trait ascribed to an ethnic group is true or accurate. This very question tends to reflect a misunderstanding of humor itself.

This does not, of course, mean that one has no right to object to certain ethnic jokes. As we saw in the previous chapter, Ted Cohen believes that we have a right to our own moral objections to a particular joke and that we are not under any obligation to explain or account for this objection. The jokes he cited in this regard were predominantly ethnic jokes. This does not mean, however, that all ethnic jokes are morally objectionable. Cohen prefaces one joke with the observation that "some people are bothered by this joke," a second joke with, "Probably more people are bothered by this one," and a third joke with, "But many more people are bothered by this one" (76–77). As all three of these jokes are ethnic, the implication is that while anyone may object to all three, there are degrees of offensiveness in ethnic humor, and whether and to what extent one takes offense depends, in part, on how one interprets it. A joke that illustrates this point is the following:

A man was very unhappy that he had no romance in his life whatsoever. So he went to a Chinese sex therapist, Dr. Chang, who looked at him and said, "OK, take off all your crose." Which the man did. "Now get down and crawl reery fass to the other side of room." Which the man did. "Okay, now crawl rerry fass to me." Which the man did. Dr. Chang said, "Your probrem velly bad. You haf Ed Zachary disease." The man said, "What is Ed Zachary disease?" "It when your face rook Ed Zachary rike your ass."

This joke derives much of its humor from its imitation of the speech patterns of an ethnic group, especially when the individual in question is attempting to speak English. Some may find it offensive because it seems to make fun of the fact that the English letter *l* is difficult for Asians to master. There also may be an implied innuendo that Chinese doctors are less qualified than their American counterparts to practice medicine because their methods are not state-of-the-art. On the other hand, one *could* view this as a joke that makes fun of the American practice of consulting a therapist when one is not experiencing sexual satisfaction, which, to an Asian, is likely to seem an odd way to address the problem. Also, by instructing the man to remove all his clothes and crawl very fast away and then toward him, it is the doctor who places his presumably American patient in a demeaning position and who then adds the further insult that his face and his ass are indistinguishable. Because the joke's punch line plays on the speech pattern issue and the patient is not identified by nationality or ethnicity, however, I would suspect that the greater offense would be taken by Asian-Americans.[2]

I will go out on a limb here, but I suggest that the *least* offensive ethnic jokes are those that represent a member of an ethnic group as stupid or ignorant. Why? Because as Apte points out, stupidity may be attributed to any ethnic group (127). The precise nature of the stupidity may, of course, play on ethnic stereotypes, so that even an ethnic joke that employs the theme of stupidity may be offensive either to a member of the ethnic group in question or to a person who has protective feelings toward this ethnic group. Still, the fact that stupidity is a universal theme in ethnic humor means that no single group is being targeted.

Conversely, while certainly not all humor about stupidity occurs in ethnic jokes, we miss a golden opportunity to reflect on the positive uses of stupidity humor if we object to all expressions of ethnic humor. As I now want to show, stupidity humor can be a healing balm for those who are afflicted with failure anxieties.

The Theme of Stupidity in Ethnic Humor

In the following discussion of the theme of stupidity in ethnic humor, I will focus on two important chapters from Christie Davies' *Jokes and Their Relation to Society* (1998). The central point of Davies' book is that ethnic humor makes the butts of ethnic humor appear either stupid or canny, the Scottish expression *canny* being a convenient way of suggesting that a group is crafty, stingy, or both. The primary reason for this focus on stupidity and canniness lies in the nature of work in modern societies, which threatens everyone with two kinds of failure: "First, there is always present the threat that one will fail to master some aspect of the world of work and be regarded as stupid in consequence, particularly at a time of rapid technical and commercial change" (1). The second mode of failure "and the one that awaits the canny is that one will be so absorbed with working, calculating and making money, as to lose out on the pleasures of life and to forfeit the trust and esteem of others by being too clever and too calculating" (1).

Davies suggests that stupidity jokes are pinned on a familiar group, "one similar to the joke-tellers but who live at the periphery of the joke-teller's country or culture. The people at the center are thus laughing at what appears to them to be a slightly strange version of themselves; almost as if they were to see themselves in a distorting mirror at a fair ground. The butts of stupidity jokes are not a distant or alien group" (1). Sometimes "the two groups may be hostile or in a state of conflict, sometimes they live as amicable neighbors and sometimes they are indifferent to one another," and the jokes "are essentially the same in all three cases and cannot be related easily to the presence or absence of conflict or hostility" (1). In fact, earlier studies have shown "that it is futile to search for an explanation of stupidity jokes in terms of intergroup conflict or tensions. The key explanation of these jokes is always the center-edge relationships of the jokers and the butts of their jokes" (1).

Davies provides a table in which he identifies the country where stupid and canny jokes are told, the identity of the stupid group in the jokes, and the identity of the canny group in the jokes (see pp. 120–21). While the table demonstrates that, in general, the joke tellers do not make themselves the butts of their own jokes, it also indicates that those who *are* the butts of their jokes are typically a subgroup of themselves (as when Canadians tell jokes about Newfoundlanders, the Irish tell jokes about Kerrymen, and Indians and Pakastanies tell jokes about the Sikhs). This is an example, then, of what Freud has called "the narcissism of minor differences" (1921/1960, 41–42; 1930/1960, 61). Thus, while Davies' book is about jokes and their relation to *society*, it is a book that may be read as a study in the psychoanalysis of joking, as the joke tellers *project* onto other members of their own group the failures and inadequacies over which they themselves have anxieties.

Davies' chapter on fooltowns is especially relevant in this regard, as it provides insight into the anxieties that underlie ethnic humor, anxieties that are exacerbated in times of rapid and extensive technological change. Here he observes that jokes about stupidity have always been pinned on people from a particular village, town, region, or nation: "The jokes told today in Egypt about the simplicity of the Nubians from the far south are based on a comic script about Nubians that is thousands of years old. The Nubians then, as now, lived on the southern periphery of Egyptian civilization, a group of distant rustic provincials, neither entirely foreign nor wholly Egyptian" (p. 11). A similar joking tradition can be traced to ancient Greece, with Boetians being the butt of ethnic jokes that originated among the Athenians: "These ancient jokes of the city dwellers of Athens about the predominantly pastoral and agricultural Boetians survive, even today, in the adjective 'Boetian,' meaning an illiterate rustic, and so do the jokes about Abdera, which have given us the terms 'abderite' and 'abderitic' for a foolish simple-minded person" (11).

Jokes about foolish communities were later to be found all over Europe. So "just as today, every country has its own ethnic jokes about stupidity, so in the past every region had a foolish town or village whose 'stupidity' formed the basis of many jests and anecdotes" (12). Davies cites many examples of such fooltowns and notes, for example, that tales of the foolish men of Gotham in England can be traced back to a fifteenth-century manuscript, though the tradition itself is certainly earlier than this. He also suggests that jokes about stupidity were attached to local communities in the past for much the same reason that they are attributed to ethnic minorities and neighboring nations today. That is, "an undesirable quality is rendered comic and exported to another group who live on the edge of the joke-tellers' social universe. When people define who they are in terms of their membership of a local community, then they will tell jokes about the stupidity of the people of *some other local community*, defining *who they are not* in terms of a social unit similar to the one which gives them their basic identity" (12, his emphasis). Thus, "in traditional societies, where people derive one of their most important social identities from their membership of a local community, the jokes are told about the members of a group that is recognizably similar and who, to the joke-tellers, look like themselves as seen in a distorting mirror. Just as we laugh at the reflections of ourselves we see in a hall of curved mirrors, so too we laugh at jokes about the stupidity of our nearest neighbors" (12–13). In effect, Davies writes, "The members of a joke-telling and joke-sharing group enjoy a 'sudden burst of glory' as the stupidity of the others is unveiled and their own superiority is briefly confirmed" (13).

Against those who would argue that ethnic humor is inherently aggressive and hostile, Davies counters:

TABLE 1. Stupid and Canny Jokes by Country

Country where stupid and canny jokes are told	Identity of the stupid group in the joke	Identity of the canny group in the joke	Country where stupid and canny jokes are told	Identity of the stupid group in the joke	Identity of the canny group in the joke
United States	Poles (and others locally, e.g., Italians, Portugese)	Scots, Jews, New England Yankees	Finland	Karelians	Laihians (from Laihia), Scots
Canada (Central and Maritime Canada incl. Ontario and Quebec	Newfoundlanders ("Newfies")	Scots, Jews, Nova Scotians	Bulgaria	Šopi (peasants from the hinterland of Sofia)	Gabrovonians (from Gabrovo), Armenians
Canada (West)	Ukrainians, Icelanders	Scots, Jews	Greece	Pontians (Black Sea Greeks)	Armenians
Mexico	Yucatecos (from Yucatan)	Regiomontanos (citizens of Monterrey)	Russia	Ukrainians, Chukchees	Jews
Columbia	Pastusos (from Pasto in Narifio)	Paisas (from Antioquia)	India	Sikhs (Sardarjis)	Gujaratis, Sindis
England	Irish	Scots, Jews	Pakistan	Sikhs (Sardarjis)	Hindus, especially Gujaratis
Wales	Irish	Cardis (from Cardigan-shire/Ceredigion), Scots, Jews	Iran	Rashtis (Azeris from Rasht)	Armenians, people from Isfahan/Tabriz

TABLE 1. Stupid and Canny Jokes by Country (continued)

Country where stupid and canny jokes are told	Identity of the stupid group in the joke	Identity of the canny group in the joke
Scotland	Irish	Aberdonians (from Aberdeen), Jews
Ireland	Kerrymen	Scots, Jews
France	Belgians, French Swiss (Ouin–Ouin)	Auvergnats (from the Auvergne), Scots, Jews
Netherlands	Belgians, Limburgers	Scots, Jews
Germany	Ostfrieslanders	Swabians, Scots, Jews
Italy	Southern Italians	Milanese, Genovese, Florentines, Scots, Jews, Levantinis
Switzerland	Fribourgers from Fribourg/Freiburg	Genevois, Balois (from Geneva and Bâle/Basel), Jews
Spain	People from Lepe in Andalucia	Aragonese, Catalans
Nigeria	Hausas	Ibos
South Africa	Afrikaners	Scots, Jews
Australia	Irish, Tasmanians	Scots, Jews
New Zealand	Irish, Maoris (North Island), West Coasters (South Island)	Scots, Jews, Dutch

We should not mistake the glee of the winners in this successful piece of playful aggression for real hostility. In the past it was often the people of the next village, township or parish who were seen as rivals, a group known to be essentially *similar* to one's own and yet also held to be *inferior*, though perhaps only by location. If the sense of superiority to one's rival is or was buttressed by the recognized advantages that a community on the main routes of transport and trade has over a more remote community at the periphery, or that an urban center has over the rural hinterland, then jokes about the alleged stupidity of the latter are likely to emerge. (13, his emphasis)

The Gotham jokes are a case in point, as they seem to reflect its position as a relatively isolated village seen in contrast to the busy market and manufacturing town of the "smiths" of Nottingham. Similarly, in the busy manufacturing, market, and university town of Reading in England, people in their eighties still remember the time when jokes akin to present-day Irish jokes or American Polish jokes were told about the people of the village of Tadley. Tadley jokes of the 1920s seem to have stemmed from the remoteness of the village, whose people worked as log cutters and wore more distinctive "pattens," a kind of wooden clog for walking through the muddy woods around Tadley. These wooden clogs became "a comic occupational badge equivalent to the present day jokes about the rubber boots, known as 'wellies' of Irish laborers on English building sites or the long rubber boots worn by Newfoundland fishermen" (13).

Davies observes, however, that jokes about these fooltowns are going out of vogue. He suggests that in the case of England, this is partly because of the creation of national media networks, together with a corresponding decline in the vitality of the local theaters and music halls where the touring comedians performed: "Comedians now tend to tell jokes which latch on to ethnic scripts and joke-conventions which are widely understood, and to abandon comic references which only have a very local and restricted meaning. Economies of scale have likewise led to the replacement of local joke-books by nationally available books of ethnic jokes" (14). But a more deeply rooted reason for the switch to ethnic jokes (such as Irish jokes in Britain) "is the decay of people's sense of being primarily members of a local community, and its replacement by ethnic nationalism as the basis of their identity" (14). Furthermore, "people's sense of what they are *not* has also become ethnic. Accordingly, comic stupidity has to be exported into the domain of another ethnic group rather than that of another local community. Also, the expansion of the urban world into rural areas has forced once-remote villages to become part of an integrated economy of increasingly mobile people" (14). Tadley jokes, for example, have little meaning for younger citizens of Reading because Tadley is now a commuter village and many of the people who live there are scientists and technicians in the nearby atomic weapons research establishment. Thus, jokes from Reading now export stupidity to Ireland, as it would hardly do to locate it in a community where atomic weapons research is being conducted!

In a variant form of the same process, in countries in which the inhabitants of towns or districts are depicted as either foolish or canny, "the small community referred to in the jokes may simply symbolize a large region or a deeper ethnic division" (16). Davies cites in this connection "Danish jokes about the people of the town of Aarhus (which is very close to Mols, a remote rural settlement that was traditionally the butt for Danish jokes about stupidity) [which] may well refer to Jutes in general, for Aarhus is the capital of Jutland, one of the three major seagirt subdivisions of Denmark" (16). Thus, traditional jokes about the people of Mols are now applied to residents of Aarhus, and Aarhusian jokes probably refer to Jutlanders in general. Thus, there is the same universalizing tendency here as the one that Carroll noted in his review of Cohen's book. The idiosyncracies of the people of Mol are attributed to the residents of the capital city of Aarhus, which stands for Jutland.

My friend Troels Norager, who teaches at the Institute for Systematic Theology at the University of Aarhus, confirmed, in a letter in response to my query, that the "stupidity" of the people of Mols has, in recent decades, been ascribed more generally to the inhabitants of the town of Aarhus, despite the fact that Aarhus boasts a major university. He sent me a book, *Old Stories from Denmark*, containing twenty-five stories translated into English about the Mol people. The book cover bears the heading "Old Stories from Denmark Hayseeds and Bumpkins." It notes that "every country has its stories about simple folk like the traditional yokel, bumpkin and gawby of England or the hayseeds and hicks of America. Sometimes the stories are generalized and told about simple people in any part of the country; but they often come to be identified with some small town or country district. In Denmark the people of Mols were singled out for this dubious honor some two centuries ago, and they have had the good sense, which goes with a humor-loving people, to be proud of the old stories, and they are nowhere more popular than in Mols itself."

One story suggests the town rivalry that Davies identifies in his analysis of fooltown humor, as it involves a few men of Mols going over to Aarhus to buy a musket after having been told by a practical joker that war had recently broken out. They purchased a rusty old gun "at a rather high price for what it was," a fact that suggests the people of Aarhus were far more "canny" than the Mol folks. No one wanted to test the gun to see if it would shoot, so finally the men agreed that one would fire it and the others would stand behind him, each holding on to the other in a solid row. The leading man aimed the gun at Mols in the far distance and pulled the trigger. The old gun kicked so hard it knocked them all to the ground. When they came to, they witnessed a terrible sight. Their beloved town of Mols, off in the distance, was a glowing red. Concluding that their shot had set the town on fire, they threw the gun into the sea, scrambled into their boat, and rowed home. As they approached the town, they realized they had mistaken the red glow of the moon for a fire and concluded that they had been a little hasty in throwing the old gun away.

If the people of Mols were the subject of such humor in centuries past, it now appears to be the people of Aarhus who are being targeted, and this is a recent phenomenon. Troels observed that to the best of his recollection, "they only go back two or three decades." After relating several Aarhusian jokes (for example, two Aarhusians decide to drive their truck under a road bridge bearing the sign MAX. 2.5 METERS even though their truck measures 3.5 meters high because "there's no police in sight"), he concluded with this one: "Why don't Aarhusians get angry at jokes directed at them? Because they don't understand them!"

Thus, in today's world, the very proximity of Aarhus to the remote rural settlement of Mols has gained it the dubious honor of an association to Mols that would have been unthinkable in earlier days. One suspects that the very humor that "canny" Aarhusians heaped on the "stupid" Mol people has come back to haunt them, for if the book cover of the storybook is to be believed, the people of Mols are cannily exploiting their *historical* reputation as simpletons while the Aarhusians have become the butt of contemporary stupidity humor.[3]

Finally, Davies points out that even though ethnic jokes have replaced jokes about smaller communities or groups, "the latter often survive locally, and the ethnic jokes that prevail across a nation or even internationally still get adapted for local use" (17). For example, in the United States, the ubiquitous Polish jokes are adapted locally and become transferred to the Italians of New Jersey, the Norwegians in the Dakotas, and the Finns in northern Michigan. In Britain, the standard pair of ethnic jokes about the "stupid" Irish and the "canny" Scots have a local equivalent in the north, where jokes about "stupid" Lancastrians and "canny" Yorkshiremen have a long history and have outlived the shires that gave rise to them. Thus, while the most common shift has been from local community to ethnic minority, there is also a reverse movement from ethnic minority to local community, a "community" that for all intents and purposes no longer exists. Also, the very fact that Polish humor is so readily adaptable to other ethnic groups supports the view that humor about stupidity has universal application, that no ethnic group is immune, and this also means that no single ethnic group is its unique or special target. It may, in fact, be argued that the only ethnic groups that might be immune are those viewed as "canny," and as Davies points out, "canniness" is no less problematic than "stupidity," for it too reflects failure anxieties, only of a different kind, that is, the failure to live a full, contented life. Charles Dickens's Ebenezer Scrooge is a case in point.

Davies concludes that jokes about fooltowns are essentially similar to ethnic jokes about stupidity because ethnic jokes "are rooted in such universal sociological contrasts as center versus periphery, urban versus rural, white-collar versus blue-collar, skilled versus unskilled and competition versus monopoly" (20). The fact that ethnic humor is thus rooted in such universal sociological contrasts needs to be emphasized "because so many scholars with some slight knowledge of the folklore of jokes claim that modern jokes about stupidity are 'hostile' in a way that fooltown jokes of the past were not, and imply that the modern jokes are rooted in bitter inter-ethnic conflicts, apparently unknown in an idyllic past, when folk lived in contented self-sufficient communities and exchanged gentle jests about Gothamite drolleries, numskulls and noodles" (20). He disputes this view in part because it romanticizes the past, failing to take into account the fact that it was often unsafe for individuals to venture alone from their own local community into the territory of another village or small town, but also and more importantly because it creates an exaggerated, even false conflict between the "gentle, good-natured" jokes of earlier times and today's "angry, insulting hate" jokes.

While he does not deny the fact that hostility and hate are expressible through ethnic humor, he believes that there is no simple relationship between the perceived threat that an ethnic group poses for the joke tellers and the fact that it is the butt of stupidity jokes. He cites the example of American Polish jokes as a case in point. Conceivably, Poles were a threat to other ethnic groups in the United States in the late nineteenth and early twentieth centuries when there was a huge wave of immigration to America of poor peasants from the most underdeveloped parts of Poland. But if so, there were few stupidity jokes about Poles. In the period after World War II, the Polish-Americans were not a threat to anyone: "The children and grandchildren of the original immigrants had been Americanized, spoke English, revered cleanliness and were absorbed into the well-paid, blue-collared, hard-hatted American working class" (22). Davies thinks that the reason Poles have been the butt of stupidity jokes is not, therefore, that they constituted a threat to other groups, but that their rate of upward social mobility out of the American working class was slow and gradual, "for they valued security rather than success" (22). In other words, Poles were easy to classify among the stupid because they were *not* taking the risks that are associated with marked upward mobility from one generation to the next. Thus, they became the targets of the failure anxieties of those who were living riskier lives, who, in the terms of my model of the person, were privileging spirit over soul.

Davies' discussion of fooltown humor and of its development into ethnic humor is of vital significance to the theme of this chapter—humor as soul maintenance—because it makes clear that the primary motivation behind this humor is not hate or aggression but the joke teller's own anxieties about failure, especially in times of rapid social change and technological development. Time and time again, Davies emphasizes that "ethnic jokes about stupidity are not told about a people who are very distant, different or alien from ourselves, but always about a neighboring and similar people, whom we can perceive as a comic imitation of ourselves, just as we might visit a hall of mirrors to laugh at our own distorted reflections" (29). In this sense, stupidity jokes are a special case, for in Davies' view, "Ethnic jokes about *other* negative qualities such as craftiness, brutality, cowardice, greed, stinginess, or perverse sexuality are ascribed to other peoples on the basis of *quite different* sets of principles" (29, his emphasis). Thus, stupidity jokes are likely to be the most valuable expressions of ethnic humor as far as soul maintenance is concerned, as they reflect a rather benign way of acknowledging the anxieties that we ourselves experience as we negotiate the demands that are placed on us—as we honor the urgings of the spirit and its aspirations.

Stupidity humor reminds us of the fact of our own limitations and of the foibles of the soul. As Davies puts it, "We laugh at the ignorance of others because we are conscious of our own." After all, "most people in an industrial society cannot give a coherent account of how even such 'old' and familiar items as a telephone or a telescope work. I can remember everyone in a high school physics class laughing at a friend of mine who refused to believe that sound could not travel through a vacuum, because in that case how was it that we were able to communicate with space satellites" (28–29). He suggests that "the jokes about Irish stupidity possibly exist in part at least to reassure the joke tellers (i.e., in this case the British) that *they* themselves aren't stupid" (29, his emphasis). He cites the following joke at the expense of the Irish as a case in point: "The observatory took on a new Irish night-porter who watched with amazement one of the astronomers setting up and operating a large telescope. Presently, as the astronomer moved the telescope into position, a shooting star shot across the sky, falling rapidly. 'Begorrah,' said the porter to the astronomer, 'I've never seen such foine shooting!'"

Stupidity and Difficult Thinking

Davies expands on this theme of anxiety in his later chapter "Stupidity and Rationality: Jokes from the Iron Cage." In effect, this chapter addresses the third of Freud's concerns in his economical theory of humor, that of difficult (i.e., rational and logical) thinking. As Freud emphasizes, humor saves in the expenditure of psychic resources relating, in this case, to the demands that modern society places on its members to engage in highly rationalized forms of thinking. Davies observes, "One of the most outstanding features of the jokes told in industrial societies is the enormous and universal popularity of jokes told at the expense of allegedly stupid groups of people" (63). He considers the range, durability, and popularity of jokes about stupidity a "remarkable phenomenon": "Why, for instance, do people in Western industrial societies prefer jokes about 'stupid' ethnic minorities to almost any other kind of joke?" On the basis of our forgoing discussion, it is not surprising that he attributes this preference for stupidity jokes to the joke tellers' own psychological needs: "By telling jokes about the stupidity of a group on the periphery of their society, people can place this despised and feared quality at a distance and gain a brief sense of reassurance that they and the members of their own group are not themselves stupid or irrational" (64).

There is a correlation, in his view, between the increased popularity of stupidity jokes and "the intensely and increasingly 'rational' character of industrial society. . . . Modern industrial societies are dominated by a belief in technical and economic efficiency, by the view that all institutions should be 'rationally' organized via the interplay of the key impersonal forces of the market place, bureaucracy and modern science so as to maximize the stated goals of these institutions from the means at their disposal" (65). Thus, on one level, "we may see jokes about stupid outsiders as an affirmation of the value of rationality, efficiency and applied intelligence on the part of the joke-tellers, for any failure to live up to and conform to these qualities is ascribed to outsiders and then subjected to severe ridicule. It is *they* who are comically stupid and irrational and *we* who are intelligent, skilled and organized" (65, his emphasis).

But a full explanation of the popularity of these jokes also requires us to consider "the negative impact of rational social organization on the individual," and the key question that must be asked is "What aspect of such a rational social order is likely to make individuals anxious about their position in the rational world in which they live and to want to indulge in jokes about stupid outsiders as a temporary release from this anxiety?" (65). In Davies' view, the answer to this question "probably lies in the high degree of specialization and division of labor imposed on them by the market, bureaucracy and modern science" (65). The mass market encourages individuals to become specialists, bureaucratic organizations emphasize the division of labor, and modern science demands specialization owing to the enormous and increasing body of scientific knowledge. Thus, no single individual can know and understand more than a fraction of it, and even the most highly skilled and intelligent individuals are aware that they are a minor part of a system that contains far more skill and knowledge than any single individual can ever master: "Under these circumstances even the most knowledgeable and skilled person is aware of how little he or she knows and how little he or she can do in a world that puts an enormous emphasis on skill and knowledge" (66). In such a world, "everyone needs to be reassured that they are not really stupid" and that stupidity is "safely restricted" to some other group.

Davies finds it suggestive that many ethnic jokes have as their setting an airplane, submarine, or space rocket where everyone is locked in a technically sophisticated artificial environment and dependent for survival on the intelligent behavior of highly skilled specialists. The introduction of a stupid outsider into the artificial situation of the joke has disastrous but comic results. There's the Polish helicopter pilot who gets cold at 15,000 feet so he turns off the fan; or the Belgian submarine crew who hear a knock on a porthole and open it to find out who's there; or the Swedish rocket with a crew consisting of a chimpanzee and a Norwegian—the chimp is there to handle the flight instructions while the Norwegian's job is to feed the chimp when he gets hungry.

Davies also observes that in a society with a high degree of occupational specialization and division of labor, people are divided into diverse and unequal groups that are differentiated by the degree of skill, training, and acumen demanded by their work. At one extreme are highly skilled specialists who "simply must get it right most of the time, if they are to survive in their chosen profession. For such people jokes about stupid outsiders are a release from the strain of having to exercise a perpetual intelligent vigilance, of having to live by one's wits. Jokes about other people's stupidity can serve to dissipate any anxiety about losing their skill or intellectual powers at a crucial moment" (68). At the other extreme are persons who perform extremely simple, repetitive tasks that require the exercise of hardly any skill or intelligence at all. These persons also are likely to be anxious about stupidity because they feel insecure about their low status in a society that prizes skill, intelligence, and rationality, and they "are anxious lest the complex and baffling society in which they live should make unexpected demands on them which they will not know how to fill. Such anxieties are relieved by jokes about ethnic groups reputedly so stupid that they cannot even reach the level of social and economic competence attained by the least skilled of the occupational groups created by the division of labor" (69). Jokes about the stupidity of the first group are also popular among members of the second group, especially jokes that satirize the first group's sophistication and know-how or their inordinate investment in work at the expense of a happy, contented life. That is, they are too "canny" for their own good.

Finally, Davies points out that a careful study of the world of ethnic jokes would reveal an awareness that the rational world we have created is, at a deeper level, irrational. It is a world in which work, for many people, is tedious, monotonous, and uncreative, and in which leisure is all too often simply a mirror image of such work. While ethnic jokes about those who are too stupid to survive in this highly rationalized work world are far more numerous than those that seek to expose its own irrationalities, the latter do exist. There are jokes about work-addicted Americans, about rigid, pedantic, over-obedient Germans, and about stingy, over-rational, humorless Scotsmen: "In each case the joke-tellers mock the members of another ethnic group for their excessive subordination to the world of work, money, and duty. They are portrayed as senseless beings who have locked themselves in the iron cage and thrown away the key. Their very rationality is irrational, for their methodical manipulation of means towards ends robs their lives of the possibility of human joy and freedom" (71). The comforting message of the jokes "is that it is the others who are irrationally rational while we are wise enough not to be trapped in the constricting formal and technical rationality" of our age (77).

The Childhood Origins of Failure Anxiety

Davies introduced his discussion of the anxiety over failure in the adult world with a story about a friend of his in high school who was laughed at in a high school physics class for wrongheaded thinking. So, anxieties about failure certainly precede our entry into the highly rationalized work world, and perhaps this explains why the readers I am most likely to encounter when I visit the humor section of a local bookstore are preadolescent boys and girls. Thus, Martha Wolfenstein's chapter "Riddles and the Legend of the Moron" in her book *Children's Humor: A Psychological Analysis* (1954) is relevant to our discussion of humor as a form of soul maintenance because it points to the ways in which children make use of humor to address the anxieties that arise in their own "work" world, that of school.

A detailed discussion of Wolfenstein's analysis of moron jokes is beyond the scope of this chapter, but her emphasis on the humor of schoolchildren suggests that an important traditional locus of stupidity humor besides that of town rivalry (as in fooltown humor) is the school. My wife, who is a preschool teacher, tells me that three- and four-year-olds sing the following ditty with great gusto: "I ain't been to Frisco, / I ain't been to school, / I ain't been to college, / But I ain't no fool!"

Wolfenstein's on-site studies of schoolchildren were carried out in the early 1950s, when moron jokes were exceedingly popular. While the word *moron* no longer appears in joke books, the dictionary, interestingly enough, defines *moron* as "a retarded person mentally equal to a child between eight and twelve years old; an obsolescent term," which is precisely the age of the children in Wolfenstein's study who enjoyed moron jokes. The dictionary has another definition of moron as "a very foolish or stupid person," and as Wolfenstein's study shows, this is actually how the children themselves understood the word. That is, they were either unaware of or oblivious to its association with mental retardation. Rather, they related it to a classmate, a parent (typically a father), or more tentatively, themselves. A typical moron joke of the period was, "Why did the moron put the television set on the stove? Because he wanted to see Milton Boil, to see Arthur Godfrey, and to see Hopalong Cassidy ride the range." In light of our earlier discussion of the popularity of stupidity jokes during periods of rapid technological change, it may not be accidental that this moron joke involved a television set, a virtual icon of technological development in the early 1950s.

Wolfenstein points out that a great number of the riddles of the children she studied had to do with the behavior of a moron as "someone who does stupid things that the child would not do. In contrasting himself with the moron, the child again feels how smart he is. Children at this age are peculiarly preoccupied with the issue of who is smart and who is dumb. They are especially sensitive to being put in the wrong or not knowing what someone else knows. . . . Any advantage is apt to be felt as smartness, any disadvantage as dumbness" (93). Thus, the riddle form itself "stresses the issue of who knows and who doesn't," and "the figure of the moron represents all that the child repudiates in his aspirations to smartness" (33–34). Children seem to acquire a store of joking riddles "with striking punctuality" at the age of six. At six and seven, about three times as many joking riddles are told as jokes in any other form. By eleven and twelve, riddles are beginning to be discarded in favor of anecdotes. Thus, for several years, young children can express their anxieties about not knowing what others know by relating a riddle in which something is concealed, in which there is something hard to guess, but when the answer is produced, it turns out to be absurd. A rational answer is thus the wrong answer, and the riddle is therefore a parody of what normally goes on in the classroom.

While the following joke is not a riddle, it reflects the failure anxiety that originates in childhood and is carried into the adult working environment:

A kid is flunking in public school, so his parents send him to a Catholic parochial school. All of a sudden, in this environment, his grades sky-rocket to all As. One night at the dinner table, his parents ask, "Why were you doing so bad in public school? Since we switched you to a Catholic school, you've been doing so well! Is it because the nuns are stricter than your teachers were in public school?" The kid responds, "No, it's not that, exactly. It's because I know they're serious about school. The first day I walked in they had a guy nailed to a plus sign."

In the terms of my model of the person, the age at which children become obsessed with riddles marks the onset of the tension between spirit and soul, of self-enlargement versus self-regeneration. School tends to become identified with the former, while the home environment is identified with the latter. The riddle is the preadolescent's attempt to negotiate the tension between them.[4]

The Kid Who Knows Too Much for His Own Good

There is a form of humor that is especially popular among adults, and it has par-ticular bearing on the theme of this book. This is humor in which children make factual mistakes that an adult is unlikely to make. We saw an illustration of this in chapter 1 where I relate the story Freud tells about the play that children had created about a husband who went off to sea while his wife remained home. When he returned with a big bag of money, she announced proudly that she too had been productive, pointing to twelve large dolls lying asleep on the floor of their little hut. Children's answers to questions about religious matters are amus-ing to adults perhaps, in part, because the adults are aware that their own knowl-edge of religion is none too secure. If anxieties about sexual matters (such as doubtful paternity) can be humorously dispelled by ascribing them to very old men and women, so anxieties about religious knowledge can be similarly dispelled by displacing them onto young children. Here is an especially fine example:

One Easter morning, a Sunday school teacher asked her class if they knew the origins of this special day. One boy responded immediately, "It's opening day for the Yankees and Mets!" Not wishing to stifle creative thinking, the teacher responded, "Yes, that is correct! But I had some-thing else in mind." A girl's hand shot up, and the teacher called on her. "This is the day we get nice new clothes and go find the eggs from the Easter Bunny." "That's right," said the teacher, "but there's something else just a little more important." Another boy jumped up and yelled, "I know! After Jesus died on the cross, some of his friends buried him in a tomb they called a sepulchre. Then three days later Jesus arose and opened the door of his tomb and stepped out." "That's right," said the teacher, "and what does this mean for us today?" The boy replied, "Well, if he sees his shadow, we have six more weeks of winter."

If grades were given out in Sunday School, this kid would have flunked because he knew so much he got his facts confused. I identify with him (and maybe you do too). A poem I wrote a few years ago explains why. It all began when I ran across an advertisement of a book titled *Is God a Vegetarian?* by Richard Alan Young (1998), a very thoughtful treatment of animal rights and the effects of meat-eating on human health. The title, however, gave me pause. Is God a vegetarian? How should I know? Does anyone know? In fact, for all we know, God is actually a vegetable. This led to speculation that Moses misheard God's response to his query about who should he say had sent him in the burning bush story (Exod 3:14)—"I YAM THAT I YAM"—and a poem titled "Thanksgiving Dinner" that contained the lines: "God, I believe, is a Golden Yam, / And what a blessing to the soul! / Best with lots of marshmallows, / In a baked casserole."

If God is a Golden Yam, what about Jesus? I guessed that Jesus might be a tomato, and the poem that resulted, titled "The Fruit of the Vine," revealed anxieties and confusion going back to my Sunday School days. I worried, "If Jesus were a tomato, / I wouldn't know how to pray. / Would I address him with a dentist's 'ah,' / Or a musician's note of 'A'?" And how would Jesus understand himself? "Would he call his Father 'Abba'? / Or rule as the Cosmic Christ / Over the whole Enchilada?" Finally, in a heroic effort at solid conviction, I concluded: "Truth is, he *was* a tomato, / Who ripened in three days. / Then he became the rosy eggs / The Easter Bunny lays."

Like the children in the joke cited above who are trying to respond with some degree of intelligence to the Sunday School teacher's question about the origins of Easter, the final stanza of this poem is a hopelessly confused attempt to integrate the two Easter traditions of the resurrection of Jesus and the Easter Bunny. Among the various errors committed here, the one that seems somewhat defensible is the confusion between the fact that Jesus "rose" from the dead and the supposition that the eggs the Easter Bunny lays are "rosy."

A couple of more poems added to the realization that I knew too much for my own good. The first, titled "The Man with the Keys," reflects a confusion between the story of David and Bathsheba (2 Sam 11:1–6) and the story of Jesus giving Peter the keys to the kingdom (Matt 16:19). It claims, "When David espied Bathsheba, / He said, 'I've got to meet her!' / So he gained entrance to her apartment / Through the landlord, Simon Peter." The second was a limerick about Daniel and three other men being thrown into a pen (Daniel 6):

THE DOGGING OF DANIEL

There was a bad king named Nathaniel,
Who hated a fine fellow named Daniel.
    So Dan and three men
    Were thrown in a pen,
To be mauled by a mean cocker spaniel.

This limerick is replete with errors: The king was not Nathaniel but Darius, and he was a good king, having been tricked into signing an edict that forced him to throw Daniel into a lion's den. The three men, Shadrach, Meshach, and Abednego, were not thrown into the lion's den with Daniel but had earlier been cast into a fiery furnace by Darius's father, King Nebuchadnezzer (Dan 3:13–23).[5] But perhaps the most egregious factual error of all is the suggestion that a cocker spaniel could be mean. Confusion about biblical facts, while unfortunate, is understandable, but confusing a cocker spaniel with a pit bull is an error that no schoolboy, however dull-witted, should make. This is almost as bad as assuming that since the Easter Bunny brings the eggs, he's also the one who lays them in the first place.

The point of this excursus on humor that focuses on children's errors about God and the Bible is that such humor enables adults to displace onto children their own anxieties about their ignorance in these matters. On the other hand, the fact that their anxieties about ignorance regarding religion are modest in comparison to their anxieties relating to subjects they began to learn about in school—where flunking *was* possible—is reflected in the fact that jokes in which St. Peter requires the applicant to heaven to answer a question correctly to be admitted to heaven do not concern religion. Instead, they usually involve spelling a word correctly or using a word in a sentence. For example, St. Peter asks a woman to spell *love*, which she easily accomplishes. When he is suddenly called away, he asks her to sit in for him and instructs her that if anyone should come along while he is gone she is to require this person to spell a word, just as she had done. To her surprise, the next person to approach the gates is her husband, who explains that he had a few drinks after her funeral and got into an automobile accident. Declaring his intention to join her in heaven, she replies, "Not so fast. First, you must spell a word: Czechoslovakia." Here's another example: When required to use the word "Timbuktu" in a sentence, one applicant replied, "My friend Tim and I were walking down the road, and along came three beautiful women, and before you knew it, I had bucked one and Tim bucked two!" These jokes suggest an emotional link between failure anxieties and death anxieties, a link reflected, on the one hand, by one's tendency to feel "mortified" after making a mistake in public and, on the other hand, by the use of the word *failing* to refer to someone who is nearing death.

Conclusion

The point of this chapter, however, is that ethnic jokes that focus on stupidity are a potentially valuable form of soul maintenance. They enable the tellers to express their personal and collective anxieties about failure by dissociating themselves from the stupidity displayed in the joke itself, thereby expressing the tension that exists between the spirit and the soul. If the spirit is that part of ourselves that aspires to greater heights, and the soul is that part of ourselves that keeps us rooted in place, these stupidity jokes are the soul's attempt to comfort the spirit: It is all right if you fail, for no matter how far you fall and how much it hurts when you land, the truth is that you cannot fall out of this world. In fact, the place where you land is not a bad place to be.

The critical point about ethnic humor is that it is much more about ourselves—those who tell the jokes—than about those whom it ridicules, satirizes, or makes fun of. Thus, attempts to determine whether the traits ascribed to the ethnic group in question are objectively true are beside the point, at least insofar as the trait of stupidity is concerned, for the real identity of the butt of the joke is one's negative self, that is, the negative self as viewed from the perspective of spirit. Thus, if Holland views humor as a means of recreating one's positive identity, ethnic humor is a means of exposing one's anxieties regarding one's negative identity, the fearful, frustrated, or failing self over against which we affirm our positive identity. If this is the case, however, then it is the soul that accepts this negative self, finds a room for it, and even breathes life into it so that it will not wither and die.

Perhaps the best illustrations of the humor of soul maintenance, therefore, are those that Davies judges to be the least common, namely, ethnic jokes that express "the revolt against rationality" (71). Instead of making fun of those who cannot keep up with the demands of a highly rationalized, highly specialized society, these jokes make fun of those who have spiritualized, as it were, the world of work, money, and duty. Here's an example: "A couple of French tourists winding up an extensive trip around the United States passed an old folks' home. The inmates were rocking back and forth vigorously in their chairs on the porch. 'Regardez, Clarinda,' remarked the French husband, 'these crazy Americans keep up their mad pace to the very end.'" Jokes like this one reflect Freud's argument that in civilized society, we are pressured to live beyond our psychic means, and humor is therefore a method by which we save in the expenditure of these means. In general, ethnic humor focuses especially on the third of Freud's three savings—that of difficult or rational thinking. But in the jokes that represent a "revolt against rationality," the second savings—that of costly inhibitions—also plays a major role, for these jokes suggest that a life devoted exclusively to the world of work, money, and duty is an inhibited life. It is one in which one may gain the world but lose one's soul.

Two jokes that illustrate Davies' point that ethnic jokes are like looking at ourselves in a distorted mirror are worth mentioning in conclusion. The first is a joke about Norwegians and Swedes:

> Two Norwegians dressed a hog in overalls and placed it between them in their pickup truck as they crossed the Swedish border. Their motive was to avoid paying a special livestock tax. The border guard eyed the trio, asking their names. "Ole Johnson." "Knute Johnson." Then the hog, "Oink." Passing them on, the guard remarked to his assistant, "I've seen some bad-looking people in my time, but that Oink Johnson has got to be the ugliest Norwegian I've ever seen!"

Because the setting is a border crossing, this joke places the members of the receiving country in a position of superiority. Swedish guards have the right and authority to question the Norwegians and the Norwegians are obligated to submit to their authority as a condition of being allowed to enter the country. But they outsmart this particular guard and thus save themselves the price of the livestock tax. The Swedish guard is therefore shown up as stupid and the Norwegians come off as the canny ones. On the other hand, they outsmarted the guard by passing a hog off as one of them, so they don't come off looking terribly good either. After all, passing a hog off as a Norwegian does not reflect a very flattering self-image.

Then there is the following joke about a traveling ventriloquist:

> A young ventriloquist is touring the clubs and stops to entertain at a bar in a small town. He's going through his usual stupid redneck jokes when a big burly guy in the audience stands up and says, "I've heard just about enough of your smart-ass hillbilly jokes; we ain't all stupid around here." Flustered, the ventriloquist begins to apologize when the big guy pipes up, "You stay out of this, mister, I'm talking to the smart-ass little fella on your knee!"

This joke suggests that defending one's group against the suggestion that it is stupid is itself a rather stupid idea, as this is really beside the point. In light of the argument presented here, such a defense is likely to deprive the joke teller—in this case, the young ventriloquist—of a valuable exercise in self-recognition. In fact, ventriloquism is itself a metaphor of the tension that exists between spirit and soul and of the need to reduce the tension as much as possible. For the spirit may aspire to glorious heights, but it dare not ignore the dummy on its knee.

Motoring through the Bible Belt

We Recommend Fleece Lining

> Now John wore clothing of camel's hair, with a leather belt around his waist, and his food was locusts and wild honey.
> *Matthew 3:4*

> John the Baptist
> Wore camel's hair.
> He scratched himself
> 'Til he was bare.
> *Burma-Shave*

5. Humor as the Gentle Art of Reframing

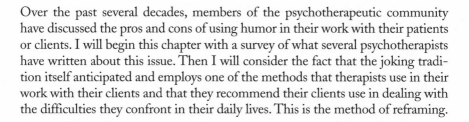

Over the past several decades, members of the psychotherapeutic community have discussed the pros and cons of using humor in their work with their patients or clients. I will begin this chapter with a survey of what several psychotherapists have written about this issue. Then I will consider the fact that the joking tradition itself anticipated and employs one of the methods that therapists use in their work with their clients and that they recommend their clients use in dealing with the difficulties they confront in their daily lives. This is the method of reframing.

Humor and Psychotherapy

Most of the literature on the uses of humor in psychotherapy has expressed a positive view of its use but with various cautionary notes. *It's a Funny Thing Humor: The International Conference on Humor and Laughter,* edited by Antony J. Chapman and Hugh C. Foot (1977), includes several brief articles that were part of a symposium on humor as a form of therapy. In his introduction to the symposium, Jacob Levine provides an example of how humor can be helpful in facilitating the therapeutic process:

> A forty-year-old female patient constantly complained about her unfaithful and inconsiderate husband. The marriage was a failure since she disliked her husband, found sex with him disgusting, and generally considered his behavior contemptible. The therapist felt moved to comment that she still chose to live with him and did not consider divorce. The patient responded that she was afraid that she would not be able to

replace him and as bad as he was she felt that loneliness would be worse. The therapist remarked that he could understand her fears of loneliness but felt that there was another aspect of her preference for remaining married which was suggested by the story of the man who worked in the circus cleaning up after the animals and giving enemas to constipated elephants. An old friend of his, observing the menial type of work that he was doing, offered to help him get another job. To which he replied, "What, and give up show biz?" The patient at first was indignant about this analogy but then began to laugh about it. She was able to come to grips with some of her covert motives in her complaints about her husband. She came to recognize that despite these constant complaints her marriage had some redeeming features and did satisfy some of her needs, not the least of which was the opportunity to complain and to blame others for her unsatisfied needs. (Levine 1977, 133)

Levine suggests that in a symposium on therapy, a distinction should be made between the claim that humor is inherently therapeutic (which he believes it is) and the ways that humor is used in psychotherapy, "when the intent is to use humor for communicative purpose" (134). I will comment on two of the articles in the symposium.

The first, by Saul Grossman (1977), concerns the use of jokes in psychotherapy. He tells the following story of a therapist who used a joke as an interpretive device:

The patient was a very intelligent, well-educated thirty-year-old man, who had been unable to achieve his professional goal of becoming an attorney because of a very severe obsessive character disorder. He was always able to rationalize and intellectualize any and all interpretations. He found fault with the behavior of others but always had "logical" reasons for his own behavior. . . . In short, he used his intellect to avoid insight. After failing his bar exams he proceeded to ruminate about a new system that would make it possible for him to pass the bar without any further real effort; or he ruminated as to whether he wanted to be a lawyer in the first place. The therapist had to cut through the rumination and came up with the following joke. A dog was playing along a railroad-track and a train came by and cut off a piece of his tail. The dog was very upset by the situation and sat down on the track and contemplated what life would be like with a shorter tail; how would it be to live without the tail he had known all his life? As he was sitting and ruminating an express train came along and killed the dog. (Grossman 1977, 150)

The patient's initial response to this little anecdote was, "You mean I was wasting all my life thinking about things rather than doing anything?" The therapist said, "Yes." The patient replied that he was going to write down this joke and try to refer to it in different situations; then he immediately went on to obsess about how other people treat him. So the therapist said, "You're sitting on the track again." At the next session, the patient reported that he spent a great deal of time thinking of ways to avoid rumination and do things instead, and the therapist responded, "You're sitting on the track again." For the first time in four years of therapy, the patient allowed himself to cry and said, "This is something I have been trying to avoid seeing about myself all my life." Grossman concludes, "A new phase of therapy was beginning," and adds, "Here the joke was used as an interpretive device in less threatening fashion, to a point where it could be understood by the patient and utilized in a creative way" (150).

Grossman also tells about a twenty-four-year-old teacher who told a joke that "alerted the therapist to a problem that the patient had not mentioned when he came into therapy":

> There were two men hiking in a desert and it was very hot. They approached an oasis that had a spring-fed lake that seemed cool and inviting. On one side of the lake there was a group of people picnicking. The two friends chose a secluded area and proceeded to get undressed to get into the water for a swim. Suddenly one of the men was bitten on the penis by a rattlesnake. They both were very upset and did not know what to do. The man who was bitten begged his friend to do something to help him. The friend said, "I don't know what to do but I will go right across the lake and find out, from the people there, if anyone can be of help." He put on his trousers and ran quickly to the other side of the lake and spoke to the people there, telling them that his friend had been bitten by a snake. What is the best way to apply first aid and what should he do? He was told by the people that the best way to treat this emergency was to take a sharp knife and cut across where the fangs had penetrated and suck the poison out and then take his friend to the hospital. Without this first aid his friend could possibly die. He went back to his friend on the other side of the lake. His friend asked, "What did they tell you? What can you do for me?" His friend responded, "You are going to die!" (150)

The patient's problem was his concern that he might not be able to control his homoerotic desires toward one or more of the boys on the basketball team he coached after school. As Grossman observes, "Here the existence of a problem area was communicated through a joke while the patient was not yet consciously aware of the cause of his anxiety" (150–51). Because of the patient's "poor ego-organization," the therapist did not bring up the topic of the patient's homosexual problems "but waited until the patient brought up his homosexual thoughts. Instead [the therapist] worked on his difficulty in dealing with closeness and poor self-concept" (151). The interesting thing here is that the joke, much like a dream, revealed more than the patient was actually conscious of. It was as if the joke knew more than the patient did about his struggles and was taking the therapist into its confidence. The joke was attempting to be helpful.

In the first illustration, the therapist introduced a joke into the therapeutic process. In the second, the patient volunteered the joke. In both cases, however, the joke served the therapeutic process where more direct communications may have been too threatening and anxiety-producing. In a third illustration, the patient told the following joke:

> This man comes to a doctor, complaining that his voice was too deep and his penis too long. He tells the doctor that his wife complains of the way he sounds and that he would like to be able to speak in a softer and higher-pitched voice. The doctor examines him and tells him that he can help him by cutting off several inches from his penis. The man agreed and the operation is a success. Soon after the operation he returns to the surgeon, and speaking in a well-modulated voice tells him that although his voice is everything he wanted it to be, still his wife was not happy. She would like him to have his long penis again. The doctor replies, in a very deep voice, "That would be a very difficult operation." (151)

This joke communicated the patient's fear that therapy would take something very important away from him, and it was therefore not too surprising that the patient left therapy after a short period of time "with the feeling that he would rather keep his problem than change" (151).

Grossman concludes his brief article with a few cautionary notes about the therapist's use of humor. He emphasizes that the therapist must not "use the joke as a harmful or aggressive instrument." He adds, "Comments about jokes or punchlines, like all interpretations, have to be very carefully timed so that they are made at the most opportune moment in treatment." Humor "should be a mature means of communication which does not seek to overwhelm or threaten the patient. Rather, it should make the patient aware of the understanding that the therapist has for his feelings" (151). He also cautions that "one should not assume that one's favorite joke is always directly connected with a patient's problem" and should therefore be careful not to tell a joke to a patient simply because it is a sure laugh-getter. It needs to be both relevant and sensitive.[1]

The second article in the symposium, "Humor in Psychotherapy" by Harold Greenwald (1977), begins with his assertion that he is currently engaged in studying happy people. He reports that happy people have experienced as many traumas, difficulties, and problems as the most neurotic and even psychotic patients. The difference is in the way they have chosen to deal with their problems: "As one of the happy people I interviewed said when I asked her how she managed to be happy: 'Well, at a certain point in my life, I decided I could laugh or I could cry. I chose to laugh'" (161). Greenwald emphasizes that he does not force his patients to laugh: "They can cry if they want to. It's their choice. But if they want to laugh at some of their problems, [I] try to help them see that if you're stuck with a lemon, it's a good idea to make lemonade" (161). Here is an illustration of his use of humor with a patient:

> I had one man who had been a wonderful analytically trained patient. He had gone to an orthodox analyst before he came to see me. He was a very proper gentleman, and he always wore his dark suit, white shirt, narrow tie, black shoes, well-shined. He would come in and he would carefully lie down on the couch and say, "I had the following dream; one, two, three. These are my associations, one, two, three. They relate to my present life, one, two, three." But nothing happened and I didn't know how to break through this, until one day he was complaining about his wife and her inordinate sexual demands on him. . . . Always complaining, you know, his wife was always complaining, and finally in desperation to break through the complete system he had, I said, "You know, if you're having so much trouble with your wife, I've met your wife, she's very attractive, next time you bring her in, I'll be glad to help you out." It's the first time I ever saw anybody get off the couch horizontally. Levitation! He turned to me and in a furious voice said, "Dr. Greenwald, someday you'll go too far." After that we had a more human interchange and eventually he even came in a sports shirt which was for him a tremendous breakthrough. (183)

Like Grossman, Greenwald concludes with an "important warning," namely, that therapists should use humor only with patients they like. Otherwise, "it can become destructive. Then it turns from irony, then it turns from understanding, to a remembrance of the old days when humor was used to attack the child, as it so frequently was used. For so many children that is more traumatic than being beaten. So I can't use humor unless I like the person concerned" (164). While we might want to know why Greenwald agrees to treat individuals whom he doesn't like, his point about humor is an important one, as it takes note of the fact that, as Levine points out, humor is employed in therapy because it can be useful, not merely because it affords pleasure. In this sense, humor in therapy is always intentional—always has an aim or purpose—and this being the case, there is the danger that it will be used aggressively, as a subtle means to ridicule or even punish the person who has come seeking help.

In a major article titled "Humor in Psychotherapy: Past Outlooks, Present Status, and Future Frontiers" (1983), Waleed Anthony Salameh identifies the several therapeutic approaches that explicitly incorporate humor, reviews the existing research on the therapeutic uses of humor, reports on his own Humor Rating Scale designed to evaluate the quality of therapists' use of humor, and offers his own classification of therapeutic humor techniques. The rating scale consists of five levels: (1) destructive humor; (2) harmful humor; (3) minimally helpful humor; (4) very helpful humor; and (5) outstandingly helpful humor. The clinical vignette that illustrates the outstandingly helpful response occurred during a group therapy session and involved a progression from the therapist's initial use of humor to challenge a manipulative member of the group, followed by another member's insightful use of the therapist's humor, which produced a laughing response by the manipulative group member that signaled his acceptance of the truth of the therapist's initial humorous comment, and concluded with a unison response by the group as a whole. One guesses that the other group member's comment allowed the manipulative member time to consider the therapist's comment and to formulate his own humorous response. Perhaps, then, humor is especially effective in a situation in which the person has some time to assimilate the message contained within the humorous communication and thereby respond more insightfully and less reactively.

In my view, Salemeh's most valuable contribution is his classification of therapeutic humor techniques. The table on pages 142–43 identifies the twelve techniques, defines them, and provides illustrative clinical vignettes. This table indicates the many different ways that humor can be used in a therapeutic context, and it suggests that one should make an effort to vary the techniques employed so that one's use of humor does not become routinized and one-dimensional. Even as one can overuse a favorite joke, so one can overuse a particular humor technique to the neglect of others.

Finally, Salemeh suggests that humor can be helpful in several ways, two of which I would like to highlight here: defining problems and helping patients develop greater awareness of creative alternatives. Regarding the first, he notes that he repeatedly says to clients, "We cannot defy your problems until we define them." In this regard, "humor can be a potent communication tool to help define problems in a quick, flexible, economical, and easily retrievable format" (79). He cites the following example, which has to do with a patient

> whose dynamics centered upon the theme of being rejected and feeling helpless about it. During his third therapy session, the patient was relating some material about feeling rejected by his peers and how this constituted a repetition of earlier life experiences. Suddenly a rattling noise could be heard outside the therapy room, at which point I [Salemeh] said, "Don't worry; you see, when people stop rejecting you the ghosts will too," at which point the patient interrupted his favorite self-absorbed tirade and engaged in loud laughter. The aforementioned comment had defined his dynamic of constantly seeking rejection as well as creating rejection in situations where it did not exist. (79)

In another case, Salameh responded to a male patient's failure to "convince" his previous night's date to have intercourse with him by commenting, "Listen, you can't possibly go to bed with her because *you* have to go to bed with power." This comment triggered the patient's laughter, "but also registered with him as a concise definition of his problem, his need to control people instead of simply enjoying one another's company" (79).

Concerning the second issue of helping patients develop greater awareness of creative alternatives, Salemah does not provide any clinical examples, but he cites several studies that have "clearly substantiated the creative nature of the process of humor production and its similarity to the creative processes operating in other forms of artistic expression"; he suggests that "healthy humor can be considered as a creatively therapeutic problem-solving modality representing the human capacity for survival, continuity, and adaptation" (81). In the second part of this chapter, I will present my own view that humor is especially useful for educating persons in the use of the art of reframing in their efforts both to define and to defy their problems.

Like the other authors, Salemah concludes his article with a discussion of harmful humor, and he notes that his humor rating scale reveals that therapists whose humorous interventions are at levels 3, 4, and 5 are persons who "do not feel the need to express anger at their clients since they are not angry at themselves. They do not experience humor as a retaliatory maneuver but as a unique opportunity to facilitate clients' growth and expand their horizons. They use humor out of a sense of inner richness, not out of a feeling of depletion. They do not look at life or at interactions in terms of vengeance but in terms of gratitude and continuing self-exploration" (83). He cites in this connection a doctoral dissertation by Barbara Killinger on the place of humor in adult psychotherapy. Killinger's research "suggests that therapists' level of maturity may be a more important factor than their level of experience with respect to determining how often humor is used. Killinger also has found that [effective] therapist humor usually focused on clients and their problems, stayed with the topic of interaction, facilitated client self-exploration as well as a positive therapist-client attitude, and communicated therapeutic messages non-defensively" (83). Thus, when used responsibly, humor can have a major impact on the therapeutic process and its outcome.

An important book on the use of humor in psychotherapy is *Humor and Psychotherapy* (1984) by Thomas L. Kuhlman. A particularly valuable chapter focuses on humor and "insight processes." Kuhlman points out that the meaning of "insight" varies according to the psychotherapeutic theory and method involved: "In psychoanalytic psychotherapies it is making the unconscious conscious; in client-centered therapy it refers to moving toward a more self-enhancing way of perceiving oneself; in rational-emotive therapy it is understanding the irrational assumptions mediating one's behavior" (27). Yet, however it is understood, the primary use of humor in psychotherapy is that it helps to facilitate mastery of "a problem that requires an insightful solution" (28). As Kuhlman points out: "Humor has long served as an insight vehicle in political satires and cartoons which seek to change or shape attitudes and beliefs. Many psychotherapists have discovered that humor can serve similar purposes as an intervention tactic during the psychotherapy hour" (28). After all, writes Kuhlman, " 'Getting' a good joke and 'achieving' new insight into one's behavior have much in common" (28).

TABLE 2. Therapeutic Humor Techniques

Therapeutic technique	Definition	Clinical vignette
Surprise	Using unexpected occurrences to transmit therapeutic messages.	Drilling noise outside office. Patient is talking about his domineering wife. Therapist: "Your wife is talking to you *now!*"
Exaggeration	Obvious overstatement or understatement regarding size, proportions, numbers, feelings, facts, actions.	To patient who romanticizes his depression while refusing to consider alternatives: "I could help you, but I guess that wouldn't do any good anyway. You know we all die eventually."
Absurdity	That which is foolish, nonsensical, inane, irrationally disordered. That which *is* without having any logical reason to be.	A young businessman is spending inordinately long hours at the office and on business trips. He reports that his wife has complained about his increasing lack of interest in their sexual relationship. Therapist responds: "It sounds like the best way for you to get more invested in your sex life is to make it tax deductible!"
The human condition	Refers to problems of living that most human beings encounter, viewed from a humorous perspective to stress their commonality.	Therapist to a perfectionistic patient who worries that he is not being "totally honest" in communicating *all* his feelings to others: "As the holy books have indicated, it is difficult for mankind to be honest at all times. But if you want to be a phony, you should be honest about it."
Incongruity	Linking two or more usually incompatible ideas, feelings, situations, objects, etc.	Oppositional female patient reacts to therapist interpretation by stating that she has "already entertained that possibility." Therapist responds: "You've entertained it, but you didn't go to bed with it."
Confrontation/ affirmation humor	Confronting patients' maladaptive and self-defeating behaviors while simultaneously affirming their personal worth as individuals. Assumes that patient confrontation is best digested by patients when coupled with affirmation.	A patient in group therapy is confronted by other group members regarding his compulsive nose-blowing behavior. He passionately defends his need to "breathe clearly." Therapist responds: "You know, we can see that you've got a lot of intensity, but you don't have to blow it out your nose!"
Wordplay	Using puns, double entendres, witticisms, song lines, and well-known quotes or sayings from popular culture to convey therapeutic messages.	Therapist to patient who keeps depriving himself of what he really wants: "You know what Oscar Wilde said, 'I can resist anything but temptation.'" To another man who prevents himself from enjoying life or other people because he refuses to take small acceptable risks: "Mae West said, 'When I choose between two evils, I always like to take the one I've never tried before.'"

TABLE 2. Therapeutic Humor Techniques (continued)

Therapeutic technique	Definition	Clinical vignette
Metaphorical mirth	Using metaphorical constructions, analogies, fairy tales, and allegories for therapeutic storytelling to help patients assimilate new insights or understand old patterns.	Patient is talking about how his interpersonal communications are becoming less confused as he really listens to others and gives relevant feedback. Therapist: "It's like that lion you see at the zoo who always growls at you but you don't know what he means. And one day you go to the zoo and he smiles and says, "Hi there, I've been fixin' to talk to you.' And you talk to each other and become pen pals."
Impersonation	Humorously imitating the typical verbal response or maladaptive style of patients and of significant others they may bring up in therapy.	Patient repeats a characteristic "Fssss" sound with his tongue whenever he experiences sadness or other "vulnerable" emotions, so as to block the expression of such feelings. Therapist imitates this "Fssss" sound when patient displays it. Patient gradually shifts from suppression to acknowledgment of his feelings.
Relativizing	Contextualizing events within a larger perspective so that they lose their halo of absoluteness. Relativizing gives the message that nothing is as serious as we fear it to be, nor as futile as we want to believe it to be.	Patient recounts his painful struggle with his "weight problem" even though his physician has informed him he is only 3 to 5 pounds overweight. Therapist: "Well, I notice you've lost some weight behind the ears since last week."
The tragic-comic twist	A delicate humor technique requiring almost surgical precision that consists of a transformation of patients' detrimental tragic energies into constructive comical energies. It begins with a well-timed implicit or explicit juxtaposition of the tragic and comic poles of a given phenomenon followed by a reconciliation of the two poles in a humoristic synthesis that triggers laughter.	Patient who has chosen depression and crying as a behavioral mode of response to any environmental stressor is crying during the session about feeling rejected and tense. Therapist reponds: "I guess you're trying to relax now." Patient's crying turns into frantic laughter as he replies: "That's one thing I do really well; I know how to cry." Therapist asks patient why he is laughing. Patient: "I suppose there are other ways of releasing tension besides crying." The entire session then focuses on the above issue.
Bodily humor	Using the entire body or specific muscle groups in physical activity aimed at imitating or creating nonverbal reflections of typical maladaptive mannerisms in order to encourage their extinction.	Patient exhibits a typical rotational hand movement to express disillusionment with others' behavior when it does not meet his "requirements." Therapist uses this same hand movement in therapy whenever patient's behavior does not meet his expectations.

Kuhlman suggests that one of the most valuable uses of humor in psychotherapy is that it helps the therapist "circumvent resistance." Resistance refers to "the warding off by the client of interpretations, reflections, functional analysis, or advice—any intervention attempts of the therapist" (37). It originates in the fact that while people seek psychotherapy in order to feel better, they often are less than enthusiastic about the changes required to achieve that goal. They tend to cling to established perspectives and belief systems because they are familiar, "second nature," self-protective, and so on. Thus, "new ways of constructing experience which the therapist may provide offer hope—but only after the person is forced to open private skeleton closets" (37).

Kuhlman notes that the ability of humor to bypass resistance has been observed by psychoanalysts (with whom the concept of resistance originated), and he cites this example from an article by J. L. Schimel on the function of wit and humor in psychoanalysis:

Patient (*complaining*): You always point out the positive aspects
                          of everything.
Psychoanalyst: That isn't true.
Patient: Then what *is* true?
Psychoanalyst: I simply point out the areas you habitually
                          neglect.
Patient: (*Laughter*)

Kuhlman comments: "One can infer that this person was actively resisting some interpretive message of the therapist that had been presented a number of times. Or perhaps the client was resisting the therapist for some other reason" (38). In any case, the "punch line" works because it validates the client's initial complaint—the therapist *does* point out the positive aspects of everything—and this invalidates the analyst's own denial—"That isn't true"—while at the same time confronting the client's tendency to disregard an important element of his life experiences. For one who habitually perceives the negative, it can be a truly eye-opening but threatening experience to see the positive. Kuhlman guesses that Schimel's comment was preceded or accompanied by "a wry grin or some other play signal," which probably primed the client for the laughter that ensued. Schimel himself comments on the aftermath of this vignette: "The result is not necessarily insight but the opportunity for insight. The working through, consensual validation, and the repetition necessary for the acquisition of functional insight is still required" (38–39). Humor, then, cannot take the place of "functional insight," but it can circumvent the client's resistance to achieving it.

In his chapter "Humor and Detachment," Kuhlman discusses the uses of humor as a means of helping a client "desensitize" herself from an anxiety-arousing situation. He cites examples of how therapists have encouraged clients to entertain a humorous thought or imagine a humorous scene while entering a situation in which they normally would panic or, in another case, would succumb to violent temper outbursts. He also discusses the role of humor in the technique of "paradoxical intention" developed by Viktor Frankl, a technique that involves describing precisely what the client *fears* he will do or say in order to demonstrate either that the client could never do or say this, or that the catastrophic events that he imagines will follow the doing or saying of it are extremely unlikely. For example, a woman who feared she would suffer a heart attack at any moment was encouraged by her therapist to "go ahead and try as hard as you can to die from a heart attack." The therapist, of course, knew that she couldn't undergo a heart attack, as it were, on demand. This instruction, however, elicited a smile from her, and she commented, "Doctor, you are teasing" (51).

In a later chapter, Kuhlman discusses the therapeutic functions of critical humor, such as sarcasm, satire, ridicule, banter, and teasing, and while he cites examples of therapists who make effective use of sarcasm and ridicule, he tends to favor light banter and teasing. Even here, however, he contends that its effectiveness depends on there being a stable, naturally trusting therapeutic alliance. Otherwise, it is risky and dangerous. It is also most effective when it is used to counter a client's negative view of himself, as when a therapist says to a client who complains that no one likes him, "Including me!" In seeming to agree with the client, the therapist communicates a genuine liking for him because he says it in a joking manner. The message the client hears is something like, "He wouldn't joke about it if he didn't like me" (69). But if the therapist went on to explain, "After all, you pay me to like you," the spontaneous effect of the first humorous comment probably would be undermined. Thus, unlike the case of the stand-up comic, one joke does not necessarily beget another. In fact, the therapist should be suspicious of his own resistances when he experiences the feeling that he is "on a roll."

Kuhlman's concluding chapter focuses on the risks and dangers of the use of humor in psychotherapy. As a case in point, he cites his own "nonempathic" use of humor in a counseling session with a very sensitive and introverted nineteen-year-old who cut his wrists after a verbal altercation with his father, an alcoholic who was given to drunken rages. John saw himself as his mother's protector and buffer from the abuses of his father. On the night of his suicide gesture, however, his mother had joined forces with his father in the middle of the altercation and demanded that John stop defending her and show some respect for his father. It was at this point that he took a knife from the kitchen drawer and ran to the bathroom to slash his wrists.

The initial counseling sessions focused on John's disillusionment with both his mother and his father, and then began to shift to his noninvolvement in peer relationships, due largely to self-confidence problems. In the seventh session, during discussion of various reinvolvement strategies, John reported that he had called a male friend of his and suggested that they go out together Friday evening. The atmosphere was light and pleasant as he proceeded to inventory the various bars and hangouts to which they might go. He brought up a dance-hall type of place and speculated aloud as to what could happen to him there:

John   (*Talking matter-of-factly at first; speech growing progressively more tentative*): You know, a lot of neat girls go there. Sometimes they ask the guys to dance! (*Pause*) If I made a fool of myself there, I know I'd want to just jump out the window.

Therapist   (*Lightly*): Well, if you do, put it off until our next session and I'll let you use one of the windows in my building here. It would probably work better here anyway; we're seven stories off the ground.

John   (*Brief laughter; breaks eye contact by looking down at the floor. Continues matter-of-factly*): Or maybe we could go down to the baseball game if the Reds are playing at home this week. . . .

John's inventory of social outlets continued, and ultimately a choice was made. But Kuhlman noticed that the light atmosphere that preceded his quip had changed slightly. What he did not realize at the time was how deeply his seemingly harmless quip affected John. John canceled their next appointment and failed to reappear for the appointment that Kuhlman's secretary rescheduled. Kuhlman contacted him directly and they met again. He indicated to John that he felt something had gone wrong in their previous session and that perhaps he had said something to offend him. At first, John protested this idea with considerable vigor; then he admitted he may have felt that Kuhlman was being a little sarcastic but that he, on his part, was being too sensitive. But when asked for specifics, he did not mention the offending humor and instead recounted an earlier time when he thought Kuhlman was making fun of him for kicking the wall when he got mad. Then he changed the subject and began, in effect, to treat Kuhlman, assuring him that everything was okay between them and that he was grateful for what he had done for him. The session, which was their last, ended in a distanced and formal fashion.

Kuhlman provides a detailed analysis of what went wrong in the earlier session and how his humor both reflected and caused his loss of contact with the sensitive vulnerability that John had exhibited in the earlier sessions. He also suggests that it was more than a coincidence that his sudden adoption of a humorous attitude toward John took place during the week following his signing of the publishing contract for his book on humor and psychotherapy (92)!

This case may be a sufficient explanation for why Kuhlman, like the other authors reviewed here, feel obliged to discuss the risks and dangers of the use of humor in psychotherapy. But another reason is that virtually everyone who writes on humor in psychotherapy is familiar with an article by psychoanalyst Lawrence S. Kubie titled "The Destructive Potential of Humor in Psychotherapy," published in 1971. As Kuhlman's own discussion of Kubie's paper indicates, there was a very strong response to it by the journal's readership: "Many psychiatrists were intensely critical of Kubie's position, and some attacked him personally. Kubie's rejoinder . . . was equally bitter" (87). The fact that "the highly charged polemics" concerned the subject of humor was especially ironic.

In the article itself, Kubie concedes that humor sometimes expresses true warmth and affection. At other times, however, "it is used to mask hostility behind a false facade or camaraderie or to blunt the sharpness of disagreement. Thus, even in social situations humor is not always kind. And since both kinds of humor can occur simultaneously, it is not always easy to be sure which is dominant" (861–62). If this ambiguity is true in ordinary social situations, it is even more likely to be true of humor employed in the therapeutic context. Kubie also notes that in the therapeutic setting, the patient has little choice but to laugh when the therapist makes a humorous comment, and because this is true, "the secret devastation that goes on inside comes to light only much later" (864). Kuhlman's case bears out the truth of this critique. Additionally, the therapist is unlikely to know much about how humor has been used by one or more of the patient's family members in the past, and the therapist's use of humor may therefore be reminiscent of a family member's aggressive or insensitive use of humor toward the patient.

Kubie cites the case of a female patient who was praised by her older brothers and their friends for her tomboy behavior until they moved on into adolescence. Then they began to make fun of her tomboy traits, teasing her about the very behaviors for which they had earlier praised her. As a result, she developed "a rigid intolerance to humor." No therapist, in Kubie's view, could have known of this personal background at the beginning of her treatment. She came to him after leaving two therapists, both of whom had tried to "heal lightly and teasingly the symptoms and fantasies about which she felt so deeply" (863).

Kubie notes that even humor directed at the patient's "opponents" in life may be resented, as the patient may feel that the therapist is minimizing the threats and forces that he is up against. Thus, he writes, "It is hard for any patient ever to feel sure that he is not in some unacknowledged way the butt of this humor" (863).

In his response to Kubie's arguments, Kuhlman emphasizes the importance of first establishing a "productive therapeutic alliance" in which there is interpersonal trust before any attempt at humor is made. On the other hand, he notes that even as therapists may use humor as a defense, so "excessive solemnity" also may be a defense. He cites an article on the use of banter as a psychotherapeutic intervention in which the author, J. V. Coleman, argues that "the active role which banter implies for the therapist heightens the therapist's sensitivity and ability to listen to the client. Furthermore, if a casual, friendly atmosphere is maintained, the novice [therapist] will experience comfort and security in the therapist role. As the client senses this, the therapeutic process is enhanced" (91). Kuhlmann also cites Harold Greenwald's candid acknowledgment in his article "Play Therapy for Children over Twenty-one," published in 1967, that his humorous attitude is not only for his patients' direct benefit "but also to make it possible for me to deal with their problems without undue suffering" (91). Thus, humor may enable the therapist to keep from becoming overwhelmed due to the very fact that he *has* empathic feelings for his clients. In effect, this confirms

Freud's point that humor provides a savings in the expenditure of limited or finite psychic resources.

Still, Kuhlman believes that these efforts to neutralize Kubie's criticism are not the same thing as refuting it, and in fact, he extends Kubie's contention that the therapist's use of humor may mask hostility by noting that it also may mask other therapist needs, such as relief from boredom, exhibitionism, seduction, or competitiveness (92).

For the most part, the literature I have briefly reviewed here focuses on the spontaneous use of humor by the therapist, and it suggests that when a therapist tells a joke, it is often one that conveys empathy toward the client's frustrations, fears, and sense of failure. In contrast, as Kuhlman points out, the jokes that clients tell, often at their own expense, tend to have "revelation potential." For example, the joke that his client John indicated was his favorite on an intake form prior to beginning therapy was the "a guy goes into a bar" type of joke involving a bartender telling the man that he could have a bottle of whiskey on the house if he first drank out of the spittoon that was on the floor next to the bar. Kuhlman notes that this joke was never discussed during therapy but that its "self-degradation theme was relevant to [John's] psychological condition at the time" (80). This joke is typical of the jokes that Kuhlman cites in his discussion of client humor in his chapter on humor and insight processes. Perhaps, then, therapists err on the side of empathic humor and do not make sufficient use of humor that helps clients realize that their approaches to the situations they face in life are not as effective as they could be, and that more effective ones are in fact available.

Salemah's view that humor may help to facilitate the development of goals of therapeutic action based on *the identification of problem areas* and also may help persons develop *a greater awareness of creative alternatives* invites us to consider ways in which certain jokes manifest these problem-solving capacities and creative initiatives. In other words, jokes that are explicitly about problem solving via the discovery or discernment of creative alternatives are worth considering in their own right, and jokes that exhibit the art of reframing are especially valuable in this regard. In order to lay the groundwork for an exploration of such jokes, however, I need to explain what I mean by "the art of reframing," and the best way for me to do this is to cite some of my earlier writings on reframing (Capps 1990) and on what I have called "the quest for the third alternative" (Capps 1998).

The Method of Reframing

I began my book *Reframing* (1990) with the following anecdote that I heard in a sermon on the theme of "looking to Jesus the pioneer and perfecter of our faith" (Heb 12:2):

A house painter was standing on his ladder, absentmindedly brushing paint on the siding of a house. Suddenly, feeling movement on the ladder below, he looked down and saw a little girl on the third rung of the ladder; she was climbing toward him. His heart leaped into his throat as he realized her danger. One slight misstep and she would fall. His first instinct was to shout at her, telling her to go down. But would this frighten her and cause her to lose control? Would she fall between the rungs as she reversed course? Instead, he greeted her with a friendly hello and encouraged her to continue climbing. As she proceeded upward, he reached down to her until she was within his grasp. He caught her up in his arms and together they made their descent safely to the ground. (9)

The preacher pointed out that looking up at the housepainter for confidence is a human example of what it means to look up to Jesus. This story is also an excellent example of reframing. The painter's initial instinct was to warn the little girl off the ladder. But quickly considering the possible consequences of her attempt to reverse directions, especially if done against her desire to climb, he calculated that it was safer for her to continue upward. Thus he *reframed* the situation and, in doing so, violated his instinctive reaction. To encourage her to continue upward did not appear to make much sense, but on reflection, it was the wiser course.

Such reframings are nothing new. No doubt, all of us have done reframing at some point in our lives, and reframing is deeply embedded in all cultural traditions through stories, folktales, and even jokes that we tell. The time-honored technique of reframing also is widely used in therapy. As Paul Watzlawick, John Weakland, and Richard Fisch point out in their book, *Change: Principles of Problem Formation and Problem Resolution* (1974), when a therapist tries to get a client to "think about things differently" or "see a new point of view" or "take other factors into consideration," these are attempts to reframe events in order to get the client to respond differently to them. They add that for a reframing to be effective, it has to take into account all of the known facts of the situation as well or better than the original frame, and the reframing needs to be as valid a way of looking at the world as the way the person sees things now; it needs to "lift the problem out of the 'symptom' frame and into another frame that does not carry the implications of unchangeability" (102). Thus, Schimel's comment to his patient—"I simply point out the areas you habitually neglect"—may be viewed as an effort to get the patient to perceive his experiences differently and thus to reframe them. The woman who told Greenwald, "At a certain point in my life, I decided I could laugh or I could cry. I chose to laugh," has, in effect, devised her own reframing of her experiential world.[2]

Some time ago, I was reading the ministerial case studies that students had written for my course "The Minister as Counselor." One student had talked with a young woman at his church whose mother had recently disclosed to her that she had tried to abort her because the biological father was a married man. For some reason that was unclear in the case study, the abortion attempt had failed. Distraught over her mother's disclosure, the young woman was now questioning God: "How could God have allowed this to happen?" By "this," she apparently meant the fact that she was the outcome of an illicit sexual encounter and the daughter of a mother who had tried to end her life before it even began. The student counselor admitted to her that he didn't know why God would allow such a thing to happen, but added that God does not control everything and that it was her mother and biological father who were primarily responsible. His point was that she should not blame God for this. But what he did not say, and I wanted him to say, was that either she could view God as allowing this sinful thing to occur, or she could view God as having intervened in the attempted abortion, thus enabling her to live. This, I pointed out in my written comments to the student, would have been a "reframing," and it would have been one that took account of the facts as well, or better, than the woman's original frame and would have been at least as valid. Furthermore, where the young woman's original interpretive frame was despairing, the reframing was much more hopeful, and isn't the role, I suggested, of ministers, to be agents of hope? (Capps 2002a).

A key feature of reframing is that it is designed to effect *second-order change*. Watzlawick, Weakland, and Fisch propose that there are two kinds of change: *first-order change* that occurs within a given system that itself remains unchanged; and *second-order change* that alters the system itself. To illustrate the difference, they cite the case of a person who is having a nightmare. This person can do many things in the dream—run, hide, fight, jump off a cliff—but no shift from any one of these behaviors to another would ever terminate the nightmare. This is first-order change. Second-order change involves a shift from dreaming to waking. Waking is not a part of the dream but a change to an altogether different state. Second-order change is a *change of change*. What occurs in second-order change is not merely a shift from stasis to change, but a fundamental alteration in change itself. In first-order change, the more things change, the more they remain the same. In second-order change, everything is different because the system itself is no longer the same.

There are many situations in life in which first-order change is all that we require. When the temperature in the room falls or rises to an uncomfortable level, we can adjust the thermostat until we are comfortable again. More—or less—of the same eventually achieves the desired effect. But in other situations in life, first-order change is insufficient. In these cases it may become the problem, making matters worse than they were before remedial efforts were tried. Watzlawick and his coauthors point out that the prohibition of alcohol in the United States led to the development of a clandestine alcohol-producing industry that created even more of a public health problem because of the low quality of its products and required a special police force to hunt down the bootleggers. In the process the police force became corrupt itself as some accepted bribes for not reporting the bootleggers.

Thus, a common approach to the reduction or elimination of a problem is to introduce its opposite as the logical solution. If a friend is depressed, we try to cheer her up. If our spouse is uncommunicative, perhaps even secretive, we try to get him to "open up." But these attempted solutions rarely, if ever, work. In fact, they increase the original problem and eventually become a problem in their own right. Efforts to get the husband to communicate make him more withholding and secretive, even to the point at which he refuses to make disclosures that are perfectly harmless and irrelevant, "just to teach her that she need not know everything." This behavior, in turn, adds more fuel to her worries: "If he refuses to talk to me about these little things, there *must* be something the matter." The less information he gives her, the more persistently she will seek it, and the more she seeks it, the less he will give her. In time, this very pattern of interaction becomes, itself, the problem. So efforts to deal with a perceived problem by introducing its opposite result in a first-order change, in which the more things change, the more they remain the same. What is required here is second-order change—an action that alters the interactional system itself.

From this basic distinction between first- and second-order change, Watzlawick and his coauthors conclude that there are *difficulties* and there are *problems*. *Difficulties* are a fact of human existence. Some difficulties can be reduced or eliminated, while others are inescapable and have to be accepted as the price we pay for existing at all. Suffering, evil, and death are difficulties. Diseases, oppression, and poverty are problems. *Problems* are situations that are created and maintained through the mishandling of difficulties, and there are basically three ways in which this mishandling may occur: (1) A difficulty exists for which action is necessary, but none is taken; (2) change is attempted regarding a difficulty that, for all practical purposes, is either unchangeable or nonexistent, so an action is taken when it should not be; and (3) a first-order change is attempted in regard to a difficulty that can be changed only at the second-order level, or a second-order change is attempted when a first-order change would be appropriate.

Most of our initial efforts to deal with a difficulty are of the first-order change variety. If these efforts don't work very well at first, we tend to apply them more forcefully, and their failure to effect any real change even when applied with greater force or effort leads to greater frustration and hopelessness. At such times, second-order change is needed, and this is the point when a therapist may be called into service. The therapist, at least one who is trained in the therapeutic approach that Watzlawick and his coauthors advocate, is likely to ask the client what she has tried already. This is itself a way of showing respect for the client while laying the groundwork for reflection on "creative alternatives" that she has been unable to think through for herself, perhaps because she has become frustrated and despairing. These alternatives are therefore understood as "second-order change" initiatives because they typically involve a fundamental redirection of the "first-order change" problem-solving initiatives that have already been attempted.

To illustrate the relationship between second-order change and reframing, the authors tell the following story:

> During one of the many nineteenth-century riots in Paris, the commander of an army detachment received orders to clear a city square by

firing at the rabble. He commanded his soldiers to take up firing positions, their rifles leveled at the crowd. As a ghastly silence descended, he drew his sword and shouted at the top of his lungs: "Ladies and gentlemen, I have orders to fire at the rabble. But as I see a great number of honest, respectable citizens before me, I request that they leave so that I can safely shoot the rabble." The square was empty in a few minutes. (81)

What has happened here? Second-order change was achieved through reframing. The authors explain: "The officer is faced with a threatening crowd. In typical first-order fashion he has instructions to oppose hostility with counter-hostility, with more of the same. Since his men are armed and the crowd is not, there is little doubt that 'more of the same' will succeed. But in the wider context this change would not only be no change, it would further inflame the existing turmoil" (81). How is this a reframing? "Through his intervention the officer effects a second-order change—he takes the situation outside the frame that up to that moment contained both him and the crowd; he reframes it in a way acceptable to everyone involved, and with this reframing both the original threat and its threatened 'solution' can safely be abandoned" (81).

The Quest for the Third Alternative

A useful way to think about reframing is to view it as the quest for a third alternative. Persons who seek counseling often are caught in a paradoxical situation and are seeking some way to extricate themselves from it. For example, a young woman presented this dilemma to her counselor: "If I let my boyfriend move in with me so that he can help pay the rent, I'll be able to keep my apartment. But then he will assume that I am more open to marriage than before, which I am not." The action designed to solve the problem (that is, loss of apartment) threatens to create another problem (that is, boyfriend's false assumption that she is more open to marriage than previously). Hers is a paradoxical situation, as it is based on a fundamental contradiction. She is confronted with a situation that is not unlike that which schizophrenic patients often experience. As John Weakland and Don Jackson express it in an early paper on the interpersonal circumstances of a schizophrenic episode:

> In trying to make the right choice between two alternatives, schizophrenic patients encounter a typical dilemma: they cannot, in the nature of the communicational situation, make a *right* decision, because both alternatives are part and parcel of a double bind and the patient is, therefore, "Damned if he does and damned if he doesn't." There are no actual alternatives of which the "right" one "should" be chosen—the whole assumption that choice is possible and should be made is an illusion. (Watzlawick et al. 1967, 231–32)

Weakland and Jackson add that in such cases, the solution lies in coming to the realization that there actually is an *absence* of choice, that one is not in fact being presented with any real alternatives. If real change is to occur, one will have to step outside the framework itself and find a third alternative. The therapist who is presented with the client's dilemma—"If I get my boyfriend to share the rent so that I can keep my apartment, he'll think I'm more interested in marriage"—will try to help her find or discern this third alternative. She believes that she is faced with a choice between two problematic options, but this is true only within the framework that she has constructed. Many parents have subsidized their daughter's living expenses because they want their daughters to be able to avoid compromising themselves. Or, if she believes the apartment could accommodate two persons (herself and her boyfriend), it would presumably accommodate herself and a female friend who could help to pay the rent. This alternative may not be as attractive as continuing to live in the apartment alone, but it would enable her to avoid creating a serious misunderstanding between herself and her boyfriend regarding her feelings about marriage. Her choice of a female friend over her boyfriend also may provide further evidence that she is *not* open to marriage at this time. Still another possibility, seemingly unthinkable but not necessarily so, is that she may decide she has no lasting attachment either to the apartment or to her boyfriend, and that the prospect of his moving in with her has helped her to see both things at once. In effect, her paradoxical dilemma has helped her to see that neither of them fit into her long-range plans. While she may find some fault with each of these alternatives, the important thing is that the very language used in reference to these potentially "creative alternatives" includes words such as *choose, decide* and *see things differently.* In other words, the "damned-if-I-do, damned-if-I-don't" sense of impotence has been replaced with the language of empowerment, of being able to choose for herself.

The story that Watzlawick and his coauthors tell about the French officer who is commanded to shoot the rabble may be viewed as one in which he gets himself out of an untenable situation by devising a third alternative. Another story that illustrates the value of a third alternative for breaking an immobilizing frame is the following one that Watzlawick tells in his book *Ultra-Solutions: How to Fail Most Successfully* (1988). It concerns a boy named Franzi Wokura, who lived in Steinhof, a small town in Austria:

> Franzi's trials and tribulations reached their peak when he was about thirteen years old. He was standing in the town's Beethoven Park, in front of a large flower bed, and there discovered a sign with the inscription "No Trespassing." This brought back a problem that had been bothering Franzi more and more during recent years. Once again he found himself in a situation that seemed to present only two possibilities, and both were unacceptable. *Either* he exerted his freedom in the face of this oppressive prohibition and began trampling on the flowers, at the same time risking

arrest; or he stayed off the flower bed. But the mere thought of being such a coward, of obeying a stupid sign, made his blood boil. For a long time he stood there, undecided, at his wit's end, until suddenly, maybe because he had never looked at flowers long enough, something totally and completely different came to his mind: *These flowers are beautiful.* (42)

Watzlawick asks, "Do you find this story trivial? Maybe so. But this is not how Franzi himself experienced it." On the contrary, "that realization [*These flowers are beautiful*] swept over him like a wave that lifts you up and swiftly, effortlessly carries you along. He was now aware that the world could perhaps be seen in a totally different, entirely new way. I want this flower bed just the way it is; I want this beauty; I am my own law, my own authority; he kept saying to himself over and over again. And suddenly that 'No Trespassing' sign had lost its importance, the pitfall of the Manichean opposites, 'submission or rebellion and nothing else,' had vanished" (42). Franzi was no longer caught in a hopeless double bind—to trample the flowers to assert his freedom from authority or to stay off the flower beds in deference to it. He had a third alternative, in which he neither trampled the flowers nor bowed to external authority. Instead, he affirmed his own desire that the flower bed remain "just the way it is." Watzlawick continues: "Of course, Franzi's euphoria did not last, but something fundamental was changed; there now was a faint melody in him, often quite inaudible, but sometimes clear enough just when he seemed about to sink again into the morass of either-or" (42–43). Watzlawick imagines that Franzi had found a way to frustrate the efforts of the "diabolical witch" who had controlled his mind until the episode in Beethoven Park. This witch complains: "I spend a lot of time and energy constructing what seems like a fool-proof situation with only two possibilities . . . and he somehow finds a third and walks away. I give him only the choice between cowardice and foolhardiness, and he chooses courage. I try to make him lust for something so that he may begin to dread the possibility of not attaining it, and he is indifferent to the one and to the other" (44).

Another illustration of reframing is this poem by Billy Collins (1988, 50):

ANOTHER REASON WHY I DON'T KEEP A GUN IN THE HOUSE

Billy Collins

The neighbor's dog will not stop barking.
He is barking the same high, rhythmic bark
that he barks every time they leave the house.
They must switch him on their way out.

The neighbor's dog will not stop barking.
I close all the windows in the house
and put on a Beethoven symphony full blast
but I can still hear him muffled under the music,

barking, barking, barking,
and now I can see him sitting in the orchestra,
his head raised confidently as if Beethoven
had included a part for barking dog.

When the record finally ends he is still barking,
sitting there in the oboe section barking,
his eyes fixed on the conductor who is
entreating him with his baton

while the other musicians listen in respectful
silence to the famous barking dog solo,
that endless coda that first established
Beethoven as an innovative genius.

This is a poem that doesn't ask to be taken too seriously, yet it is a wonderful illustration of the reframing of a frustrating situation. In this relatively short poem of twenty lines, Collins uses the word *bark* or *barking* twelve times. For the first two stanzas, his approach is to try to drown out the sound of the dog's barking by playing the Beethoven symphony full blast. When he can "still hear him muffled under the music, barking, barking, barking," he "reframes" the situation. Thus, the third stanza begins, "And now I can see him sitting in the orchestra, / his head raised confidently as if Beethoven / had included a part for barking dog." The fourth stanza expands on this new vision of the dog, suggesting, "When the record finally ends he is still barking, / sitting there in the oboe section barking," and in the fifth stanza "the other musicians listen in respectful / silence to the famous barking dog solo, / that endless coda that first established / Beethoven as an innovative genius."

Of course, the dog has proven his ability to outlast the Beethoven symphony and to ruin Collins's evening, as he has presumably ruined previous evenings when the neighbors have been out. But this time, Collins has gained some leverage on the situation by *imagining* the dog as a member of the symphony orchestra, sitting in the oboe section, "his eyes fixed on the conductor who is / entreating him with his baton." The title of the poem conveys, of course, that the situation is frustrating to Collins, as he sees no real way out of it short of violence. (Think here of the French officer who is commanded to shoot the rabble.) Yet the title also is humorous in itself, as it suggests that there are other reasons Collins does not dare keep a gun in the house. Clearly, other provocations that are not mentioned in this poem also exist.

It so happens that the summer before I first encountered this poem, I read in a local newspaper of a case in New Jersey (where else?) in which a man *did* shoot and kill his neighbor's dog because he had gotten sick and tired of the dog's barking on an unmercifully hot day in August. Afterwards, he was very remorseful and the neighbor also was somewhat apologetic, though he said he wished his neighbor had told him that the dog made him so upset that he could actually kill him.

Collins's initial approach to the "barking dog" difficulty involved first-order change. It was one of fighting noise with more noise. Thus, in the second stanza he writes, "I close all the windows in the house / and put on a Beethoven symphony full blast." But meeting the dog on his own terms—countering noise with noise—doesn't work. He goes on: "But I can still hear him muffled under the music, / barking, barking, barking." I suspect that the dog's muffled bark is actually more disconcerting than the loud barking sound had been. Teachers and other students may be more irritated by a couple of students whispering or conversing in low voices during a lesson than by louder noises—such as a lawnmower—coming from outside the room. The teacher may eventually interrupt the lesson and ask the two offenders, "Would you like to share what you were saying with the rest of us?"

Thus, Collins first applied a first-order change and it didn't work. The last three stanzas, however, introduce a second-order change, a "creative alternative" that occurred to him when his initial effort to drown out the dog with loud music had failed. A couple of things are noteworthy about the transition that occurs in the third stanza. The first is that Collins uses his imagination. He says, "And now I can see him in the orchestra. . . ." In reality, of course, the dog is over there in his neighbor's house and nowhere near the symphony hall where Beethoven's work is being performed. But Collins can "see" him there, and in "seeing" him there, his attitude toward the barking dog undergoes a major change. The second is that Collins uses the attempted first-order change response and creates second-order change out of *it*. In this sense, his second-order change is similar to that of the French officer. The first-order change provides the materials, as it were, for the second-order change. Thus, the first-order change attempt was not for naught and should not be disparaged. After all, it *might* have worked, and even though it didn't, Collins deserves some credit for thinking of it. (Similarly, a therapist should not ridicule the initial problem-solving efforts of a client merely because they were unsuccessful.) But the temptation in first-order change is to apply the method more forcefully or with greater precision if it doesn't work at first. It isn't difficult to think of ways that Collins might have continued to take this approach. He could play Beethoven full blast plus add a pair of earplugs, or he could go out and buy an improved stereo system that would enable him to raise the decibel level higher.

I suspect, though, that having fortified himself with earplugs or an improved stereo system, Collins would be sitting there anticipating an especially loud or prolonged bark that could penetrate his sound fortress. I doubt that he could relax enough to concentrate on his own work. There is also the likelihood that listening to a Beethoven symphony full blast is itself a bit trying. As Collins says at the beginning of the fourth stanza, "When the record finally ends he is still barking." "Finally ends" suggests more than a little frustration either with the Beethoven symphony itself or, more likely, with having to listen to a full blast rendition of it. If there are forms of music that are intended to be played at full blast, a Beethoven symphony is not one of them. In any case, there is something incongruous about a major symphony being used to drown out the sound of a barking dog. Collins might just as well go out and buy a recording of barking dogs (one, in fact, exists) and use *it* to drown out his neighbor's dog.

To his credit, perhaps, Collins does not resort to these possible refinements of his initial first-order change initiative. Instead, he reframes this approach by acknowledging that it hasn't worked. It seemed a good idea, but it failed. Because it did not completely fail—it was somewhat effective—he could have been tempted, as suggested, to improve on it. But in reality, though Collins does not exactly say this, the dog defeated him. His second-order change is therefore a bid to snatch victory from the jaws of defeat. In the fourth and fifth stanzas, a change comes over Collins that is not unlike Franzi Wokura's discovery that he finds the flowers are beautiful. That is, as he warms up to his vision of the barking dog sitting in the orchestra, with head raised confidently as if Beethoven had included a part for barking dog, Collins seems to develop a respect for the dog that was previously beyond him. He imagines the dog desiring to do a fine job performing the solo that Beethoven wrote just for him. As Collins envisions him: "His eyes [are] fixed on the conductor who is / entreating him with his baton." In other words, the dog is attentive. Then, in the final stanza, he imagines the other musicians listening in "respectful silence" to the famous barking dog solo. Collins's view of the dog has been transformed from dog as nuisance to dog performing to the very best of his ability. Of course, Collins cannot resist one final complaint in the next to last line where he refers to the barking dog solo as an "endless coda." Codas are not supposed to be "endless." In fact, an "endless" coda is a contradiction in terms, for the dictionary defines a coda as "a more or less independent passage added to the end of a section or composition so as to reinforce the sense of conclusion." Yet this is also Collins's point, for the addition of an "endless coda" that continues long after the other musicians have ceased playing is a testimony to Beethoven's "innovative genius." Imagine a coda that goes on and on and on.

Now, I myself can imagine that some readers of this analysis of Collins's poem as an illustration of the art of reframing are muttering to themselves: "The only real solution in this situation would be for Collins to talk with his neighbors about the problem and, together, work something out. Anything short of this is bound to be ineffective." But before we dismiss his second-order change here as ineffective, we should consider three important facts: First, he used his imagination to reframe the situation, and he could do this without securing the cooperation of his neighbors. Second, by employing his imagination in this way, he has written a poem. Suppose that this very evening he had sat down at his desk with the intention of writing a poem. After all, he *is* a poet. On the one hand, he could say to himself, "That incessantly barking dog is ruining my concentration. How can a person write a poem with all that racket going on?" On the other hand, he could view the dog as a blessing in disguise, as his frustration over the dog enables him to write a poem he otherwise would not have written. Should anyone argue that the dog prohibited him from writing a more important poem than the one he *did* write, it is not without significance that this poem, originally published in 1988, is the lead poem in his collection of new and selected poems published in 2001. This would seem to indicate that he is not unhappy with it.

Third, and perhaps more important, Collins has reframed his view of the dog. Initially, the dog is nothing but a nuisance, an irritant, a big pain in the neck, a stimulus for feelings of frustration, and if we are to believe the title, of seething anger. Yet by the conclusion of the poem, Collins's description of the dog has changed from that of an incessant barker to that of an accomplished musician. Collins has ascribed a dignity to the dog that is wholly missing in the earlier stanzas and has transformed him into an object of respect. Collins's own attitude toward the dog may not be one of affection—after all, he is not the dog's owner—but what he has made of this dog is even greater than this, for he has elevated the dog to the level of one who is worthy to perform a solo in a symphony by that great innovative genius, Beethoven himself.

Some Problems with Difficulties

Watzlawick, Weakland, and Fisch define *difficulties* as a fact of human existence and suggest that some difficulties can be reduced or eliminated while others are inescapable and have to be accepted as the price we pay for living at all; and they define *problems* as situations that are created and maintained through the mishandling of difficulties. One way in which difficulties are mishandled is that a difficulty exists for which action is necessary, but none is taken; another way is that change is attempted regarding a difficulty that, for all practical purposes, is either unchangeable or nonexistent—in other words, action is taken when it should not be.

But how is one to know if, in a given case, the difficulty should be acted upon or simply lived with? Do Watzlawick and his coauthors address this problem? Not really. They seem to suggest that each case needs to be judged on its own merits. Some difficulties appear to be amenable to change efforts, others not. You just have to use your best judgment and hope that you are right. I have never been very satisfied with this suggestion, and it wasn't until I happened onto *Poetic Parodies* (2001), edited by Martin Gardner, that I was able to work out a much more satisfactory answer. In reading *Poetic Parodies,* I came across a poem by Edgar Guest, "It Couldn't Be Done," and a parody of Guest's poem, "When It Can't Be Done," by Armand T. Ringer, a Martin Gardner pseudonym (49–50). What I immediately liked about the original poem and the parody is that the "it" is never specified. "It" is simply "the thing" that is said to be undoable.

We may call this "it" a "difficulty," a difficulty, moreover, that is ambiguous as far as acting upon it is concerned. Maybe "it" will lend itself to problem-solving initiatives or maybe "it" will not. But a misjudgment as to which one is true is likely to have some real consequences. Here is Guest's poem:

IT COULDN'T BE DONE

Somebody said that it couldn't be done,
But he with a chuckle replied
That "maybe it couldn't," but he would be one
Who wouldn't say so till he'd tried.
So he buckled right in with the trace of a grin
On his face. If he worried he hid it.
He started to sing as he tackled the thing
That couldn't be done, and he did it.

Somebody scoffed: "Oh, you'll never do that;
At least no one ever has done it";
But he took off his coat and he took off his hat,
And the first thing we knew he'd begun it.
With a lift of his chin and a bit of a grin,
Without any doubting or quiddit,
He started to sing as he tackled the thing
That couldn't be done, and he did it.

There are thousands to tell you it cannot be done,
There are thousands to prophesy failure;
There are thousands to point out to you one by one,
The dangers that wait to assail you.
But just buckle in with a bit of a grin,
Just take off your coat and go to it;
Just start in to sing as you tackle the thing
That "cannot be done," and you'll do it.

The "thing that cannot be done" is clearly a difficulty. Those who have defined it this way would say, "Don't try to change it. Leave well enough alone. You'll just need to learn to live with it." But not Edgar Guest. He says, "Plunge right in and don't be consumed with self-doubt. Take off your hat and coat and go to it. Sing as you tackle the thing, and by golly, you'll find that you can do it." For Guest, it's a difficulty all right, but it's a difficulty that will lend itself to efforts to do something about it.

Ringer is not convinced. In fact, he takes the opposite point of view. His protagonist knows that they are saying it cannot be done, but he plunges in just like Guest says he should, only to discover after much hefting and heaving that, sure enough, "it" cannot be done.

When It Can't Be Done

Somebody said that it couldn't be done,
But he with a chuckle replied
That "maybe it couldn't," but he would be one
Who wouldn't say so till he'd tried.
So he buckled right in with the trace of a grin.
If he worried, no friend of his knew it.
He started to sing as he tackled the thing,
And sure 'nuff, the poor chap couldn't do it.

Somebody scoffed: "Oh, you'll never do that;
At least no one ever has done it";
But he took off his coat and he took off his hat,
And the first thing we knew he'd begun it.
With a lift of his chin and a bit of a grin,
In a couple of hours he blew it.
He started to sing as he tackled the thing.
By golly! He just couldn't do it!

There are thousands to tell you it cannot be done,
There are thousands to prophesy failure;
There are thousands to point out to you one by one,
The dangers that wait to assail you.
But just buckle in with a bit of a grin,
Just take off your coat and go to it;
Just start in to sing as you tackle the thing,
'Til it dawns on you, no one can do it!

Ringer's parody is a perfect example of Watzlawick and his coauthors' second course of action, that is, attempting to overcome a difficulty which is, to all intents and purposes, unchangeable. Action is taken when it should not be.

As I reflected on these two poems, it occurred to me that they leave the dilemma exactly where Watzlawick and his coauthors leave it. Some difficulties appear to be amenable to change efforts, others not. You just have to use your best judgment and hope that you are right. One might take this answer one step further on the basis of these two poems and suggest that there are two types of people. There are the Edgar Guests of this world who will say, "It's worth a try." And there are the Armand T. Ringers of this world who will say, "You're wasting your time."

I found myself uneasy with this rather wishy-washy conclusion, so I began to think about a third alternative. The poem that I wrote is an example of "third alternative" thinking. It accepts the likelihood that Ringer is right, that it is a mistake to try to reduce or eliminate the difficulty in this case. At the same time, it challenges the idea that, therefore, there is nothing to be done. What one can do is to enlist someone else, preferably someone who fits the Edgar Guest personality type, persuading this someone to take "it" on.

IF IT CAN'T BE DONE, EDDIE WILL DO IT

Somebody said that it couldn't be done,
So I with a chuckle replied,
If that is the case, I won't be the one
Who gets blamed for having tried.

So I went to Eddie and showed him the task,
And told him another guy blew it.
"So, Eddie, I have a favor to ask,
'Cause no one but you can do it."

Well, Eddie gave it his very best shot,
But it wasn't half good enough.
He cussed and swore and sweated a lot,
But the task was just too tough.

So if you've a job of herculean scale,
And need a guy who's bound to fail,
Eddie's your man, 'cuz he'll chase his tail
As if it were the Holy Grail.

The reader of this poem may object: "But no one will fall for this trick. Your Eddie is the proverbial straw man." I disagree. In fact, I think that all of us are susceptible to it. We need only be told that "no one but you can do it," and we're hooked because we want to believe this so badly. And this, I submit, is why we spend so much of our precious lives chasing our tails as if they were the Holy Grail. And the sad fact of the matter is that those who are the oppressors of our daily lives know that we can be hooked through flattery, that is, appealing to our need to believe that we are the only one who can do it—or do it well, or do it as it ought to be done: Like the dog barking the endless coda.

Minister, Priest, and Rabbi Jokes

Collins's poem about the barking dog and Ringer's and my parody of Edgar Guest's original poem are only semi-serious. The fact that they are only semi-serious, however, draws attention to the fact that many poems and many jokes have certain features in common—that they are episodic, that they use an economy of words, and that the final sentence of each needs a certain "punch" in order for it to have its intended effect on the hearer or reader. So these poems create a bridge between the forgoing discussion of the art of reframing and the jokes that I will now introduce as examples of reframing.

I have chosen to focus on "minister, priest, and rabbi" jokes for two reasons. One is that they illustrate not only the art of reframing but also the more specific reframing method of discovering the third alternative. The other is that these jokes are about religious leaders and therefore provide a natural connection between religion and humor. These jokes typically introduce a difficulty to which the minister responds in a certain way. Then the priest responds in a somewhat different way, but his response is really one of first-order change. In fact, his response must be quite similar to that of the minister because he establishes the "frame" from which the rabbi's response will significantly deviate, thus introducing second-order change.

Of course, "minister, priest, and rabbi" jokes are not the only type of joke that employs this structure. In the preceding chapter, I cited a joke about a German, an Italian, and a Norwegian who devised ruses for getting into the Olympic Games despite the fact that the seats were all sold out. But in that particular case, the explicit content of the joke runs precisely counter to the creative problem-solving that psychotherapy seeks to foster, for the first two ruses were effective while the third one was bound to fail. This joke may then serve the purpose of providing insight into the client's tendency to fail where others succeed, into the liabilities and disadvantages of being the third-born sibling, and so forth ("I'm just like that hapless Norwegian"), or it may serve to make the point that in some situations first-order change is all that is needed. In any case, "minister, priest, and rabbi" jokes invariably result in the creative alternative to which Salemah refers. While this may be attributed, in part, to the fact that the rabbi, after all, is Jewish, and Jews, like Scots, are typically identified as "canny" (cf. Davies 1998, 2), for our purposes here it is the reframing structure itself that is of primary importance. The joke itself "works" if the listener or reader does not anticipate the rabbi's response, and this fact is what makes this joke type important for problem-solving purposes. If the rabbi's response is readily predictable, then it is not counter-intuitive and therefore represents first-order change ways of thinking about problematic situations. If it comes as a surprise and violates expectations even when the listener is prepared for the *fact* that it will break the pattern set by the minister and priest, then we may assume that it exemplifies second-order change.

The following "minister, priest, and rabbi" joke is a particularly fine example of reframing a rather dicey situation:

A minister, a priest, and a rabbi went for a hike one day. It was very hot. They were sweating and exhausted when they came upon a small lake. Since it was fairly secluded, they took off all their clothes and jumped in the water. Feeling refreshed, the trio decided to pick a few berries while enjoying their freedom. As they were crossing an open area, who should come along but a group of ladies from town. Unable to get to their clothes in time, the minister and the priest covered their privates and the rabbi covered his face while they ran for cover. After the ladies had left and the men got their clothes back on, the minister and the priest asked the rabbi why he had covered his face rather than his privates. The rabbi replied, "I don't know about you, but in my congregation, it's my face they would recognize."

Part of the humor of the joke is in the fact that the rabbi prefaces his explanation with a disclaimer, "I don't know about you," thus implying that for all he knows, the women in these two men's congregations *would* recognize their privates, in which case the two men were probably doomed from the start, as they couldn't cover both their faces and their privates at the same time. But the reframing in this case is expressed in the simple fact that the minister and priest cover their privates and the rabbi covers his face, for the issue, as he sees it, is not that of shameful exposure to the women's gaze but of recognizability.

Here's another example of reframing, one in which the minister acts in a certain way, the priest comes up with a slight variation, and the rabbi breaks the frame that the first two have established:

A minister, a priest, and a rabbi were all stuck on a God-forsaken island for a number of years. One day they found a magic lamp! A genie came out and said that since there were three of them, they each got one wish. The minister said, "After all these years on this miserable island, I want to go back to San Francisco," and *poof!* he disappeared. The priest said, "I agree with the minister, but send me to the Vatican," and *poof!* he disappeared too. The rabbi said, "Well, I really don't have any place to go. No family, no friends, and I sort of like this island and just wish my two buddies were back." *Poof!*

The minister begins to set the frame by requesting what one would assume anyone stuck on a God-forsaken island for a number of years would most dearly want, a chance to get off the island. In following suit, but with a variation more appropriate to his Catholic affiliation, the priest reinforces the frame. Anticipating that the rabbi will request a different destination (New York? Jerusalem?), the listener is not prepared for the rabbi's observation that, after all, he doesn't have any place to go or anyone to go to and that he sort of likes the island. But not without his buddies. So he uses his wish to negate theirs. This joke is a variant form of the traditional genie story in which three wishes are totally wasted because the third wish is used to reverse the stupidity or impetuousness of the first two, and the outcome is the restoration of the status quo that prevailed prior to the genie's offer of three wishes. But whereas the traditional genie story is an exercise in futility and lost opportunity, in this joke the rabbi uses his wish to restore what, in his opinion, was the best of all possible worlds. He seems not to have shared his companions' assumption that this was, in fact, a "God-forsaken island." Not, at least, as long as he had his two buddies for companionship.

If the forgoing joke employs the three wishes device, the following one employs a similarly traditional device of the last request:

> A minister, a priest, and a rabbi are traveling in the Old West. Suddenly they are ambushed and captured by blood-thirsty Indians. All three are tied to stakes. Then out comes the Big Chief. He walks up to the minister and says, "We're going to torture you, burn you, skin you alive, and then use your skin to make a canoe. I will grant you one last request." Without a second thought, the minister asks for a knife. As soon as he gets the knife, he slashes his own throat and dies. "Very brave man," says the Chief. He then walks over to the priest and says, "We're going to torture you, burn you, skin you alive, and then use your skin to make a canoe. I will grant you one last request." Without a second thought, the priest asks for a knife. As soon as he gets the knife, he slashes his own throat and dies. "Very brave man," says the Chief. He then walks up to the rabbi and says, "We're going to torture you, burn you, skin you alive and then use your skin to make a canoe. I will grant you one last request." The rabbi thinks about it for a little bit and finally says, "Bring me a fork!" The entire tribe bursts out laughing. The Chief, laughing himself, commands that a fork be given to the rabbi. The rabbi grabs the fork, starts poking himself all over the chest and stomach, and screams, "I hope your canoe sinks!"

Some of the humor in this joke is due to the fact that the knives that are given to the minister and priest are capable of killing. When the rabbi asks for a fork, there is a shift from deadly knife to the more benign category of ordinary silverware (knife, fork, and spoon). So the Chief and his men break out laughing. The rabbi's request evokes no anticipation of the kind of bravery that the minister and the priest had displayed. But the fork enables the rabbi to stand up to his captors in a way that neither the minister nor the priest had done. He will meet the same fate, but *his* body will be of no use to his captors.

The three "minister, priest, and rabbi" jokes that I have presented here (plus the "he's moving" joke presented in chapter 1 as illustrative of the theme of death anxiety) present scenarios in which the rabbi comes up with a second-order change based on his awareness of the first-order change initiatives of the minister and priest. In the "I hope your canoe sinks" joke, the first-order responses are represented as accepting the inevitable, whereas the second-order response involves a creative alternative. Moreover, if the actions of the minister and priest are acts of bravery, the rabbi's action reflects the very fact that, as Freud points out, humor is rebellious. I think it is also noteworthy that, of the three men, the rabbi comes off as being not only more "canny" than the other two, but also more in touch with his emotions. This is especially true in the "God-forsaken island" joke, in which he is aware of the fact that a bond had formed between the three men during their exile, but it is also true of the "I hope your canoe sinks" joke, in which he is in touch with his feelings of rage and is willing to accept ridicule as the price one pays for depriving the Chief of the power to accomplish his stated goals. This very fact should caution us against the assumption that a reframing merely involves mental agility, as if one were playing chess, for these jokes also suggest that reframing needs to take into account our emotions as well. They are matters of spirit (escape in the first case, bravery in the second), but even more importantly, they are matters of the soul (longing for community in the first case, avenging one's predicament in the second).

One *could*, perhaps, derive a moral lesson from each of these three "minister, priest, and rabbi" jokes, concluding, for example, that the joke about the three clergymen marooned on an island for several years teaches us that our present circumstances may not be as negative as we think they are. But this, in my view, is to miss the more fundamental point that these jokes are about reframing and, more specifically, about finding a third alternative that does a better job of problem solving than the first two. All three responses take into account the facts of the situation, but the third one is more clearly a "creative alternative."

Here is one last "minister, priest, and rabbi" joke in which the creative alternative is not what the rabbi does but how an onlooker reframes the situation in a way that favors the priest:

> Two Irishmen were digging a ditch directly across the street from a brothel. Suddenly they saw a rabbi walk up to the door, glance around, and duck inside. "Ah, will you look at that?" one ditch digger said. "What's our world coming to when men of the cloth are visitin' such places?" A short time later, a Protestant minister walked up to the door and quietly slipped inside. "Do you believe that?" The workman exclaimed, "Why, 'tis no wonder the young people today are so confused, what with the example clergymen are setting for them." After an hour went by, the men watched as a Catholic priest quickly entered the house. "Oh, what a pity," one of the diggers said, leaning on his shovel, "One of the poor lasses must be ill."

This joke indicates that the "minister, priest, and rabbi" pattern need not be an invariant one, but for this revised pattern to work, some new condition—that is, the fact that the onlookers are Irishmen—needs to be introduced. Also, there are many examples of exclusively Protestant clergy jokes (typically involving an Episcopalian, a Methodist, and a Baptist).

Not all jokes that link reframing and religion, however, involve clergy trios. Here is one involving a young penitent that suggests there are other than spiritual benefits that might accrue from confessing one's sins:

Tommy O'Connor went to confession and said, "Forgive me, Father, for I have sinned." "What have you done, Tommy O'Connor?" "I had sex with a girl." "Who was it, Tommy?" "I cannot tell you, Father. Please forgive me for my sin." "Was it Mary Margaret Sullivan?" "No, Father. Please forgive me for my sin, but I cannot tell you who it was." "Was it Catherine Mary McKenzie?" "No, Father. Please forgive me for my sin." "Well, then, it must have been her sister, Sarah Martha McKenzie." "No, Father. Please, Father, please forgive me; I cannot tell you who it was." "Okay, Tommy, go say five Hail Marys and four Our Fathers and you will be absolved of your sin." Tommy walked out to the pews, where his friend Joey was waiting. "What did ya get?" asked Joey. "Well, I got five Hail Marys, four Our Fathers, and three good leads."

"Five Hail Marys" and "four Our Fathers" set the frame of penitence and absolution, while "three good leads" introduces a new frame of opportunism that negates the original frame.

Obviously, once we begin to view jokes from the perspective of the art of reframing, it is rather easy to find jokes that fit this model. The ones presented here are intended to show how jokes portray human resourcefulness. This, in my view, is why these jokes have relevance to human problem solving, as they make a case for using our imaginations—a combination of thought and emotion—in order to come up with creative alternatives that otherwise might not occur to us when we are struggling with a difficulty or problem. And don't forget: When Freud needed a good reframing, he turned to jokes.

Conclusion

I began this chapter with a discussion of literature concerned with the role of humor in psychotherapy. It seems appropriate to conclude it with a brief comment on another article that reports on the use of humor in a psychiatric ward. The article, "Laughter in a Psychiatric Ward" by Marc Gelkopf, Shulamith Kreitler, and Mircea Sigal (1993), reports on an experiment with thirty-four resident patients in two chronic schizophrenic wards who were exposed to seventy movies during a three-month period. The residents in the first ward were exposed to humorous movies only, while the residents in the second ward were exposed to different kinds of movies, only 15 percent (eleven films) of which were comedies. The researchers wanted to see if humor would have a noticeable effect on the patients and predicted that the patients exposed only to comedies would manifest the most positive changes. They found some evidence in support of this prediction, as there were significant reductions in these patients' use of verbal hostility and in anxiety and depression, and significant increases in activation (i.e., less passivity and inaction). But the major and unexpected finding was the effect of exposure to seventy comedies over a three-month period on the ward staff, as the patients in the first ward received "a higher level of social support from the staff" (288). The authors conclude that, whereas the patients, despite the research findings, did not perceive any change in themselves due to their having been exposed to comedies, "there is evidence for changes in the way the staff observed the patients," a change that the patients *did* perceive and mention in the social support questionnaire they were asked to fill out.[3]

This study, then, is itself illustrative of the art of reframing, as an experiment intended for the patients' benefit proved even more beneficial for the staff. Needless to say, there's a lesson in this for anyone who is engaged in an occupation or profession intended to help others. In my view, it underscores the importance of the helping person's own soul maintenance. Which is perhaps why a minister, a priest, and a rabbi entered a bar, eliciting this query from the bartender: "Is this some sort of joke?" Or why the same trio, after an exhausting hike and vigorous swim, were picking berries in the altogether.

Motoring through the Bible Belt

A Sorry Sight

> But when he came to himself he said, "How many of my father's hired hands have bread enough and to spare, but here I am dying of hunger! I will get up and go to my father, and I will say to him, 'Father, I have sinned against heaven and before you; I am no longer worthy to be called your son; treat me like one of your hired hands.'"
> *Luke 15:17–19*

> "Father, I've sinned
> And misbehaved.
> And worst of all,
> I haven't shaved."
> *Burma-Shave*

Epilogue

In the foregoing chapters, I have made the case that religion may be enriched by humor by focusing on five of humor's gifts. I have not attempted to make a systematic argument on behalf of these gifts' capacity to enrich religion, for I believe that an effort to do so would lead to the sorts of generalizations and abstractions that theologians tend to delight in but that leave more ordinary religious people gasping for air.

In identifying a handful of humor's gifts, I have tried to make the case that some forms and expressions of it—and more than we think—are good for religion. Throughout this study I have emphasized one form of humor—jokes—because they have a very long history, because they are found in all social strata, and because they are a form of humor that lends itself to citation in a book on religion and humor. Another reason more intrinsic to religion, however, is that even as there is music that is explicitly religious, so there are jokes that are explicitly about religion, ones that work with religious themes, issues, and problems. While jokes about religion frequently make light work of religion, challenging its pretensions and flights of grandiosity, this does not mean that they are not in service of religion.

In fact, there is an uncanny resemblance between Freud's economic theory of humor, with its emphasis on the saving of the expenditure of our limited psychic resources, and Jesus' invitation, "Come to me, all you that are weary and are carrying heavy burdens, and I will give you rest. Take my yoke upon you, and learn from me; for I am gentle and humble in heart, and you will find rest for your souls. *For my yoke is easy, and my burden is light*" (Matt 11:28–30, my emphasis). The dictionary defines *yoke* as "something that binds, unites, or connects" (as in the *yoke* of matrimony). Religion itself means to bind together, and as we saw in chapter 3, humor too is a means by which shared beliefs and dispositions are expressed and amplified in shared feelings (Cohen 1999, 28). So I can imagine an old hard-of-hearing fellow in the crowd turning to the fellow standing next to him and asking, "Did the preacher say, 'My joke is easy?' and the other fellow wisely responding, "Well, you heard it wrong, but you got it right."

Another uncanny resemblance between Freud's economical view of jokes and the central message of Jesus himself occurs at the very end of Freud's book. After pointing out that the pleasure we derive from humor is due to an economy in the expenditure of painful emotions, costly inhibitions, and difficult thinking, he suggests that humor is a method "of regaining from mental activity a pleasure which has in fact been lost through the development of that activity" (Freud 1905/1960, 293). When did we lose it? When we began to pass from childhood into adulthood. Freud continues: "For the euphoria which we endeavor to reach by these means is nothing other than the mood of a period of life in which we were accustomed to deal with our psychical work in general with a small expenditure of energy—the mood of our childhood, when we were ignorant of the comic, when we were incapable of jokes, and when we had no need of humor to make us happy in our life" (293).[1]

It seems hardly necessary to remind readers of this book of Jesus' charge to his disciples, "Let the children come to me, and do not stop them; for it is to such as these that the kingdom of heaven belongs" (Matt 19:14), and of this cautionary note, "Truly I tell you, unless you change and become like children, you will never enter the kingdom of heaven" (18:3). Paraphrasing Freud's oft-stated observation that dreams are the royal road to the unconscious,[2] humor is the royal road to the kingdom of God.

There is a related statement of Jesus' that has particular bearing on the approach that I have taken toward humor and its relation to religion in this book. In Matthew 6:34, Jesus says, "Therefore do not be anxious about tomorrow, for tomorrow will be anxious for itself" (RSV).[3] In the preceding chapters I have explored how humor addresses anxieties relating to death, bodily functions, intimacy, and failure. In *Childhood and Society* (1962), Erik H. Erikson makes a useful contrast between anxieties and fears. Fears, he says, "are states of apprehension which focus on isolated and recognizable dangers so that they may be judiciously appraised and realistically countered," whereas anxieties "are diffuse states of tension which magnify and even cause the illusion of an outer danger, without pointing to appropriate avenues of defense or mastery" (406–7).

Erikson further observes that the major impediment to adults' inner sense of integration or integrity is the fact that their childhood fears continue to manifest themselves in adulthood, now in the form of inexplicable anxieties. If the child was justified in having fears (after all, the child *was* vulnerable), the adult's anxieties are less explicable, as they are typically experienced even when there is little or no real external threat. If there *is* such a threat, the adult reacts, as did the child, with fear. But by definition, anxieties involve a sense of being threatened that has no clear justification and thus no identifiable solution in the external world. To be sure, fears and anxieties sometimes occur together, and when they do, the anxieties have basis in reality. But there is a fundamental distinction to be made between fear and anxiety, for it is not "the fear of danger (which we might be well able to meet with judicious action) but the fear of the associated state of aimless anxiety which drives us into irrational *action*, irrational *flight*—or, indeed, irrational *denial* of danger. When threatened with such anxiety we either magnify a danger which we have no reason to fear excessively—or we ignore a danger which we have every reason to fear" (407).

In conclusion, I want to add one additional type of anxiety to those that I have discussed in previous chapters. This is the anxiety of boredom, another form of anxiety that humor is also in a position to moderate or reduce. This form of anxiety comes to mind because as researchers cited by Vasillis Saroglou have shown, there is a rather strong correlation between humor and "novelty, sensation seeking, and risk" (Saroglou 2002a). In *Boredom* (1995), Patricia Meyer Spacks suggests that boredom, "the internal experience of paralyzing monotony," often impels its victims "to dramatic action in an attempt to evade what they feel" (166). In reviewing the literature on boredom, she cites psychoanalyst Otto Fenichel's 1934 essay "The Psychology of Boredom." Fenichel defines boredom as "an unpleasurable experience of a lack of impulse" and cites its connection with depression, loneliness, and restlessness. He emphasizes that the bored person does not experience the "lack of impulse" as a pleasurable condition. This is because boredom also includes a "need for intense mental activity." In the bored person, this need cannot find gratification by generating its own impulse but instead seeks "incitements" from the outside world. Boredom is also a state of internal tension in which instinctual aims are repressed. One turns to the external world for help in the struggle against the tension that results from such repression. Fenichel distinguishes between "pathological" and "normal" boredom. Common to both states is that "something expected does not occur." Their differences are that in pathological boredom this expected event fails to occur because one "represses his instinctual action out of anxiety," whereas in normal boredom it fails to occur because the external world does not give what "we have a right to expect" (cited in Spacks 1995, 5). Thus, in pathological boredom, the inadequacy lies within, while in normal boredom, the inadequacies are external.

The following example of how Jesus came to the rescue of bored college students may be an illustration of pathological boredom, normal boredom, or a combination of the two. The distinction does not matter very much. What *does* matter is that the victims of the boredom were in desperate need of "incitements" from the outside world, and they were willing to engage in sensation seeking and risk to make something happen. What they did to realize such incitement was more humorous than criminal, and I am quite certain that the "paternal" voice to which Jesus himself appealed would have agreed. What makes this episode significant from a religious point of view is not simply that the baby Jesus was involved, but also, and more important, that it illustrates the genial, nonpunitive side of God who takes a sympathetic view toward the human need to do something to dispel our boredom, especially when the external world does not give what we have a right to expect.

Five years ago I was thumbing through the January 27, 1999, issue of *The Christian Century,* and I came across Martin E. Marty's account of an episode that occurred in Belleville, Illinois, in early December 1998. Marty wrote:

> According to an Associated Press story, early last December a student borrowed a baby Jesus figurine from the town square nativity display in Belleville, Illinois, and took it to Applebee's Grill and Bar. "It was a case of having a couple of cocktails in a boring town," said the student. "We were driving around and it was like "Hey, let's take baby Jesus out for a drink." Applebee's hostess Haydee Gryzmala, who retains good taste in these days of bad manners, called the police, who arrested the prankster. The AP reporter learned from the Belleville Exchange Club, which sponsors the display, that "other figurines in the nativity scene are wired down, but that they can't really tie down the baby Jesus."

In his commentary on the AP story, Marty focused on the statement by the Exchange Club, saying, "Lots of people do try to keep Jesus tied down. And they try to keep him tied down as a baby. . . . The helplessness of the child is a key theme in incarnational theology. The God beyond the gods is among us in weakness. People bow before this mystery. But many turn their backs when the time comes to consider Jesus as a grown-up." He went on to note that we don't have to wait until Good Friday "to get some effects of his grown-uppedness," but "there is that death, toward which the Gospels see him marching and which an epistle describes as 'the joy that was set before him,' enduring the cross." He concluded, "There they lifted him up. The Belleville Exchange Club person was right: 'They can't really tie down the baby Jesus.' "

Marty's commentary was thought-provoking, but I found it difficult to put out of my mind the great Harry Houdini, the famous magician who, during my own youth, was able to squirm his way out of many tight spots: "They couldn't tie down Harry Houdini, either" (Phillips 2001b). Nor could I ignore the fact that an advertisement for a Doctor of Ministry degree program was placed alongside Marty's column. It read, "Don't read this if you are satisfied with stagnation and monotony in your ministry." It struck me there was another issue floating around here, begging to be tied down, and that this was the issue of boredom. The student in Belleville sought to dispel his boredom, at least for a time, by snatching the baby Jesus and taking him to Applebee's Grill and Bar, and ministers were being urged to dispel their boredom by returning to seminary where, arguably, the monotony began! (Instead, read Dykstra 2001, 24–28.) The following poem was the result of these ruminations:

JESUS' FIRST DRINK

The story doesn't say how many he downed
that evening at Applebee's.
Nor does it mention who was around
to check on patrons' IDs.

But if I saw a baby outside on the Square
on a cold December night,
I'd like to believe I'd take him somewhere,
and get him warm—and tight.

Let's never condone bad behavior
merely because one is bored,
but maybe our small, little Savior
was tired of being ignored.

So let's raise our glasses to Jesus,
this innocent kid from the stable,
and before the police come to seize us,
let's drink him under the table.

Whatever may happen next, there is no need to be anxious, because the baby Jesus—who symbolizes the small child who continues to live inside all of us—is safe and sound. And when he is safe and sound, so too are we.

Yet as Marty points out, Jesus did not remain a child, and we don't have to wait until Good Friday "to get some effects of his grown-uppedness." As proof

of this point, there is an unusual example of Christian iconography overlooking the street of the north wall of the Surajmal Banthia Haveli in Churu, India, which portrays Jesus smoking a cigar (see figure on page 173).[4]

A crucial event in Jesus' "grown-uppedness"—his own coming of age—was his transfiguration, when "his face shone like the sun, and his clothes became dazzling white" (Matt 17:2). He was joined on that occasion by two biblical greats, Moses and Elijah, and the three of them engaged in spirited conversation together. Then the Heavenly Father also spoke from out of the bright cloud that overshadowed the three men, saying, "This is my Son, the Beloved; with him I am well pleased; listen to him!" (v. 5). Hearing the voice of God, the disciples fell to the ground and were overcome by fear, but Jesus came and touched them, and said, "Get up and do not be afraid" (v. 6). To capture the "grown-uppedness" of this occasion, I wrote the following short poem:

TRANSFIGURATION

Jesus brought the bottle,
Elijah brought the cup.
Moses brought the stogie,
And they all lit up.

As "minister, priest, and rabbi" jokes have taught us, whenever three religious men appear together, we should anticipate that some sort of joke is in the off-ing.[5] But the transfiguration story is a special example of this fundamental truth, for this was the day when Jesus told his disciples to set aside their anxieties and, for God's sake, lighten up!

Motoring through the Bible Belt

"Mary, It's Me!"

Jesus said to her, "Woman, why are you weeping? Whom are you looking for?" Supposing him to be the gardener, she said to him, "Sir, if you have carried him away, tell me where you have laid him, and I will take him away." Jesus said to her, "Mary!" She turned and said to him in Hebrew, "Rabbouni!" (which means Teacher).
John 20:15–16

"Mary, O Mary,
What's the trouble?
Could it be
My three day stubble?"
Burma-Shave

Notes

Acknowledgments

1. My boyhood interest in Burma-Shave poetry led me to paste into my scrapbook when I was ten years old an excerpt in *The Readers' Digest* of an article by David E. Scherman from *Life* magazine on Allan Gilbert Odell, who in 1926 persuaded a Minnesota farmer to allow him to erect a few signs on the edge of his property, thus "letting loose upon America a torrent of doggerel from undercover poets throughout the country. He also put his father's almost moribund Burma-Vita shaving cream company in the black and, incidentally, brightened the lives of motorists." In the early days, Odell "scared up most of the jingles himself, basing his selections on time-tried vaudeville and radio gags." As business picked up, he tried to get big-name poets to write the jingles, but they wanted too much money for their efforts, so the company settled instead on a nationwide contest that brought in 50,000 poems annually, from which senior company officials selected the top 25 and paid contributors $100 each. The article goes on to note that the most popular jingles were ones that involved courtship ("The wolf who starts to roam and prowl / Should shave before he starts to howl"), but safety jingles also were popular ("Passing school zones take it slow, / Let our little shavers grow"). The article concludes that Odell is firmly convinced of one thing, namely, that his signs are never ignored ("If you don't know whose ads these are, / You can't have driven very far").

Introduction

1. In a series of important empirical and theoretical studies, Vassilis Saroglou (see bibliography entries) has demonstrated that exposure to religious videos has a negative effect on humor production in response to frustrating situations (as devised by Rosenzweig, 1950) and that despite the fact that humor is present in all religions, religions tend to promote a suspicion of humor because humor has features that are disfavored by religion, such as the

tolerance of ambiguity, suspension of moral judgment, social risk-taking, loss of self-control (i.e., uncontrollable laughter), and aggressive and sexual features that religion opposes.

2. An oft-cited article in this connection is Reinhold Niebuhr's "Humour and Faith" (1990). That Niebuhr wrote an article on humor is clearly to his credit, as theologians and religious thinkers have tended to neglect the subject of humor altogether. Yet while for Niebuhr humor has a place in religion, it is clearly a subordinate one. He notes that the "intimate relation between humor and faith is derived from the fact that both deal with the incongruities of our existence," but then goes on to make a distinction between the immediate incongruities of life, with which humor is concerned, and the ultimate incongruities of life, with which faith is concerned. Thus, he writes, "Laughter is our reaction to immediate incongruities and those which do not affect us essentially," and "faith is the only possible response to the ultimate incongruities of existence, which threaten the very meaning of our life" (10). With this distinction between that which does not affect us essentially and that which does, Niebuhr effectively downplays and even downgrades humor while elevating faith to a position of highest importance and significance. Little wonder, then, that he concludes his essay with this highly qualified endorsement of humor: "Insofar as the sense of humor is a recognition of incongruity, it is more profound than any philosophy which seeks to devour incongruity in reason. But the sense of humor remains healthy only when it deals with immediate issues and faces the obvious and surface irrationalities. It must move toward faith or sink into despair when the ultimate issues are raised. That is why there is laughter in the vestibule of the temple, the echo of laughter in the temple itself, but only faith and prayer, and no laughter, in the holy of holies" (15).

3. I discovered an excellent illustration of religion's tendency to wear the long face in *Martin Gardner's Favorite Poetic Parodies* (Gardner, ed., Amherst, New York: Prometheus Books, 2001). The original couplet by Robert Louis Stevenson is parodied by Armand T. Ringer, a Martin Gardner pseudonym (note anagram). Following Ringer, I have contributed my own parodies. These show that when religion is invoked, unhappy thoughts of evil, of a better world than this, and of moral conflict are sure to follow:

Happy Thought

> The world is so full of a number of things,
> I'm sure we should all be as happy as kings.
> *Robert Louis Stevenson*

Further Thoughts

Prayerful Thought
> The world is so full of violence and sleaze,
> We should all bow our heads and get down on our knees.

Theological Thought
> The world is so full of things that appall,
> I wonder if God is aware of it all.
> *Armand T. Ringer*

After Thoughts

Food for Thought
> My mind is so full of a number of things,
> Three celery sticks and six buffalo wings.

Theological Thought
>   This world is so full of a number of things,
>   Kinda makes you wonder what the next world brings.

Prayerful Thought
>   The world is so full of pretty young things,
>   Please help me, O Lord, think of buffalo wings.
>   *Donald Capps*

Chapter 1: Humor as Saving Psychic Resources

1. George L. Christie, in a fairly recent essay titled "Some Psychoanalytic Aspects of Humour" (1994), quotes James Strachey, the editor of Freud's collected works, as saying in his introduction to Freud's essay that "here for the first time we find the superego presented in an amiable mood" (481). Christie observes, however, that, except for a brief controversy in the 1950s over the very notion of "the benevolent superego," little has been written about it; he comments, "In later reviews of the superego concept I have found no references to Freud's 'Humour' paper. . . . We still have a great deal to learn about the nature of the superego" (482).

2. Once when I was sitting in the dentist's chair for a root canal, the dentist and her assistant were listening to a local talk show, the subject of which was making donations to the poor and needy. Considerable debate was generated by a caller's account of how she had organized a project to provide needy individuals and families with a nourishing Thanksgiving dinner plus cans of food and so on. In exchange, she asked that the recipients write a brief note of thanks, presumably so that she could use these comments to inspire others to participate in the project the following year. Because no thank-you notes were received, she said that she felt the recipients did not exhibit the appropriate gratitude and that she therefore would not organize the project the following year. As my dentist and her assistant came down on opposite sides of the question of whether she was justified in feeling the way she did, I wanted to chime in and cite the story of the ten lepers in Luke 17:11–19, as it seemed to make a difference that one of the ten who had been healed returned to give Jesus thanks. It seemed to me that if the woman had received just one thank-you note, she would have decided to repeat the project a second year. Unable to join in the conversation, I did the next best thing, which was to thank the dentist and assistant for a conversation between them that distracted me from the root canal procedure itself.

3. When I told this joke in class, only a few students laughed, leaving me to wonder whether the joke itself isn't especially funny or whether seminarians today wouldn't know that Ole and Lars lived in an era when the third person of the Trinity was more ghostly than spirited, and that when people died, they "gave up the ghost." Another possibility, of course, is that they understood the joke, thought it was pretty funny, but were inhibited about laughing because it made humorous use of a venerable Christian doctrine.

4. The fact that "fanny" is a slang word for the buttocks and that "Fanny" is a diminutive for the feminine name Frances makes a woman bearing this name a rather inevitable character in jokes. In jokes, of course, the humor is intended. There is unintentional humor, however, in William Makepeace Thackeray's poem "The Cane-Bottom'd Chair." In *Victorian Parlour Poetry: An Annotated Anthology* (1967), editor Michael R. Turner refers to "the relic or souvenir school of poetry," a type of poetry "in which a possession of a deceased loved one is the subject of tearful nostalgia. Chairs are particularly favored" (186). Thackeray's poem tells the story of how a young woman sat on his cane-bottom'd chair one fair morning years ago, and because she did, he treasures this chair over all his other, more valu-

able possessions. Unfortunately, her name happened to be Fanny, so there is a bit of unintended humor in that unlucky thirteenth stanza:

> When the candles burn low, and the company's gone,
> In the silence of night as I sit here alone—
> I sit here alone, but we yet are a pair—
> My Fanny I see in my cane-bottom'd chair.

An out-of-body experience, perhaps? In any case, the humorous effect is heightened by the fact that the poem is about the chair's own bottom, that fannies, too, are a pair, and that when Thackeray was a boy, his bottom was probably caned.

5. In his discussion of dream symbolism in his *Introductory Lectures on Psychoanalysis* (1917/1966), Freud observes that the male organ finds symbolic substitutes in things that resemble it in shape, such as sticks, umbrellas, posts, and trees, and in objects that represent the characteristic of penetrating into the body and injuring it, such as knives, daggers, spears, and sabres. He also notes that the male organ can be replaced in dreams by objects from which liquid flows, such as fountain pens, and by objects that are capable of being lengthened, such as extensible pencils (190). To illustrate Freud's point, I wrote a poem about a hapless Norwegian foot soldier who accidentally jammed his rusty old lance down the leg of his Norse Army pants and cut off an inch of his penis. The poem concludes: "Due to its foreshortening menace / The sword is mightier than the pen is!"

Chapter 2: Humor as Stimulus to Identity Creation

1. In *The Prostitute in the Family Tree: Discovering Humor and Irony in the Bible* (1997), Douglas Adams adopts the view of biblical scholar James A. Sanders that "biblical stories are mirrors for identity and not models for morality" (6). He suggests that Jesus' parables presented his listeners with the following challenge: "With whom do you identify in the story?" He also observes that our tendency to try to derive a moral from these stories leads us to overlook the fact that they are open-ended. If we connect the fact that the parables are "mirrors for identity" with the fact that they are open-ended, we can see that the identity question raises the issue not only of our actual selves but also of our potential selves, or not only who we are but also who we are in the process of becoming.

2. Erikson also cites Luther's advice to would-be authors: "Thou shalt not write a book unless you have listened to the fart of an old sow, to which you should open your mouth wide and say 'Thanks to you, pretty nightingale; do I hear a text which is for me?'" (Erikson, 1958, 33). Luther's association of authorial inspiration and a sow's flatulence prompted me to imagine that the original words to Luther's well-known hymn, "A Mighty Fortress Is Our God," went something like this:

> A mighty fartress is our sow,
> She warbles forth with wonderful poise.
> Compared to her, a German Hausfrau
> Backdrafts but indiscriminate noise.
> Her harmonies doth swell,
> On a colossal scale.
> None other can compare
> With her majestic flair,
> On earth is not her equal

A mighty fartress is our sow,
Her anthems are uncommonly rich.
Didst God an angel ever endow,
Such lovely tone and marvelous pitch?
'Tis true there is a cost,
On noses it's not lost.
But rather than complain,
We'll list for her refrain,
The smell's harmonious sequel.

I considered submitting a scholarly article to a church history journal supposedly written by Professor Assh Oleson of the University of Oslo and Dr. Anahl Kaboom, Professor of Christian Studies at the University of Kabul. The article would announce their astounding discovery of this original version among Luther's personal papers and would claim that Philip Melancthon was responsible for the sanitized version. On reflection, however, I decided it would be better in this case to let sleeping sows lie.

3. While Luther's identification with the sow was very positive, Cotton Mather's identification with a dog was quite negative. Consider this entry from his diary: "I was once emptying the *Cistern of Nature,* and making *Water* at the Wall. At the same Time, there came a *Dog,* who did so too, before me. Thought I: 'What mean, and vile Things are the Children of Men, in this mortal State! How much do our *natural Necessities* abase us, and place us in some regard, on the same level with the very *Dogs!*'" Then, however, his thoughts continued, and he declared: "Yett I will be a more noble Creature; and at the very Time, when my *natural Necessities* debase me into the Condition of the *Beast,* my *Spirit* shall (I say, *at that very Time!*) rise and soar, and fly up, towards the employment of the *Angel*" (Mather, 1911, 357). Mather's spiritual struggle prompted me to write the following short verses:

Fido Makes Personal Appeal

When you and I come here to pee,
I wish, kind sir, that you could see,
An angel doth inhabit me.

Cotton has Theological Insight

When the dog joined yours truly to pee,
He stood not on two legs but three.
   This canine tripod
   Brought deep thoughts of God,
Three persons in one Trinity.

I felt however, that Mather's struggle warranted a more sustained poetic effort, and inspiration came from Adelaide Anne Procter's "A Lost Chord," victim of many parodies (see Gardner, ed., 2001, 155–59). I imagined that Mather might suffer from urine retention (a problem to which I briefly alluded in the preceding chapter). Thus, in the following parody, the focus shifts from the fact that our natural necessities place us on the same level with the very dogs, and concerns instead the fact that our bodies do not always perform as our Creator intended. I imagined Mather reciting Psalm 98 because verses 7–8 read: "Let the sea roar, and all that fills it. . . . Let the floods clap their hands; let the hills sing together for joy." First the Procter poem, then the Mather parody:

A Lost Chord

Seated one day at the Organ,
  I was weary and ill at ease,
And my fingers wandered idly
  Over the noisy keys.

I do not know what I was playing,
  Or what I was dreaming then;
But I struck one chord of music,
  Like the sound of a great Amen.

It flooded the crimson twilight
  Like the close of an Angel's Psalm,
And it lay on my fevered spirit
  With a touch of infinite calm.

It quieted pain and sorrow,
  Like love overcoming strife;
It seemed the harmonious echo
  From our discordant life.

It linked all perplexed meanings
  Into one perfect peace,
And trembled away in silence
  As if it were loth to cease.

I have sought but I seek it vainly,
  That one lost chord divine,
Which came from the soul of the Organ,
  And entered into mine.

It may be that Death's bright angel
  Will speak in that chord again,—
It may be that only in Heaven
  I shall hear that grand Amen.
    Adelaide Anne Proctor

Praise God from Whom All Blessings Flow

Standing one day at the cistern,
I was not feeling exactly chipper,
As my fingers struggled to open
My shirt-catching rusted old zipper.

I do not know what I was praying,
Or what I was dreaming then;
But gone was my urine retention,
And I shouted a hearty Amen!

I flooded the cistern that morning,
While reciting the 98th Psalm.
Released from my poor fevered spirit,
I felt an infinite calm.

Thus ended pain and sorrow,
Like love overcoming strife,
I wanted to shout to the rooftops,
And go home and make love to my wife.

Gone were all perplexed meanings,
Replaced by perfect peace.
I stood there in holy silence,
Amazed how the flow did not cease.

I've returned on subsequent mornings,
To recapture that moment divine,
Which came from the soul of Life's Organ,
And entered into mine.

It may be that Death's bright angel
Will bequeath that moment again,—
It may be that only in Heaven
I will shout that hearty Amen!
  Cotton Mather

4. For example, a three-year-old gave my wife a painting on which she had worked dili-
gently for twenty or thirty minutes. "I want you to have this, Mrs. Capps, and I want you
to keep it forever. Keep it in a very safe place where no one else can find it. But if they do
find it and try to take it away from you [long pause], shoot them!" What was humorous to
my wife was the fact that the little girl thought long and hard before the idea of "shooting"
occurred to her. Also, because she is rather shy and reserved, the very idea that she would
suggest violence was completely unexpected. What was humorous to me when my wife
reported the incident is that art theft is a popular theme in literature and film, and at that
very time, I was writing an article on the theft in 1911 of Leonardo da Vinci's *Mona Lisa*.
Somehow, this little three-year-old seemed to be aware that people like to steal precious art,
especially when, as in the case of her own painting, it is one of a kind.

5. A student about to graduate also identified with this joke. She said that while she can
hardly wait to leave the seminary, which she considers an unhealthy environment, she also
anticipates that after she has been away from it for a spell, she will feel a lot like the rabbit
when he found himself dying for a cigarette.

6. This chapter has focused on jokes involving animals and birds. Humorous verse about
animals and birds would lend itself to a similar exploration of identity themes. It once
occurred to me that even though the Japanese haiku has been taught in American schools,
it has not succeeded in capturing the hearts of the adult American public, nor have any
major American poets written more than a couple of haiku. I believe that the reason the
haiku has not become popular in the United States is that it is unrhymed, usually lacks a
title, and is rather placid. Furthermore, animals and birds are underrepresented in Japanese
haiku. In a recent collection of haiku (Washington, ed., 2003), only 35 of the 530 Japanese
haiku are about animals and birds. If Americans have been able to domesticate the Japan-

ese automobile, there is no reason in principle why they can't do the same to the haiku. The following are illustrative of what the American haiku might look like:

O Little Crow, Head Hanging So Low

> Pity poor jackdaw,
> Eyes vacant and face slack-jaw,
> Neck sev'ring hacksaw.

I Lost My Heart in San Francisco

> Little polliwog,
> Body caught in trolley cog,
> Short life, folly frog.

Sailing Over the White Cliffs of Dover

> Poor English sheepdog,
> Not good playing sheep leapfrog
> On day of deep fog.

Fast Forward

> Like mouse-crazed feline,
> Haiku poet makes beeline
> To end of three line.

Chapter 3: Humor as Expression of Intimacy

1. In "What's So Funny? A Scientific Attempt to Discover Why We Laugh" (2002), Tad Friend reports on the efforts of British psychologist Richard Wiseman to identify the world's funniest joke. Responses to Wiseman's announcement of the study on the Internet poured in, and this joke won. Friend says that it was "submitted by a psychiatrist from Manchester who often tells it to cheer up his patients" (93). In chapter 5, I will provide evidence that psychotherapists tend to tell jokes primarily to reassure their clients: "If you think your life is a mess, consider the guy who . . ." Friend also comments on a feature of the joke that has particular relevance to a central issue in the present chapter, what Cohen calls the "conditionality" of jokes. Friend observes that "the gratuitous inclusion of 'New Jersey' " was clearly "a shrewd play for the American vote, tapping social-identity scorn for the Garden State" (93). In the first version of this joke that I heard, the hunters were Texans.

2. Here is a variation on the "Anderson Nails" joke: Jesus was really exhausted after the resurrection. So when he came to an inn, he put three nails on the counter and said to the innkeeper, "Can you put me up for the night?"

3. As the biblical text suggests that Sarah denied having laughed because she feared she would be punished for her laughter, and also implies that her fears in this regard were groundless, this story is illustrative of Freud's view that humor is under the aegis of the superego, which is normally associated with the parental function (the internalization of the parental voice) and thus with conscience. But in contrast to the punitive voice of conscience, humor is the genial side of the superego, the side that lets the one who joked or laughed off the hook. The feared punishment does not take place. Cohen himself seems aware of this side of the superego when he mentions that in cracking a joke we "get away with" something we possibly ought not to have gotten away with.

4. "Texts of terror" is the phrase made popular by Phyllis Trible's *Texts of Terror: Literary-Feminist Readings of Biblical Narratives* (1984). Following a brief introductory chapter on the telling of sad stories, Trible explores the stories of Hagar, Tamar, the unnamed woman in Judges 19, and the daughter of Jephthah, victims of rejection, rape, dismemberment, and ritual sacrifice. Nearly a decade later, in *New Adam: The Future of Male Spirituality* (1992), which is dedicated to Trible, Philip Culbertson explored three biblical narratives from the perspective of male experience, viewing them as men's texts of terror. He focused on the Abraham-Ishmael, David-Absalom, and Jonathan-David relationships, the first two concerning father-son relations, the third having to do with love between two men. Both authors note their selective use of biblical narratives. Given the sheer number of such narratives, they could hardly have done otherwise. But given their respective hermeneutical lenses, a "terror" story that was destined to fall between the cracks is the story of Rebekah and Jacob in Genesis 27.

5. In *The Prostitute in the Family Tree* (1997), Douglas Adams suggests that the story about Jesus turning water into wine at the wedding in Cana (John 2:1—11) is intentionally humorous. There is hyperbole in the sheer amount of wine that the miracle produced (Adams guesses it would have equaled from six hundred to nine hundred bottles of wine); in the steward's declaration that this wine was superior to what had been served previously (Adams guesses that by this time the steward was probably too drunk to tell; in fact, he may have been the one responsible for the wine shortage in the first place); and in the fact that this was the sign that first inspired the disciples to believe in Jesus. Another humorous element, one that has bearing on my earlier discussion of the "bad-enough mother," is Jesus' response to his mother when she tells him there is no wine left. Jesus responds, "Woman, what concern is that to you and to me?" (2:4). Adams notes, "If my mother asked me to take out the garbage and I said, 'Woman, what concern is that to you and to me? My hour has not yet come,' she might have responded, 'Your hour is closer than you think!' In the story, however, Mary's response shows that she took no offense but was accustomed to this type of banter; she tells the servants, 'Do whatever he tells you' (v. 5)." Adams concludes, "Such a story is not the stuff of conventional Mother's Day Sermons, which idealize the relationship of mothers and sons, but it makes it much easier to live with our imperfect relations between mothers and sons" (63). Well, maybe. But what are we to make of the fact that Mary simply assumes that her son will respond to her concern? Is this a case of a son who resorts to humor when he would dearly love to tell his mother to go take a hike? If so, it may illustrate the use of humor as a temporary relief from costly inhibitions. It is also worth noting that the miracle at Cana has produced its own joke tradition, such as the following: A minister is pulled over by the state trooper for doing 90 in a 65-mile-an-hour stretch of the New York State Thruway. The trooper smells alcohol on the minister's breath and sees an empty wine bottle on the floor. He asks, "Sir, have you been drinking?" "Just water," the minister replies. "Then why do I smell wine?" The minister looks down at the bottle and says, "Good Lord, he's done it again!"

6. A colleague, John W. (Jack) Stewart, goes fishing every summer in northern Michigan while I typically remain in New Jersey. One summer he sent me the "Quotes about Fishing" which had appeared in the county newspaper where he does his fishing. I responded with "The Miraculous Catch of Fish":

Quotes about Fishing

When two fishermen meet . . .
"Hiymack"
"Lobuddy"
"Binearlong?"

"Coplours"
"Cetchanenny?"
"Goddafew"
"Kinarthay?"
"Bassencarp"
"Enneysizetoom?"
"Cuplapowns"
"Hittinhard?"
"Sordalike"
"Wachozin?"
"Gobbawurms"
"Fishanonaboddum?"
"Rydononaboddum"
"Watchadrinkin?"
"Jugajimbeam"
"Igoddago"
"Tubad"
"Seeyaroun"
"Yeahtakidezzy"
"Guluk"

The Miraculous Catch of Fish

(Loosely Based on John 21:1–14)

Cetchanenny?
Zilch.
Gotathought.
Whazzit?
Starboardside.
Thinkit'llhelp?
TrustmeI'mthebrainsofthisoutfit.

(A short interval as the nets are moved from the left to the right side of the boat.)

Whataboodle!
What'dItellyou?
You'rethegreatest!
Oyeoflittlefaith.

(Another time lapse.)

Ferchrissakewho'sgotthejug?
VerilyIsayuntoyouhewhodoesthethinkin'getstodothedrinkin'.
Fairnufflord.
Writeitdownforfuturereference.
Heyanyonegotapencil?
Ifiguredasmuch.

Chapter 4: Humor as Soul Maintenance

1. Ethnic humor is one form of local or particularistic humor. Regional humor is another. (Garrison Keillor's *Pretty Good Joke Book* [2003] has several pages of regional jokes about Iowa, Minnesota, and South Dakota). Also, as indicated by Cohen's example of the "com-

monplaces" associated with university professors, humor that occurs among members of an occupational group or profession is yet another. I have chosen to focus here on ethnic humor because it enables me to address the role of humor in the neutralizing or relativizing of our anxieties about failure. I view such anxieties as a major issue in society today and attribute them to the "spirit" of the times in which we live.

2. I asked an Asian-American student who has a wonderful sense of humor what he thought of this joke. Was it funny? Was it offensive? He found it mildly funny, noting that mastering English speech patterns is something that he and his Asian-American friends often joke about, but that he takes offense when a comedian makes fun of Asian speech patterns on TV. What inhibited his enjoyment of the joke, however, was that the term "Ed Zachary" was puzzling to him. Did it have some cultural reference? Was there a famous American named Ed Zachary? I informed him that to the best of my knowledge the name was contrived to sound like an Asian saying "exactly" and that there was no greater significance to it than that. I added, however, that there might be some humor in the fact that Zachary's first name is "Ed," not "Edward" or "Edwin," as this adds to the undignified nature of this particular disease as compared with diseases that bear only the surname of the physician who first discovered it (Hansen's disease, Alzheimer's disease, etc.). In the course of our conversation, he noted that this joke, while problematic on ethnic grounds, would be even more problematic on religious grounds (i.e., among Asian-Christian groups) because of its sexual and physiological references. This observation has direct bearing on a central theme of this book, namely, that religion is unduly suspicious of humor.

3. A variation on this reversal is direct counterattack, as reflected, for example, in Rick Trask's *Toronto Jokes* (1989). Born in Newfoundland, Trask "felt the sting of countless 'Newfie jokes'" when he moved to Toronto in 1964. So he decided to give Torontonians "a taste of their own medicine."

4. In *Jokes and Their Relation to the Unconscious* (1905/1960), Freud notes that the philosopher Franz Brentano, whose lectures he had attended during his first year as a student at the University of Vienna, "composed a kind of riddle in which a small number of syllables had to be guessed which when they were put together into words gave a different sense according as they were grouped in one way or another" (34). Because the examples that Freud cites are in German, the editor, James Strachey, provides an English illustration: "Burglars had broken into a large furriers' store. But they were disturbed and went off without taking anything, though leaving the show-room in the greatest confusion. When the manager arrived in the morning, he gave instructions to his assistants: 'Never mind about the cheaper goods. The urgent thing is to get the *********.'" The correct answer is "first-rate furs straight" (296). Paul Dickson's *Dickson's Joke Treasury* (1984) has several pages of "What's the Difference?" riddles that employ the same device, such as "What's the difference between a cat and a comma?" Answer: "The cat has claws at the end of his paws, while the comma has its pause at the end of its clause" (288). Or this: "What's the difference between a photocopy machine and the Hong Kong flu?" Answer: "The one makes facsimiles, the other sick families" (238). A variant form is one in which the second half of the answer is implied but not directly stated. For example, "What's the difference between a bad marksman and a constipated owl?" Answer: "A bad marksman shoots and shoots and never hits" (240). Or this one, another indication that lawyers are the most disagreeable of all professionals: "What's the difference between a rooster and a lawyer?" Answer: "A rooster clucks defiance."

5. While I am not a lover of puns, I lament the fact that there is a dearth of biblical puns. Here is my modest attempt to address this lack: Fergus went into a bar and sat down next to a fair Scottish lass. They immediately hit it off, and as they got up to leave some three hours later, it was clear that they would spend the night together. She said, "We could go to my place, but I live with my mother and she does not approve of me having men over."

So they piled into Fergus's truck and headed for his place. As he drove into the lot, he apologized, "It's a sad shack, but it's me shack, so a'bed we go."

Chapter 5: Humor as the Art of Reframing

1. Interestingly enough, these two criteria also apply to the use of the Bible in pastoral counseling. In "The Bible's Role in Pastoral Care and Counseling: Four Basic Principles" (Capps 1984), I note that the first two principles for deciding whether to cite a biblical verse or story are those of *relevance* and *sensitivity*.

2. In a footnote in their chapter "The Gentle Art of Reframing," Watzlawick et al. observe: "Reframing plays an important role in humor, except that there the second frame, usually introduced by the punchline, is a *non sequitor* that unexpectedly gives the whole story a funny slant" (85). They cite an old joke that illustrates this technique: "In 1878 Austro-Hungary occupied Bosnia very much against the will of the Bosnians, who soon began to show their displeasure by sniping at Austrian officials. The situation grew so bad that according to an untrue story, a Draconian law was drafted in Vienna which read: For shooting at the Minister of the Interior: two years hard labor; for shooting at the Foreign Minister: three years hard labor; for shooting at the War Minister: four years hard labor. *The Prime Minister must not be shot at all.*" Since a *non sequitor* is a conclusion or inference that does not follow from the premises, a therapeutic reframing may share even this characteristic in common with jokes, because such reframings challenge the premises on which clients have based or drawn conclusions.

3. While Gelkopf et al. used humor as a potentially useful therapeutic method with schizophrenic patients, Max Levin suggested in his article on "Wit and Schizophrenic Thinking" (1957) that "some jokes are identical in structure with the thinking disturbances found in the psychoses, notably in schizophrenia, a fact that seems to have biological meaning" (917). While schizophrenic thinking disturbance takes many forms, it can be summed up, in his view, as a confusion of form and substance. He illustrates the confusion with an account of a patient who, one day in April, was asked the date by a member of the hospital staff, to which he replied, "The first week in December." "Then, will Christmas soon be here?" "No, that's already gone." "Then this can't be the first week in December." "Then it must be the *second* week in December." Levin suggests that "many a professional gag writer has done worse than that" (917). One is reminded here of Abbott and Costello dialogues, which involve a similar confusion of form and substance (e.g., their famous "Who's on first?" routine). Recently, a schizophrenic man who has hung around the downtown area of Princeton for many years and is well known to shop owners and longtime residents asked me if I had watched "the game" the previous evening. I said no and asked him who won. He answered, "The other team." I doubt that he intended his answer to be funny, but in its formal structure, it isn't very different from the following joke:

> Drunk: "Taxi?"
> Driver: "Yes, Sir!"
> Drunk: "I thought so."

Epilogue

1. Freud does not specify the year or years when this transition began, but Robert Provine (2000) indicates that "joking becomes prominent and intentional" at age five or six (93). So we may conclude that it was around five years of age that we began to adopt the method of humor to regain the very mood of childhood, when we had no need of humor to make us happy.

2. More precisely, he wrote, "The interpretation of dreams is the royal road to a knowledge of the unconscious activities of the mind" (Freud 1899/1965, 647). One might add that the interpretation of jokes was, to Freud, the low road to the unconscious.

3. I have chosen the RSV translation of this verse over the NRSV because the NRSV uses the word *worry* instead of *anxious*. In his article "An Investigation of Worry and Sense of Humor" (2002), William E. Kelly reports that humor was effective in reducing anxiety, but so was worry. This book is concerned with humor and its role in reducing or inhibiting anxiety. A book that makes a similar case for worry is Julie K. Norem's *The Positive Power of Negative Thinking* (2001).

4. I am indebted to Richard Fox Young, professor of world religions of Princeton Theological Seminary, for this piece of iconography.

5. As young boys, we intuitively knew this. While the adults sang the Christmas favorite "We Three Kings," we surreptitiously sang our own version: "We Three Kings of Orient are, / Trying to smoke a rubber cigar. / It was loaded, it exploded, / Now we're on yonder star."

Motoring through the Bible Belt

Caution: Wait until You Can See Your Face!

Saul got up from the ground, and though his eyes were open, he could see nothing; so they led him by the hand and brought him into Damascus. For three days he was without sight, and neither ate nor drank.
Acts 9:8–9

For three days
After he was saved,
Paul neither ate
Nor drank nor shaved.
Burma-Shave

Bibliography

Abel, Millicent H. 1998. Interaction of Humor and Gender in Moderating Relationships between Stress and Outcomes. *The Journal of Psychology* 132:267–76.

Adams, Douglas. 1997. *The Prostitute in the Family Tree: Discovering Humor and Irony in the Bible.* Louisville: Westminster John Knox.

Anonymous. 1998. *Old Stories from Denmark.* Ebeltoft, Denmark: Elles Forlag.

Apte, Mahadev. 1985. *Humor and Laughter: An Anthropological Approach.* Ithaca, N.Y: Cornell University Press.

Bakan, David. 1966. *The Duality of Human Existence: An Essay on Psychology and Religion.* Chicago: Rand McNally.

Baker, Russell, ed. 1986. *The Norton Book of Light Verse.* New York: W. W. Norton.

Bizi, Smadar, Giora Keinan, and Benjamin Beit-Hallahmi. 1988. Humor and Coping with Stress: A Test under Real-Life Conditions. *Personality and Individual Differences* 9:951–56.

Capps, Donald. 1984. The Bible's Role in Pastoral Care and Counseling: Four Basic Principles. *Journal of Psychology and Christianity* 3:5–15.

———. 1990. *Reframing: A New Method in Pastoral Care.* Minneapolis: Fortress.

———. 1993. Sex in the Parish: Social-Scientific Explanations for Why It Occurs. *Pastoral Psychology* 47:350–61.

———. 1994. The Soul as the "Coreness" of the Self. Pages 82–104 in *The Treasure in Earthen Vessels: Explorations in Theological Anthropology (In Honor of James N. Lapsley).* Edited by Brian H. Childs and David W. Waanders. Louisville: Westminster John Knox.

———. 1997a. *Men, Religion, and Melancholia: James, Otto, Jung, and Erikson.* New Haven, Conn.: Yale University Press.

———. 1997b. Power and Desire: Sexual Misconduct Involving Pastors and Parishioners. Pages 129–40 in *Women, Gender, and Christian Community.* Edited by Jane D. Douglass and James F. Kay. Louisville: Westminster John Knox.

———. 1998. *Living Stories: Pastoral Counseling in Congregational Context.* Minneapolis: Fortress.

————. 1999. Don Quixote as Moral Narcissist: Implications for Mid-Career Male Ministers. *Pastoral Psychology* 47:401–23. Repr. pages 66–92 in *The Spirituality of Men: Sixteen Christians Write about Their Faith.* Edited by Philip L. Culbertson. Minneapolis: Fortress.

————. 2002a. *Agents of Hope: A Pastoral Psychology.* Eugene, Ore.: Wipf & Stock.

————. 2002b. *Men and Their Religion: Honor, Hope, and Humor.* Harrisburg, Pa.: Trinity Press International.

Carroll, Noël. 2000. Intimate Laughter. *Philosophy and Literature* 24:435–50.

Chapman, Antony J., and Hugh C. Foot, eds. 1977. *It's a Funny Thing, Humour.* Oxford: Pergamon.

Christie, George L. 1994. Some Psychoanalytic Aspects of Humour. *The International Journal of Psychoanalysis* 75:479–89.

Cohen, Ted. 1999. *Jokes: Philosophical Thoughts on Joking Matters.* Chicago: University of Chicago Press.

Collins, Billy. 1988. *The Apple That Astonished Paris.* Fayetteville: University of Arkansas Press.

————. 2001. *Sailing Alone around the Room: New and Selected Poems.* New York: Random House.

Cousins, Norman. 1979. *Anatomy of an Illness as Perceived by the Patient: Reflections on Healing and Regeneration.* New York: Bantam Books.

Culbertson, Philip. 1992. *New Adam: The Future of Male Spirituality.* Minneapolis: Fortress.

Davies, Christie. 1998. *Jokes and Their Relation to Society.* Berlin: Mouton de Gruyter.

Dawson, Jim. 1999. *Who Cut the Cheese? A Cultural History of the Fart.* Berkeley: Tenspeed.

Deaner, Stephanie L., and Jasmin T. McConatha. 1993. The Relation of Humor to Depression and Personality. *Psychological Reports* 72:755–63.

Dickson, Paul. 1984. *Dickson's Joke Treasury: An Anthology of Gags, Bits, Puns, and Jests—And How to Tell Them.* New York: John Wiley & Sons.

Dykstra, Robert. 2001. *Discovering a Sermon: Personal Pastoral Preaching.* St. Louis: Chalice Press.

Erikson, Erik H. 1958. *Young Man Luther: A Study in Psychoanalysis and History.* New York: W. W. Norton.

————. 1959. *Identity and the Life Cycle.* New York: W. W. Norton.

————. 1963. *Childhood and Society.* 2nd rev. ed. New York: W. W. Norton.

————. 1964. *Insight and Responsibility.* New York: W. W. Norton.

————. 1968. *Identity: Youth and Crisis.* New York: W. W. Norton.

————. 1981. The Galilean Sayings and the Sense of "I." *The Yale Review* 70:321–63.

Filkins, Kenn. 1994. Funeral for a Funny Lady: Humor and the Funeral Message. *Preaching* 9:25–26.

Freud, Sigmund. 1899/1965. *The Interpretation of Dreams.* Repr. translated by James Strachey. New York: Avon Books.

————. 1905/1960. *Jokes and Their Relation to the Unconscious.* Repr. translated by James Strachey. New York: W. W. Norton.

————. 1913/1997. The Theme of the Three Caskets. Repr. pages 109–21 in Sigmund Freud, *Writings on Art and Literature.* Edited by Werner Hamacher and David E. Welberry. Stanford, Calif.: Stanford University Press.

————. 1915/1957. Thoughts for the Times on War and Death. Repr. pages 273–302 in *The Standard Edition of the Complete Psychological Works of Sigmund Freud.* Edited and translated by James Strachey. Vol. 14. London: Hogarth.

————. 1917/1966. *Introductory Lectures on Psychoanalysis.* Repr. translated by James Strachey. New York: W. W. Norton.

————. 1921/1960. *Group Psychology and the Analysis of the Ego.* Repr. translated by James Strachey. New York: Bantam Books.

————. 1925/1952. *An Autobiographical Study.* Repr. translated by James Strachey. New York: W. W. Norton.

————. 1926/1989. *Inhibitions, Symptoms and Anxiety.* Repr. translated by Alix Strachey. New York: W. W. Norton.

————. 1927/1963. Humor. Repr. pages 263–69 in *Character and Culture.* Edited by Philip Rieff. New York: Collier Books.

————. 1930/1961. *Civilization and Its Discontents.* Repr. translated by James Strachey. New York: W. W. Norton.

Freud, Sigmund, and Josef Breuer. 1895/1953. *Studies on Hysteria.* Repr. in *The Standard Edition of the Complete Psychological Works of Sigmund Freud.* Edited by James Strachey. Vol. 2. London: Hogarth.

Friedman, David M. 2001. *A Mind of Its Own: A Cultural History of the Penis.* New York: The Free Press.

Friend, Tad. 2002. What's So Funny? A Scientific Attempt to Discover Why We Laugh. *The New Yorker,* November 11, 2002, 78–93.

Gardner, Martin, ed. 2001. *Martin Gardner's Favorite Poetic Parodies.* Amherst, N.Y.: Prometheus Books.

Gelkopf, Marc, Shulamith Kreitler, and Mircea Sigal. 1993. Laughter in a Psychiatric Ward: Somatic, Emotional, Social, and Clinical Influences on Schizophrenic Patients. *The Journal of Nervous and Mental Disease* 181:283–89.

Greene, Mel. 1999. *The Greatest Joke Book Ever.* New York: Avon Books.

Greenwald, Harold. 1977. Humour in Psychotherapy. Pages 161–64 in *It's a Funny Thing, Humour.* Edited by Antony J. Chapman and Hugh C. Foot. Oxford: Pergamon.

Gross, John, ed. 1994. *The Oxford Book of Comic Verse.* New York: Oxford University Press.

Grossman, Saul A. 1977. The Use of Jokes in Psychotherapy. Pages 149–51 in *It's a Funny Thing, Humour.* Edited by Antony J. Chapman and Hugh C. Foot. Oxford: Pergamon.

Harris, Henry F. 1908. The Absence of Humor in Jesus. *Methodist Quarterly Review* 57:460–67.

Hillman, James. 1975. *Re-Visioning Psychology.* New York: Harper & Row.

————. 1979. Peaks and Vales: The Soul/Spirit Distinction as Basis for the Difference between Psychology and Spiritual Discipline. Pages 54–74 in *Puer Papers.* Edited by James Hillman et al. Irving, Tex.: Spring Publications.

Holland, Norman N. 1982. *Laughing: A Psychology of Humor.* Ithaca, N.Y.: Cornell University Press.

James, William. 1902/1982. *The Varieties of Religious Experience.* New York: Penguin Books.

————. 1992. *William James: Writings 1878–1899.* Edited by Gerald E. Myers. New York: Library of America.

Jastrow, Morris, Jr. 1912. The Liver as the Seat of the Soul. Pages 143–68 in *Studies in the History of Religions.* Edited by David Gordon Lyon and George Foot Moore. New York: Macmillan.

Kaminsky, Joel S. 2000. Humor and the Theology of Hope: Isaac as a Humorous Figure. *Interpretation* 54:363–75.

Keillor, Garrison. 2003. *Pretty Good Joke Book.* 3rd ed. Minneapolis: Highbridge.

Kelly, William E. 2002. An Investigation of Worry and Sense of Humor. *The Journal of Psychology* 136:657–66.

King, Alan. 2002. *Great Jewish Joke Book.* New York: Crown Publishers.

Kubie, Lawrence S. 1971. The Destructive Potential of Humor in Psychotherapy. *The American Journal of Psychiatry* 127:861–66.

Kübler-Ross, Elisabeth. 1969. *On Death and Dying.* New York: Macmillan Company.

Kuhlman, Thomas L. 1984. *Humor and Psychotherapy.* Homewood, Ill.: Dorsey Professional Books.

Lefcourt, Herbert M., and Rod A. Martin. 1986. *Humor and Life Stress: Antidote to Adversity.* New York: Springer-Verlag.

Levertov, Denise. 1992. *Evening Train.* New York: New Directions Books.

Levin, Max. 1957. Wit and Schizophrenic Thinking. *American Journal of Psychiatry* 113:917–23.

Levine, Jacob. 1977. Humour as a Form of Therapy: Introduction to Symposium. Pages 127–37 in *It's a Funny Thing, Humour.* Edited by Antony J. Chapman and Hugh C. Foot. Oxford: Pergamon.

Mather, Cotton. 1911. *Diary of Cotton Mather.* Vol. 1. New York: Frederick Ungar Publishing Company.

Nezu, Arthur M., Christine M. Nezu, and Sonia E. Blissett. 1988. Sense of Humor as a Moderator of the Relation between Stressful Events and Psychological Distress: A Prospective Analysis. *Journal of Personality and Social Psychology* 54:520–25.

Niebuhr, Reinhold. 1990. Humour and Faith. *Katallagete* 11:10–15. Repr. from *Discerning the Signs of the Times.* New Haven, Conn.: Yale University Press, 1946.

Norem, Julie K. 2001. *The Positive Power of Negative Thinking.* New York: Basic Books.

Oring, Elliott. 1984. *The Jokes of Sigmund Freud: A Study in Humor and Jewish Identity.* Philadelphia: University of Pennsylvania Press.

Phillips, Adam. 2001. *Promises, Promises: Essays on Literature and Psychoanalysis.* New York: Basic Books.

———. 2001b. *Houdini's Box: The Art of Escape.* New York: Pantheon Books.

Porterfield, Albert L. 1987. Does Sense of Humor Moderate the Impact of Life Stress on Psychological and Physical Well-Being? *Journal of Research in Personality* 21:307–17.

Provine, Robert R. 2000. *Laughter: A Scientific Investigation.* New York: Penguin Books.

Reik, Theodor. 1962. *Jewish Wit.* New York: Gamut Press.

Rosenzweig, S. 1950. The Treatment of Humorous Responses in the Rosenzweig Picture-Frustration Study: A Note on the Revised (1950) Instructions. *The Journal of Psychology* 30:139–43.

Salameh, Waleed Anthony. 1983. Humor in Psychotherapy: Past Outlooks, Present Status, and Future Frontiers. Pages 61–88 in *Handbook of Humor Research: Applied Studies.* Edited by Paul E. McGhee and Jeffrey H. Goldstein. New York: Springer-Verlag.

Saroglou, Vassilis. 1999. Humor, Religion, and Personality. Unpublished doctoral dissertation. Catholic University of Louvain, Belgium.

———. 2002a. Religion and Sense of Humor: An A Priori Incompatibility? Theoretical Considerations from a Psychological Perspective. *Humor: International Journal of Humor Research* 15:191–214.

———. 2002b. Religiousness, Religious Fundamentalism, and Quest as Predictors of Humor Creation. *The International Journal for the Psychology of Religion* 12:177–88.

———. 2003. Humor Appreciation as Function of Religious Dimensions. *Archive for the Psychology of Religion* 24:144–53.

———. 2004. Being Religious Implies Being Different in Humour: Evidence from Self- and Peer-Ratings. *Mental Health, Religion, and Culture* 7:255–67.

Saroglou, Vassilis, and Jean-Marie Jaspard. 2001. Does Religion Affect Humour Creation? An Experimental Study. *Mental Health, Religion and Culture* 4:33–46.

Selzer, Richard. 1974. *Mortal Lessons: Notes on the Art of Surgery.* New York: Touchstone.

Smith, Ronald E., James C. Ascough, Ronald F. Ettinger, and Don A. Nelson. 1971.

Humor, Anxiety, and Task Performance. *Journal of Personality and Social Psychology* 19:243–46.

Spacks, Patricia Meyer. 1995. *Boredom: The Literary History of a State of Mind.* Chicago: University of Chicago Press.

Stangland, Red. 1979. *Norwegian Home Companion.* New York: Barnes & Noble Books.

Sullivan, Harry Stack. 1953. *Conceptions of Modern Psychiatry.* 2nd ed. New York: W. W. Norton.

Tapper, Albert, and Peter Press. 2000a. *A Minister, a Priest, and a Rabbi.* Kansas City, Mo.: Andrews McMeel Publishing.

———. 2000b. *A Guy Goes into a Bar . . . .* New York: MJF Books.

Thorson, James A., and F. C. Powell. 1993. Relationships of Death Anxiety and Sense of Humor. *Psychological Reports* 72:1364–66.

Tibballs, Geof. 2000. *The Mammoth Book of Humor.* New York: Carroll & Graf.

Trask, Rick. 1989. *Toronto Jokes.* Port Sydney, Ontario: Upalong Enterprises.

Trible, Phyllis. 1984. *Texts of Terror: Literary-Feminist Readings of Biblical Narratives.* Philadelphia: Fortress.

Turner, Michael R. 1967. *Victorian Parlour Poetry: An Annotated Anthology.* New York: Dover Publications.

Washington, Peter, ed. 2003. *Haiku.* New York: Alfred A. Knopf.

Watzlawick, Paul. 1983. *The Situation Is Hopeless, but Not Serious: The Pursuit of Unhappiness.* New York: W. W. Norton.

———. 1988. *Ultra-Solutions: How to Fail Most Successfully.* New York: W. W. Norton.

Watzlawick, Paul, Janet Beavin Bavelas, and Don D. Jackson. 1967. *Pragmatics of Human Communication: A Study of Interactional Patterns, Pathologies, and Paradoxes.* New York: W. W. Norton.

Watzlawick, Paul, John Weakland, and Richard Fisch. 1974. *Change: Principles of Problem Formation and Problem Resolution.* New York: W. W. Norton.

Winnicott, D. W. 1991. Transitional Objects and Transitional Phenomena. Pages 1–25 in *Playing and Reality.* London: Tavistock/Routledge.

Wolfenstein, Martha. 1954. *Children's Humor: A Psychological Analysis.* Glencoe, Ill.: The Free Press.

Young, Richard Alan. 1998. *Is God a Vegetarian? Christianity, Vegetarianism, and Animal Rights.* Chicago: Open Court.

Yovetich, Nancy A., J. Alexander Dale, and Mary A. Hudak. 1990. Benefits of Humor in Reduction of Threat-Induced Anxiety. *Psychological Reports* 66:51–58.

Index